Night Vision Goggles *for Helicopter Pilots*

About this Publication

Title:

Night Vision Goggles

Series:

For Helicopter Pilots

Edition:

First published 2011, Third Edition, January 2022

Principal Author:

Mike Becker, ATPL(H), FIR, FER, Diploma (Training and Assessment)

Editor:

Bev Austen, BTech(CompSt), MEd(DTL)

Copyright

Copyright © 2022 Becker Helicopter Services Pty Ltd

Photos and Illustrations

Most photos and illustrations in this document have been sourced from Becker Helicopter Services Pty Ltd. The remainder is taken from the internet from various sources; Every effort has been made to ensure images with Creative Commons Licences have been used and/or appropriate attribution provided.

Disclaimer

Nothing in this text supersedes any operational documents issued by any civil aviation authority or regulatory body, aircraft, engine, and avionics manufacturers or the operators of aircraft throughout the world. No responsibility is taken for the interpretation and application of the information contained in this document Managing the safety of the aircraft is the sole responsibility of the pilot-in-command.

Every possible effort has been made to establish the accuracy of the information contained in this book; however, the author, Becker Helicopter Services Pty Ltd, accept no responsibility for errors or omissions.

The Publisher and the Author make no representations or warranties for the accuracy or completeness of the contents of this work and expressly disclaim all warranties, including without limitation warranties of fitness for a particular purpose. No warranty may be created or extended by sales or promotional materials. The advice and strategies contained herein may not be suitable for every situation. This work is sold with the understanding that the author is not engaged in rendering legal, accounting, or other professional services. If professional assistance is required, the services of a competent professional person should be sought. Neither the Publisher nor the Author shall be liable for damages arising therefrom.

The fact that an organisation or website is referred to in this work as a citation and/or a potential source of further information does not mean that the author or the publisher endorses the information the organisation or website may provide or recommendations it may make. Further, readers should be aware that internet websites listed in this work may have changed or disappeared between when this work was written and when it is read.

Contents

About this Publication 1
Contents 2
About this Book 10
About the Author 11

The History of Light **12**
    Electricity 13
    The Intensifier Tube 14
    Summary 14

Science of Light **15**
    A Star: The Source of Light 15
    Photons 16
    Light Spectrum 18
    Speed of Light 19
    Colours of the Spectrum 20
        White 20
        Black 20
        Grey 21
        Tints, Shades, and Tones 21
    Infrared Light 22
        Atoms, Energy and Heat 22
        Thermal Imaging 23
        Night Vision Devices (NVDs) 25

Light Terminology **26**
    Candlepower 26
    Foot-candle 27
    Lumen or LUX 28
    Newton's Inverse Square Law 29
    Radiance 30
    Illuminance 30
    Luminance 31
    Summary of Light Terminology 33
    What is a Laser 34
        Laser Classification System 35
        Laser Warning and Classification Labels 36
        Laser Type and Wavelength 36

Components of the NVG **37**
    Binocular Housings 38
        Lenses 39
            Convex Lens 40
            Convex Lens Image Inversion 40
            Concave Lens 41
            Planar Lens 42
            Compound Lens 42
        NVG Objective Focal Adjustment 43
    NVG Filters 44
        Light Intensity Filter (LIF) 45
        Class A and B Cockpits 45
            Class A and B Filters 46

Modified Class B Filters	46
Current NVG Requirements	46
NVG Eyepiece and Dioptric Focus Lens	46
Intensifier Tube	**48**
Gain	48
Tube Gain	48
System Gain	49
MTTF (Mean Time To Failure)	49
Photocathode	**50**
Geometric Distortion	51
Making a Photocathode for NVG	52
Photosensitivity	53
Generational Change	53
Vacuum Chamber	54
Microchannel Plate	**54**
Making a Microchannel Plate	57
Ion Barrier Film	58
Phosphor Screen	**61**
What are Phosphors?	61
Making a Phosphor Screen	64
Fibre Optic Inverter	**64**
What is Fibre Optics?	64
Distortion	65
S Distortion	65
Sheer Distortion	66
Electrical Supply	**66**
Anode and Cathode	66
Controlling the Amount of Light	67
Blooming	67
Halo Effect	68
Bright Source Protection (BSP)	68
Automatic Brightness Control (ABC)	68
Autogain	69
Autogating	70
Operational Defects	**71**
Unacceptable Defects	71
Shading	71
Edge Glow	72
Emission Points	72
Flashing, Flickering or Intermittent Operation	73
Acceptable Defects	73
Bright Spots	73
Black Spots	74
Fixed Pattern Noise (FPN)	74
Chicken Wire	74
Honeycomb	75
Scintillation	75
Signal to Noise Ratio (SNR)	76
Resolution	76
Figure of Merit (FOM)	**77**
Power Supply	**77**
Battery Compartment	77
Battery Usage Plan	79
Electrical Circuit Within the Intensifier Tube	80

- Low Battery Indicator ... 80
- Mounting System ... 81
  - Helmet Mounting ... 81
  - Mount Assembly ... 81
    - Locking Pin ... 82
    - Vertical Adjustment ... 83
    - Tilt Adjustment Lever ... 83
    - Fore and Aft Adjustment Knob ... 84
    - Eye Span Distance Adjustment Knob ... 84
    - Breakaway ... 85
    - Electrical Connection ... 85
  - Problems in NVG Adjustment ... 86
    - Tube Alignment ... 86
    - Collimation ... 86
    - Optical Image Differences ... 87
    - Focus Lane ... 87
- Summary ... 87

Hoffmann 20/20 Focus Box ... 88
- Controls and Indicators ... 89
- Checking NVG System Resolution and Dynamic Range ... 90
- The Resolution Pattern ... 91
- Greyscale Outer Ring ... 92
- Hoffmann 20/20 Focusing Procedure ... 94

The Generation Game ... 97
- Omnibus ... 97
- Generations ... 97
  - Full Face Goggles ... 98
  - Displaced Goggles ... 98
  - Generation 0 ... 99
  - Generation I ... 99
  - Generation II ... 100
  - Super Generation II ... 100
  - Generation III ... 100
  - Generation III Plus and Generation III Omnibus "X" ... 100
  - Generation IV ... 100
  - XR5 ... 100
  - Comparing US and European Classifications ... 101
  - More Terms ... 102
- Figure of Merit (FOM) ... 103
- Performance-based Not Technology-based ... 104
- Summary ... 106

Aeromedical Factors When Using NVGS ... 107
- Eyes When Using NVGs ... 107
  - Field of View (FOV) ... 108
  - Field of Regard (FOR) ... 110
- Scanning Techniques ... 110
  - Scanning Patterns ... 111
  - Unaided Scan ... 111
  - Ambient or Artificial Light ... 112
- NVG Eye Factors ... 112
  - Eye Stress and Fatigue ... 112

- Night Adaptation 113
  - Eyes That Need Corrective Lenses 114
- Visual Illusions 115
  - False Horizons 115
  - Flicker Vertigo 115
  - Fascination (Fixation) 115
  - Confusion of Ground Lights 116
  - Relative Motion Illusion 116
    - Lack of Motion Illusion 116
    - Wave Drift Illusion 116
    - Waterfall Illusion 117
  - Autokinesis 117
  - Structural Illusion 117
  - Height Perception Illusion 117
  - Size Distance Illusion 117
  - Altered Planes of Reference 117
  - Reversible Perspective Illusion 118
  - Crater Illusion 118
  - Light 118
    - Infrared Light 118
    - Monochromatic Adaptation 119
- Ears When using NVGs 119
- Proprioceptive System When Using NVGs 119
  - Postural Right Reflex 119
  - Vestibular Ocular Reflex 119
- Fatigue When Using NVGs 119
  - NVG Fitting 120
    - Fitting Your Helmet 120
    - Balance Your Helmet 121
  - Building Your Fitness 122
  - Side Effects 122

Terrain and Environmental Factors 123
- Illumination 123
  - Lumination 124
  - Natural Sources 124
    - Moon 125
    - Night Sky Illumination 125
    - Solar Influence 128
  - Artificial Sources of Light 129
- Terrain 129
  - Terrain Reflectivity (Albedo) 130
  - Terrain Contrast 131
  - Terrain Shadowing 134
- Weather and Atmospheric Obscurants 135
  - Atmospheric Absorption 135
    - Absorption 136
    - Scattering 136
    - Refraction 137
    - Reflection 137
  - Weather 137
  - Airborne Obscurants 138
  - Atmospheric Influence 138

- Clouds 139
- Thunderstorms and Lightning 140
- Rain 140
- Snow 140
- Haze, Mist, Fog 140
- Salt, Dust, Smoke, Ash, Pollen, Leaves, Grass and Bugs 140
- Wind 141

Aircraft Configuration 141
- Windshield 141
  - Shape 141
  - Wavelengths 141
  - Distance from User 141
  - Condition 141
- Lighting 142
  - Cockpit Lighting 142
  - External Lighting 143
- Cockpit Design 143

Risk Management for NVG Operations 144
Quick Review of Risk Management 144
Risk Management Plans 145
- Risk Management Plan (RMP) Process 145
- Risk Management Plan (RMP) Content 145
- RMP Headings 146
- Risk Matrix 147
- Consequence Rating 147
- Likelihood Rating 148
RMP Example 149
Threat Error Management (TEM) for NVG Operations 150
- Threat 150
  - External Threats 150
  - Internal Threats 150
  - Organisational Threats 151
- Error 151
- Management 151
- Pre-flight Brief 151

Crew Resource Management and Phraseology 152
Standard Phraseology 152
Crew Resource Management (CRM) 152
- Eyes Inside/Outside Drill 153
- NVG Scanning Procedures 153
  - Scanning 153
  - NVG Scanning Arcs Of Responsibility 154
- Standard Words and Phrases 155
- Standard Crew Interactions 158
- NVG Standard Phraseology 158
- Hover And Taxi Management Phraseology 159
- In-Flight Phraseology 159
- Identifying and Avoiding Obstacles Phraseology 160
- Take-Off And Landing Phase Below 500 ft AGL Phraseology 161
Checks 161
- Pre-lift-off and Pre-landing checks 161
- Hover Checks 161
- Instrument Performance Checks 162

Night Vision Goggles *for Helicopter Pilots*

- Power Wind Plan (PWP) Statement 162
- Use of Lights For NVG 162
    - External Lights in General 162
    - Position Lights 162
    - Anti-Collision Light 163
    - Strobe Lights 163
    - Landing Light / Searchlight / Night Scanner 163
    - Torch 163
    - Lip Light / Finger Light 163
- Goggle Up/De-Goggle Procedure 163
    - On the Ground 163
    - Goggle Up Procedure : On the Ground 164
    - De-Goggle Procedure : On the Ground 165
    - Goggle Up Procedure : In The Air 165
    - De-Goggle Procedure : In The Air 166
- NVG Departure Profile 166
    - Restricted Instrument Flight Take-off (RIFTO) 167
    - Constant Angle and Standard Airfield Departure 167
- Encountering Low Contrast Situations 167
- NVG Approach Profiles 168
    - Standard NVG Approach Profile 169
    - HLS NVG Pinnacle Approaches 172
- Departing an HLS 172
- Arriving at an HLS 173
- NVG Navigation 175
- NVG Low-level Flight 175
- Transition Between Flight Categories 177
    - Transition from NVG Flight to IFR Flight 177
    - Transition from IFR Flight to NVG Flight 178
    - Transition from NVG Flight to NVFR Flight 179
    - Transition from NVFR Flight to NVG Flight 180
- NVG Emergencies 181
- Helicopter Emergencies With NVGs In General 182
- NVG Specific Emergencies 182
    - Radio Altimeter (RADALT) Failure 182
    - Goggle Failure Drill 182
        - Flying Pilot Goggle Failure 183
        - Non-flying Pilot Goggle Failure 183
        - Single Tube Failure 184
    - Inadvertent IMC (IIMC) Procedure 185
        - Entering IMC (IIMC) 186
        - AHTA Drill 186
        - During IIMC 186
    - Loss of Visual Reference (Brownout/Whiteout) 187
    - Landing Techniques 188
    - Take-off Techniques 189

Planning an NVG Flight 190

- NVG Checklist 191
    - 1. NVGs 191
    - 2. AIRCRAFT 191
    - 3. CREW 192
    - 4. MISSION 192
    - 5. ROUTE 192

  6. WEATHER 193
  7. FLIGHT PLANNING 193
  8. POST FLIGHT 193

Explaining the NVG Checklist 194

 1. NVGs: Checklist Explained 194
  Serviceable And Released 194
  Mounted To Helmet And Focused 194
  Battery Life 194
  Backup If Required 194

 2. Aircraft: Checklist Explained 194
  Serviceable And Released 194
  NVFR or IFR Approved 194
  Pre-flight Inspection 194
  Ancillary Equipment 194
  Weight And Balance 195

 3. Crew: Checklist Explained 195
  Rested And Within Flight And Duty Times 195
  Stop Time Calculated 195
  Currency And Recency 195

 4. Mission: Checklist Explained 196
  Purpose 196
  Flight Timings 196
  Airspace 197
  Aerial Work Activity 198

 5. Route : Checklist Explained 198
  Route And Working Area Selected and Assessed 198
  Terrain Appreciation 198
  LSALT Calculated 199
  Wires And Obstacles Noted 199
  Best Way To Look For Wires 200
  Negotiating Wires and Obstacles 202
  Wire Maps 202

 6. Weather : Checklist Explained 203
  Australia: For NVG Operations, The Following Weather Requirements Will Apply And Are The Legal Minimums Within Australia 204
  Five Key Elements Of The Weather 204
  1. Cloud Amount and Base 205
  2. Visibility 205
  3. Freezing Level 205
  4. Alternates and Holding Fuel 205
  5. Ambient Light 206

 7. Flight Planning: Checklist Explained 207
  Flight Log 207
  Mud Map 207
  Flight Plan With Air Traffic Services (ATS). 207
  Crew Briefing and Co-Ordination 207
  Risks and Threats Discussed 208
  IIMC Recovery Plan 208
  NVG Sortie Crew Plan 208

 8. Post Flight: Checklist Explained 208

NVG Map Hints and Tips 210

 Map Marking 211
 Creating A Mud Map 214

Abbreviations and Acronyms 215

Glossary 221

Bibliography	233
Index	234

About this Book

Night Vision Goggles for Helicopter Pilots is written by Captain Mike Becker, one of Australia's most experienced helicopter instructors. With over 16,000 helicopter flight hours and recipient of the "Captain John Ashton Award for Flight Standards and Aviation Safety" by the Guild of Air Pilots and Air Navigators of London, Mike's experience provides invaluable insights and real hands-on knowledge.

Mike Becker has been operating a helicopter flight school since 1995. As Chief Pilot and Head of Training Operations, Mike has managed and operated a fleet of over 20 helicopters while employing a team of more than 30 instructors to deliver over 10,000 turbine training hours per year. This book captures his experience as Chief Pilot and Chief Flight Instructor and the breadth of knowledge of the team of flight instructors who, over the years, have contributed to the continual improvement of this book.

This experience is evident in this practical, hands-on guide to NVG civilian operations. It is written by a helicopter pilot for a helicopter pilot and demystifies the world of NVGs.

The information and teaching material in *Night Vision Goggles for Helicopter Pilots* covers the issues of sourcing and using NVGs, understanding how they work and operate, dealing with unique hazards and risks, flight planning for NVG operations, crew resource management considerations, helicopter emergencies, and establishing safe and regulatory-compliant operational systems. New terms like Omnibus, Gen III, ANVIS 9, microchannel plate, lumen, photocathode, infrared, chicken-wire, and more are clearly explained and simplified.

Although a technical theory book, it is written in plain English with easy-to-understand explanations supported by many photographs, illustrations and diagrams.

This book is a ground-breaking world-first comprehensive text. It is a must for the new and current NVG helicopter aviator, bringing you out of the dark and into the light in terms of the depth of knowledge required for civilian NVG operations.

About the Author

Mike Becker is one of Australia's most experienced helicopter instructors, with over 16,000 hours of rotary-wing flight experience. His career has taken him from the mountains in New Zealand to the outback of Australia to the jungles of Papua New Guinea. He has also worked in the United States, Italy and Borneo.

He has flown a range of helicopter types – the Robinson R22, Robinson R44, Bell 47, Hughes 269, Hughes 500, Bell 206, Bell 427, Bell 212, EC120, Dragon Fly, Brantley B2B, Enstrom EF28, Sikorsky S62A, Hiller

H12ET, Aerospatial AS350, Agusta 109E Power, Agusta 109S Grand, and the Agusta 119 Koala.

He is experienced in a comprehensive range of helicopter operations, including high altitude, remote area operations, mustering, firefighting, tourism, sling load operations, specialised long-line operations, search and rescue, and Night Vision Goggles operations.

Mike is a Grade One Flight Instructor and Flight Examiner who holds an Australian Air Transport Pilots Licence (Helicopter) and an Australian Commercial Pilots Licence (Fixed Wing).

Mike is the Chief Pilot and Head of Training for his own business Becker Helicopters, in Australia. He, and his wife Jan, established Becker Helicopters in 1997 with one Bell 47 and have grown the company through a love of helicopters, hard work, and determination.

Mike is the recipient of many awards, including the "Captain John Ashton Award for Flight Standards and Aviation Safety" by the Guild of Air Pilots and Air Navigators of London, which was awarded in recognition of over 18,000 accident-free flight training hours at Becker Helicopters. Mike has also authored "Mike Becker's Helicopter Handbook", first published in 1986, and a range of theory books and instructional videos.

Mike Becker

The History of Light

Figure 1 Possibly the first Night Vision Device [1]

Since the beginning of time, darkness has been a source of protection, whereby those who could not see in the dark could hide away in a secure place to rest and be protected, additionally, those who could see in the dark could use its protection for hunting for food or attacking an enemy. In most cases, with darkness being a source of protection, animals that were a danger to man were naturally afraid of light. Therefore light, during times of darkness, evolved as a tool for man's protection.

Therefore, the first Night Vision Device (NVD) can find its history in fire as the simple torch. This torch may have consisted of a burning stick, possibly with fat or skin wound around one end, which shed light so that it allowed the holder to see in the dark.

As history progressed, better ways of seeing in the dark were invented. This included using lanterns powered by oil, gas, and electricity to generate light, enabling man to utilise the dark for continued productivity and protection.

Oil   **Gas**   **Electricity (Battery)**

Man's greatest predator has always been another man. So, during times of war, the ability to see at night would be an advantage. The question was how to make a device that allows you to see in the dark without being seen yourself?

---

1 Shutterstock, viewed 14 February 2022, https://www.shutterstock.com/image-photo/primeval-caveman-wearing-animal-skin-exploring-1595983387 [licensed]

Night Vision Goggles *for Helicopter Pilots*

As humankind began to accelerate into the technological age during World War I and II, we discovered and utilised artificial ways to generate light. Initially, this was related to the light bulb and electricity use. Probably the most famous was the searchlight. As aviation began its steady improvement, aircraft flew night missions under the protection of darkness and height to bomb cities in enemy countries. Large searchlights would penetrate the dark to search the sky, trying to light up a plane and give their gunners something to at which to aim. The searchlight is a night vision device because it allows you to see into the darkness.

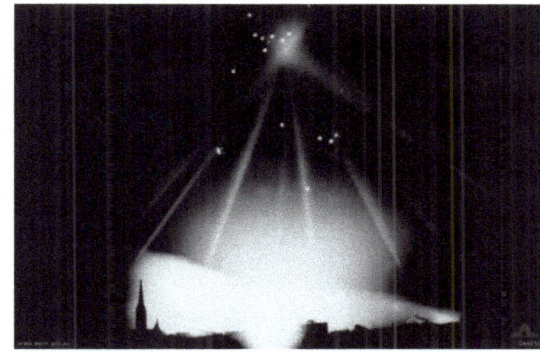

Figure 2 A Night Bombing Raid On The German City Of Bremen [2]

These NVDs are known as active night vision systems because they emit light to see. However, active night vision systems have a significant problem; they emit light, allowing the enemy to identify your position. This is not good if you don't want to be seen or shot. So, scientists began to experiment with various light types to develop a night vision system that would allow the user to see in the dark without being seen. The creation of a device that would enable you to see in the dark without emitting any form of light is known as a passive night vision system.

Electricity

Scientists began to experiment with electricity to create a passive night vision device. The original logic was that if electricity is a medium that is easily able to be modulated (increased or decreased) in strength, then if you turned whatever visible light that was available into electricity amplified the electricity before turning it back into visible light again, you might just be able to "see in the dark" by amplifying the visible image.

To prove the logic, all you had to do was look at past inventions where all sorts of electrical devices take in a small electrical current (flow of electricity) at one end and amplify it to produce a bigger flow at the other.

Example

Someone playing an electric guitar can strum strings to make a sound. That sound is picked up and passed through an electrical amplifier before it is turned back into sound so that it can be heard in a big stadium from the stage.

We know this works for sound, but what about light?

To work for light, something new had to be invented that replaced the sound amplifier. This would become the job of the *light intensifier tube*.

---

2 Australian War Memorial, digital image collection, image number 044856, viewed 20 June 2013, https://www.awm.gov.au/collection/044856?image=1 [Public Domain]

The Intensifier Tube

Although this will be covered later in more detail, in its most straightforward description, the intensifier tube is a small vacuum-sealed device that collects light in one end and converts that light into electricity. The electricity is then *amplified* before it is converted back into light that we can see as an intensified image on a viewing screen.

Summary

A Night Vision Device (NVD) is anything that will help the human eye "*see*" in the dark. This may be using either an *active* or a *passive* NVD

Figure 3 XR5 Image Intensifier tube [3]

To create a passive NVD, the *light intensifier tube* was invented, which takes whatever light available, amplifies it, then projects that intensified image onto a viewing screen so that the user can literally "*see in the dark*".

It is essential to understand that if there is no light, then there is nothing to be amplified, and, therefore, there is no image that can be seen on the viewing screen.

---

[3] Photonis.com, viewed 20 June 2013, http://www.photonis.com/en/nightvision/75-xr5.html

Science of Light

Light is something that we seem to take for granted, but we very rarely take the time to understand just what it is. We often fail to realise that it is something physical, has various components, and can manipulate it, just like we do water or air. To understand the more complex technical explanations of Night Vision Devices that will follow in this book, you need a basic understanding of what light is, how we describe it, and how it is divided.

Figure 4 Light in the Universe

The universe is made up of matter, the building blocks of matter being atoms, which are, in turn, made up of protons, electrons, and neutrons held together by an electrochemical bond. This electro-chemical bond, consisting of positively charged protons, negatively charged electrons and neutral (no charge) neutrons, is essential in understanding how we use technology to enhance light.

Some of this matter is collected into objects. These objects can be:

- as **large** as suns, planets, asteroids, moons, etc.
- as **small** as trees, animals, dust
- **artificial** objects such as a desk, a car, a building, etc.

Some of this matter, particularly within a star, is burning. However, the bulk of it is spread throughout the galaxy as hydrogen atoms, and since the universe is supposedly infinite in size, it logically means that there is an infinite supply of hydrogen atoms.

Hydrogen is the most prolific atom in the galaxy and is referred to as the building block of the universe.

A Star: The Source of Light

A star is a large celestial body of hot gases held together by gravity that radiates energy derived from thermonuclear hydrogen fusion. In essence, it is a large atomic bomb exercising the full power of Einstein's formula of $E=MC^2$.

(Energy = Mass x the speed of light squared (C2))

Our sun converts over 657 million tons of hydrogen into 653 tons of helium every second. The missing 4 million tons of mass is discharged into space as energy. It is calculated that the earth receives only about one two-billionths of this energy as the rest continues off into space.

As a star releases its power (energy), it pushes out **photons**. A photon is several atoms grouped into **packets** that we detect and describe as light. This explanation describes light as being made up of actual particles of matter (atoms) travelling outwards away from their source towards infinity.

Photons

There is much scientific debate regarding what makes up a photon. It is probably most helpful to apply an analogy or example to help grasp a basic understanding. A photon is created when two or more atoms collide.

To demonstrate this, clap your hands.

Each hand represents an atom. As the two hands (atoms) come together, energy is created.

Your hands can feel hot as they hit each other and create an energy wave. That energy wave is manifested when we clap our hands as sound. Your hands have not necessarily changed their state, but something new is created.

Light is created in the same manner. As two atoms collide, they generate heat and produce an energy wave, manifested as a photon of light.

The more hands we have clapping, the greater the energy wave and the louder the sound.

The more atoms that collide, the greater the heat and the greater the number of photons of light are created.

Our sun is only very small, but over 657 billion tons of atoms collide every second. You do not need to use your imagination to realise how much heat or light that produces; instead, we can see it moving across the sky every day.

On earth, we receive these particles as light in the form of an electromagnetic wave or electromagnetic energy. An electromagnetic wave simply describes the way the packets of atoms (photons) move. It can be imagined as a moving source of energy.

Night Vision Goggles *for Helicopter Pilots*

To give an example of a wave, simply drop a rock into a pond of water. As the rock hits the water, its energy can be seen moving outwards in the form of a wave

It is interesting to note here that the water itself is not necessarily moving away from the rock; instead, the energy wave is passed on from one particle of water to the next. This is the basis of an energy wave.

The electromagnetic wave or electromagnetic radiation emitted from our sun is classified into several types according to the frequency of its wave; these types include (in order of increasing frequency and decreasing wavelength):

Figure 5 Water waves

- radio waves
- microwaves
- infrared radiation
- visible light
- ultraviolet radiation
- X-rays
- gamma rays.

The diagram below shows the small optical window and the larger radio window of wavelengths of light that arrive on the earth's surface.

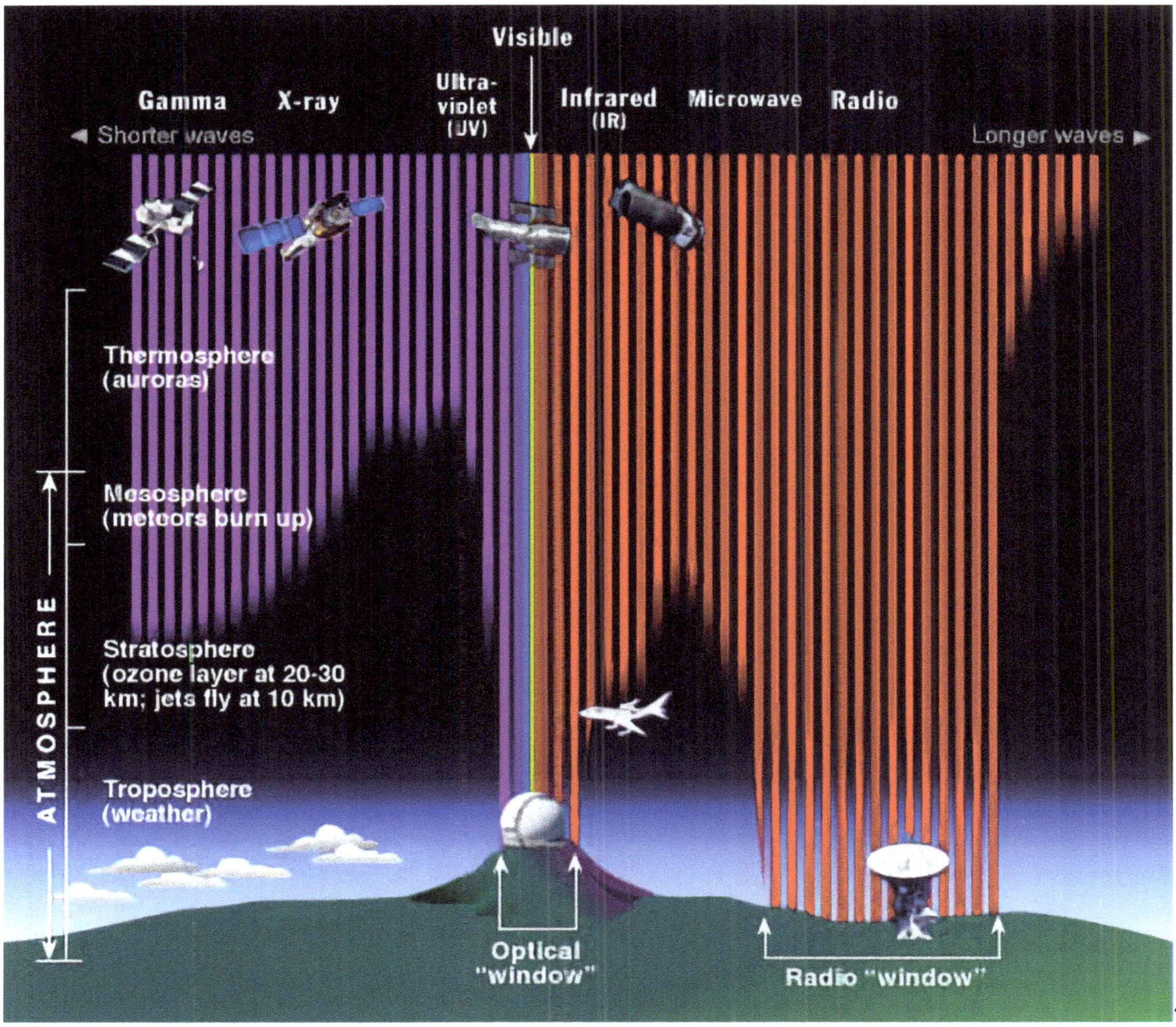

---

4 Amazing Space, online image viewed 21 November 2011, amazing-space.stsci.edu/resources/explorations/groundup/lesson/basics/g17b/

As these light particles travel through space, they will interact with objects as they reach them. With regards to the earth, some of these light particles are reflected back into space. While the rest may be absorbed by the earth, passing through various mediums such as the gaseous atmosphere, water, glass, or even a camera lens which allows us to manipulate them and transform them into another form. This transformation may be achieved by using the photons to create heat energy, grow plants, or capture an image on a camera or through an NVD.

Our closest star, the sun, is our greatest source of light energy; however, we also receive light energy from other suns or stars which are much further away. Light energy may also be reflected, such as what happens with the moon, asteroids and other planets. We can also create our own light sources (artificial light) on earth, either through fire, electricity, or chemical interaction.

Light Spectrum

All of these light sources radiate out **photons** which are packets of energy travelling at various wavelengths. The wavelengths for light are measured in **nanometres** (nm). A nanometer is one-billionth of a metre in its basic translation.

White light is the combination of the light spectrum that the human eye can see, known as the " *visible spectrum*". This can be evidenced by splitting the white light into its components which is commonly done when we see a rainbow or shine light through a prism. White light is divided into red, orange, yellow, green, blue, indigo and violet. This can often be remembered by using the acronym: **ROY G BIV**.

Figure 6 Rainbow

Figure 7 Light shining through a prism

The human eye has evolved only to see a small spectrum (or piece) of the total light spectrum being emitted from the sun and other light sources. Light travelling between **400 to 700 nanometres** (nm) is visible to humans and is referred to as the visible spectrum. The light outside this narrow spectrum, with infrared on one side between **700 to 800 nm** and ultraviolet on the other side between **400 to 300 nm**, is not visible to the human eye.

It is the infrared spectrum that allows NVDs to work (700 to 800 nm).

Some animals, for example, owls, bats, some deep-sea fish, and moths, can see beyond the human eye's spectrum, which allows them to see differently and in less light. Other animals have a more limited visible spectrum than humans.

Night Vision Goggles *for Helicopter Pilots*

Figure 8 below shows the small spectrum available to the human eye. It also shows the other wavelengths and frequencies of those light particles that we cannot see but are still reaching earth, whether the light is being radiated out from the sun or being received from some other cosmic or artificial source.

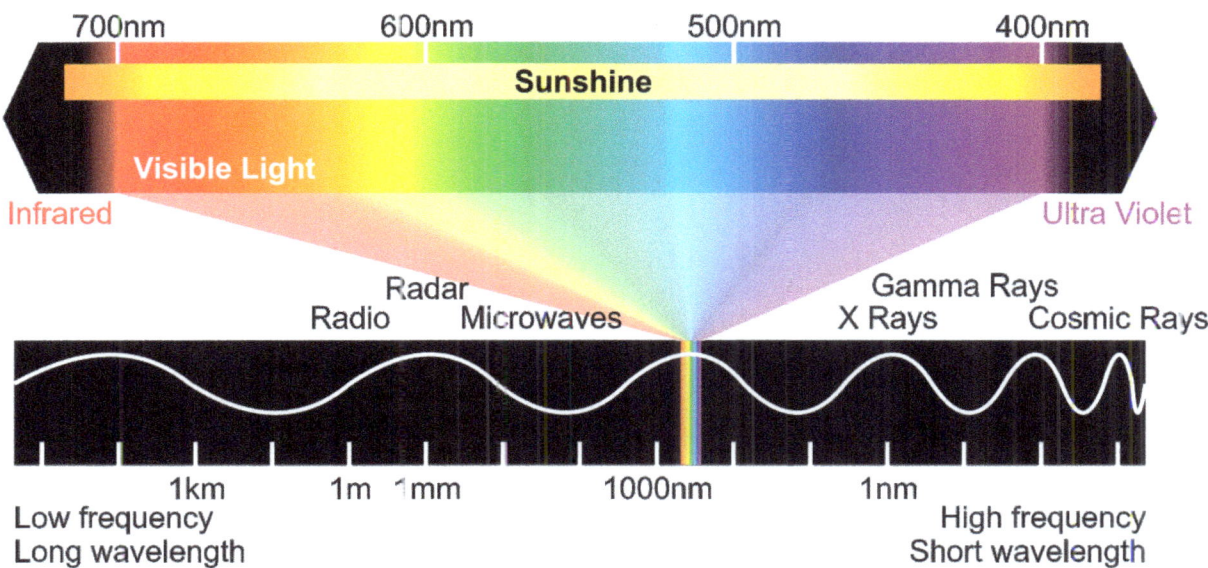

Figure 8 The Visible Spectrum available to the human eye

Speed of Light

All light (the various wavelengths) is travelling at the same speed. The speed of light is exactly 299,792,458 metres per second, equivalent to 299,792.458 kilometres per second or approximately 161,771 nautical miles or approximately 186,282 statute miles per second. The speed of light currently represents the maximum speed at which all energy, matter and information within the universe can travel.

Because it is such an important number, it is mathematically denoted by the letter **C** in calculations. You may recall Einstein's famous formula $E=MC^2$, which in its explanation describes how **E**nergy equals **M**ass times the speed of light squared (C^2)!

We now know light consists of various wavelengths that oscillate at varying frequencies as they travel together, giving us our light spectrum.

Often the question is asked, "if light is travelling at the same speed, how can we have varying wavelengths travelling at different speeds?" The best way to explain this is to give an analogy or example.

Consider two boats travelling side-by-side at the same speed on a rough ocean. One boat is very small (representing a high frequency, short wavelength), and one is very large (representing a low frequency and long wavelength).

The small boat will go up and down many times over the same distance in the rough ocean, whereas the large boat will cut through the rough ocean and go up and down at a slower rate and less frequently. Both boats will arrive at the destination at the same time because they are both going at the same speed.

Light acts in the same manner. All the various wavelengths travel at the same speed, but they will oscillate differently, giving them a different frequency and, therefore, a different wavelength.

Colours of the Spectrum

Since we have discussed the "colours of the spectrum", the next logical question is: "so what about white, black and grey?"

White

When light arrives at a surface, it will absorb certain wavelengths and reflect others. What we see is the reflected wavelength.

Example
Consider you are looking at green grass. You see the visible light within the spectrum that is green being reflected, and all the others are being absorbed.
If the object you are viewing is white, the surface reflects all of the light from the visible spectrum and absorbs none; therefore, you will see white. If white reflects all of the light, it must also reflect the energy, and the surface would appear cool to the touch.

Black

Black is the opposite of white in that none of the light in the visible spectrum is reflected; instead, all of the light is absorbed, and we then see black because nothing is reflected that we can see. If black absorbs all the light, it must absorb all the energy, and the surface would appear hot to the touch.

Grey

Grey describes the colours ranging from black to white, known as achromatic or neutral colours. Below is the standard greyscale.

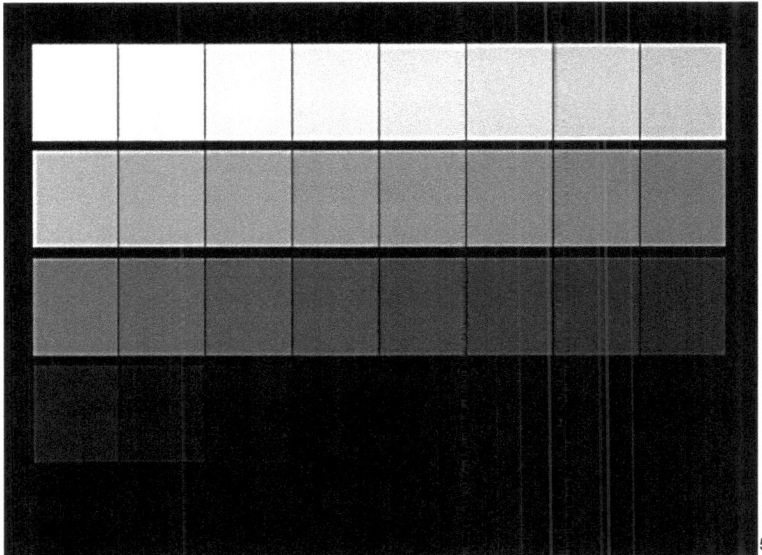

Tints, Shades, and Tones

The terms tints, shades and tones can often be misused and lead to much discussion. In general:

1. If a colour is made **lighter** by adding **white**, the result is called a **tint**
2. If a colour is made **darker** by adding **black**, the result is called a **shade**
3. If **grey** is added to a colour, the result is called a **tone**.

The arguments arise when the question is asked: "so is black and white a colour, shade, tone or tint?"

If white reflects all colours in the spectrum and is a combination of all colours, it is argued that white is, therefore, a colour.

On the other hand, black absorbs all the colours in the spectrum and, therefore, emits no colour and logically cannot be called a colour but a shade.

Grey would have to be a colour (white) with black (shade) added until there is no colour (white) left, but only the shade (black).

---

5 Black and White Digital Photography, 2010, Greyscale viewed 20 June 2013, http://www.blackandwhitedigital.com/Theory/grayscale.html

Infrared Light

As we know, the visible spectrum of light is from red to violet. The light outside this spectrum cannot be seen with the human eye.

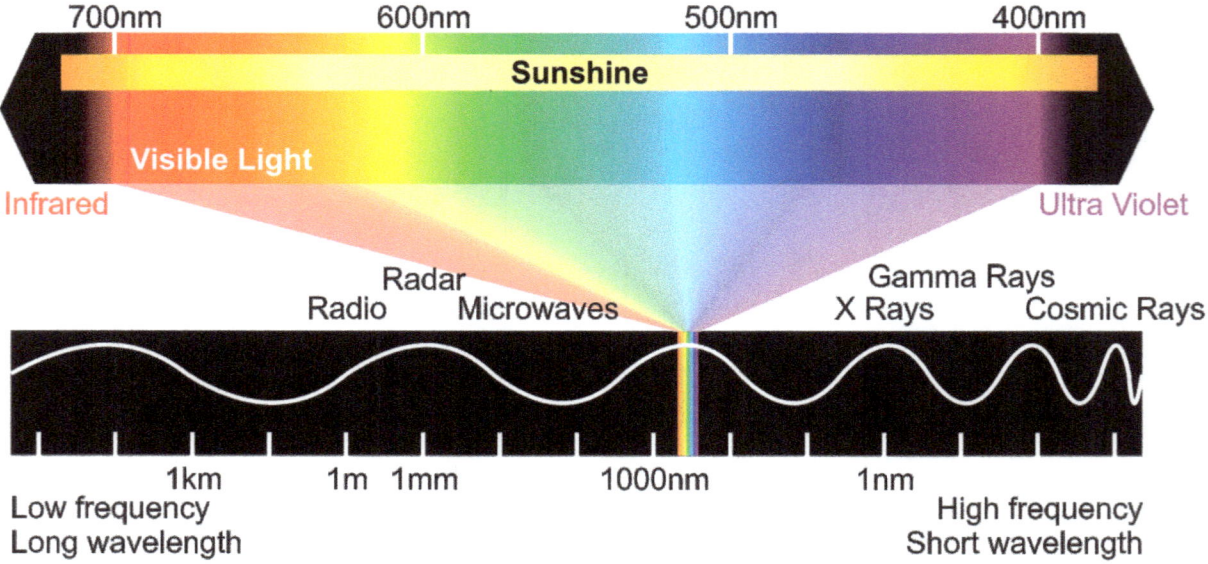

Figure 9 The Visible Spectrum available to the human eye

The term *"infra"* is Latin, meaning **"below"**. Red is the colour of the longest wavelength of visible light. Infrared light has a wavelength longer (lower frequency) than red light, which is visible to humans and hence the term infrared, which literally means ***"below red"***.

So infrared is a wavelength within the light spectrum that is just below our ability to see with the human eye, but it is a good wavelength to utilise technology to detect and, therefore, see artificially.

Technologies Using Infrared Radiation

Because infrared radiation generates both heat and a light wave, differing technologies may be used to capture either one of these for differing results.

In aviation, the two most common uses for infrared radiation are:

- Thermal Imaging
- Night Vision Devices.

Atoms, Energy and Heat

Atoms are constantly in motion, but they can be at differing states of excitation; in other words, they can have differing energies. If we apply energy to an atom, it will leave its "ground state energy level" and move to an excited level. The level of excitation will depend on the amount of energy applied in the form of light, heat or electricity.

Obviously, the atom will try to return to its ground state energy level and, in doing so, will release a photon (light energy). This photon will have a particular wavelength (colour) that will be dependent on the state of the electron energy within the atom when the photon is released.

Anything using energy, whether a living animal, a car, a helicopter, or an electric eggbeater, will generate heat that will cause atoms to release photons in the infrared spectrum.

The hotter the object, the shorter the wavelength of the photon released. Once an object starts to get really hot, it may even begin to emit wavelengths in the visible spectrum where it will begin to glow red, then orange, then yellow, blue and eventually white.

Night Vision Goggles *for Helicopter Pilots*

An example of this could be the common element on the cooking stove.

> **Example of heat-emitting light**
>
> As you turn on a stove element, electricity is supplied to it, and it starts to get warm. You do not see it at first (although if you were touching it, you would feel it getting warm), but you do not yet see any discernible change.
>
> As the atoms get more excited, you will start to see a faint red glow which intensifies to be a bright red glow and possibly even up to yellow. Stove elements are then limited to that level of excitation. To go further would probably melt the stove, but what you have witnessed is atoms being excited and emitting infrared radiation. When you turn the element off, it will return to its ground state and start cooling down again, and it will stop glowing.
>
> **A cold element** – dark colour, cold to the touch. No visible light
>
> **Warming** – still a dark colour, but will feel warm to the touch. Still no visible light.
>
>
>
>
> The element is **getting hotter** – starting to glow red, too hot to touch without burning your hand—visible red light.
>
> **Getting hotter still** – starting to glow orange as it gets hotter. If it got any hotter, it would melt. It becomes brighter as there is more visible light.
>
>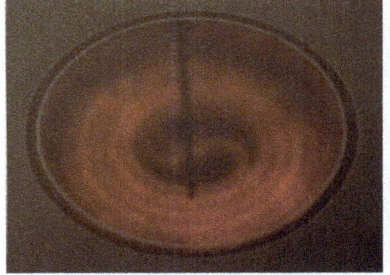
>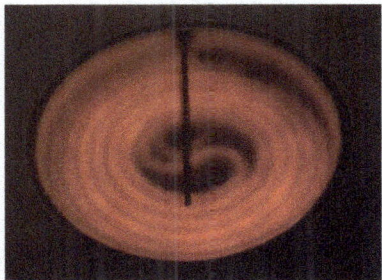

Thermal Imaging

Thermal imaging does not require any ambient light; instead, it operates on the principle that all objects emit infrared energy as a function of their temperature. The hotter an object, the more infrared radiation it will emit.

The thermal imager device collects all this information and electronically creates an image from the "heat" signatures it receives as infrared (IF) radiation and displays this on a viewing screen.

Thermal imaging is usually displayed in black and white (greyscale), with very cold objects being black and hot objects being white with various shades of grey in between. Because it is an electronically created image, the viewer can choose to reverse this so that the cold objects can be white and the hot objects can be black. Whichever way the thermal imager is orientated is referred to as "Hot". So, if white was representing a hot image, the operator would call it "White Hot". Alternatively, if black represented a hot image, the operator would call it "Black Hot".

A colour thermal imager artificially adds colour based on the heat signature to give a more representative image to the viewer. This is done by internal circuitry. Depending on the device, the colours used to represent temperature may be pre-set by the manufacturers or selected by user.

Figure 10 White hot display

Figure 11 Black hot display

Figure 12 Ironbow colour display

Another benefit of thermal imagers is that they can see through clouds, dust, smoke and haze, which is an excellent advantage for aviation use.

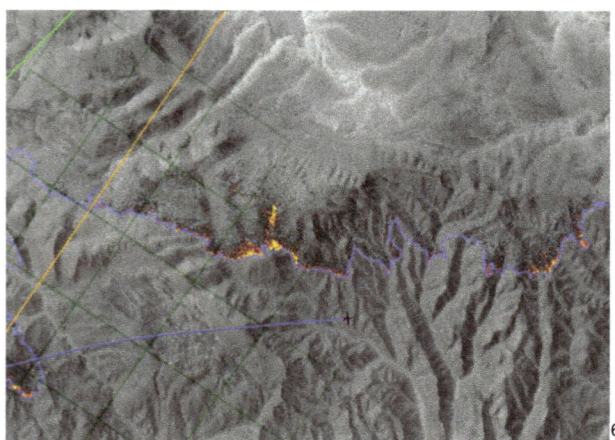

In aviation, a thermal imager installation is known as a **F**orward-**L**ooking **I**nfra**r**ed device or a FLIR. They are usually large, expensive units installed in the aircraft and using aircraft generated electrical power. The image is displayed on a remote screen for pilot and crew use. Following are examples of Thermal Imager Installations:

Figure 13 Side-mounted FLIR on a Eurocopter AS350 [8]

Figure 14 Aircrew screen [9]

6 Incaendiumavis, 2012, viewed 16 February 2022, https://commons.wikimedia.org/wiki/File:RAB_wallowV9_TIIMclip_16x9.png [Creative Commons 3]

7 Thermal-infrared imaging sensors on NASA's Ikhana unmanned research aircraft recorded this image in the San Bernardino Mountains of Southern California, viewed 16 February 2022, https://commons.wikimedia.org/wiki/File:Thermal-infrared_imaging_sensors_on_NASA%27s_Ikhana_unmanned_research_aircraft_recorded_this_image_in_the_San_Bernardino_Mountains_of_Southern_California.jpg

8 Lambert, Arnaud (2012), viewed 16 February 2022, https://en.wikipedia.org/wiki/File:FLIR_mont%C3%A9_sur_Eurocopter_AS350_%C3%89cureuil_AS-555_Fennec_de_l%27Arm%C3%A9e_de_l%27Air.jpg [Creative Commons 3]

9 FLIR used during search and rescue, https://commons.wikimedia.org/wiki/File:FLIR_used_during_search_and_rescue_operation.jpg [public domain]

Night Vision Goggles *for Helicopter Pilots*

Night Vision Devices (NVDs)

Night Vision Devices (NVDs) ***do*** require ambient light. They ***do not*** recognise heat. A small intensifier tube installed in an NVD will amplify any available light in the infrared spectrum to a level that is useful to the user and project this onto a viewing screen.

In aviation, the NVD is usually made up of two separate intensifier tubes forming a binocular goggle and collectively called a set of Night Vision Goggles (NVGs). These can be small, portable, robust and very cost-effective. They are personalised units that are independently powered, worn individually by the user, and not physically installed as part of the aircraft.

NVGs in use

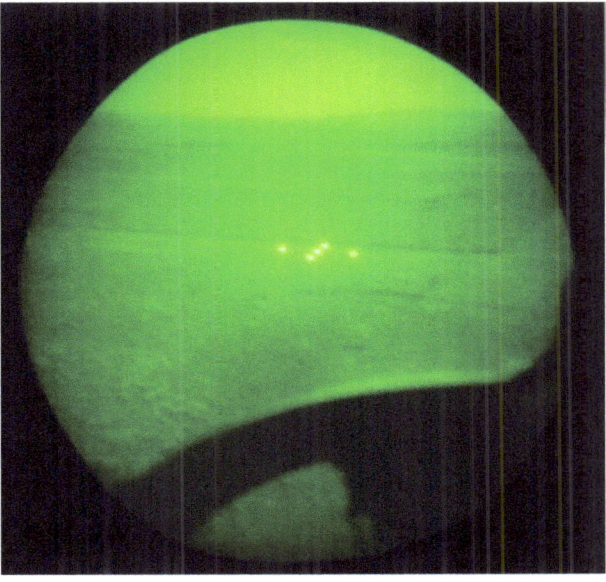

Light Terminology

To further discuss light devices in detail, we now need words and measurements that are universal and can be easily understood by everybody. Unfortunately, this has not always happened as various scientists in different countries have created their own words and units of measurement to try to understand and compare light based on their experiments.

The photometric system is based on the concept of radiated flux, where flux is defined as the total amount of radiation passing through a unit of area over a unit of time. Flux is measured in terms of its ability to stimulate the human eye.

Candlepower, watts and joules have been used to describe the **intensity** of a light source.

Foot-candles, Lumen, Lux, and Flux have been used to measure light that falls on a surface, commonly referred to as **illumination**.

Lux, foot-lamberts, and candelas have been used to measure the light that reflects off a surface, more commonly referred to as **luminance**.

Today's scientists working with NVGs have settled on the universal term **Lumen** as the standard term for light measurement.

Let's look at the history of some of these words and terms.

Candlepower

Candlepower measures the brightness of the light at its source.

The term candlepower (although no longer commonly used by scientists) was initially defined in England by the Metropolitan Gas Act of 1860. One candle power was equivalent to the light produced by a pure spermaceti candle weighing one-sixth of a pound and burning at 120 grains per hour. A grain is a measurement for mass and in the past was based on a typical cereal grain such as a barley seed. In the late 1800s, artificial light was primarily produced from whale fat and the spermaceti oil found in the head of a sperm whale was once used to make high-quality candles.

Foot-candle

Foot-candle is a standard unit of measurement based on the amount of light the spermaceti candle is giving one foot away.

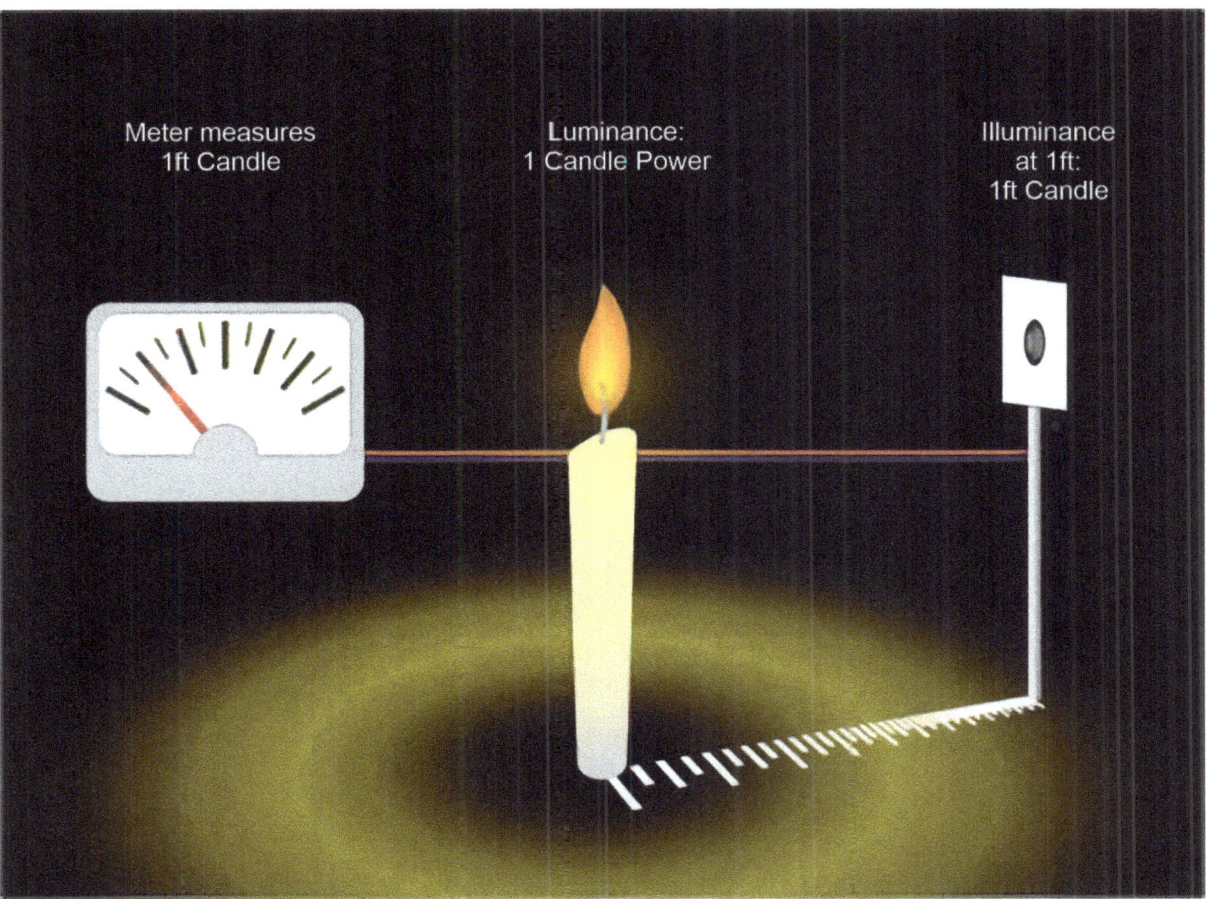

If you now have another light source, you can compare it to the spermaceti candle.

Example

You are given a lamp or a torch that produces 50 foot-candles. That means that at one foot from the lamp, the light is equivalent to 50 spermaceti candles burning. So the lamp would be said to be equivalent to 50 foot-candles.

One spermaceti candle emits light with a luminous intensity of approximately one candlepower.

So, if we are flying a helicopter with a night sun with a 1 million candlepower searchlight, it has the same power as 1 million spermaceti candles all burning simultaneously in the same spot.

Lumen or LUX

A lumen (also referred to as luminous power, or luminous flux, or a foot-lambert) is a measurement describing how much light is illuminating one square foot of area using one foot-candle.

LUX refers to the same methodology but uses metric units (metres) instead of imperial units (feet).

> **Example**
>
> You have one lit spermaceti candle placed one foot away from a wall. You then draw a 1 x 1-foot box on the wall. The amount of light within the box equals both one foot-candle and one lumen. If your box was 1 x 1 metres square, you would have 1 LUX.
>
> For a direct comparison, 10.76 Lumens equals 1 LUX.
>
> If you now get your 50 foot-candle torch and shine it at the same box on the wall, you would have 50 lumens or, based on the above formula, 538 LUX.
>
>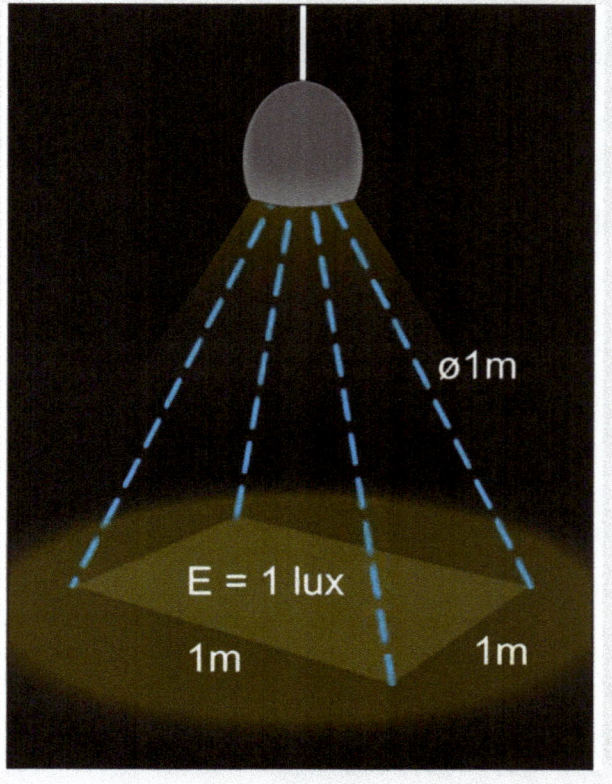

The term **Lumen** is now the universal standard measurement (and word) used by scientists when discussing and comparing the photocathodes in NVDs. Measuring how many Lumens are required to produce how much electricity (microamps) in an intensifier tube gives a microamps per lumen (uA/lm) measurement (more about that in detail later).

Night Vision Goggles *for Helicopter Pilots*

Newton's Inverse Square Law

Have you ever noticed that as you walk further away from a light source, it gets dimmer, and there seems to be less light? This is due to Isaac Newton's inverse square law, which states that:

"The intensity of the light
is related inversely to the square of
the distance from its source".

In other words, the intensity of the illumination will decrease as the light is positioned further away (or you walk further away from it).

Example

You have two rooms. One is 1 x 1-metre square, and the other is 2 x 2 metres square. Both rooms have a candle producing 1 LUX of light positioned in the middle of the room. The total amount of light striking the surface of the 1-meter wall would be the same amount of light striking the 2-meter wall, **BUT** the intensity or the density of light measured in LUXs on the 1 x 1 square meter room walls would be 4 times that of the LUXs measured on the 2 x 2-meter square room walls.

In simple terms, the light photons striking the 1 x 1-metre wall would be four (4) times as dense or thick or close together compared to the photons on the 2 x 2-metre wall that have the same amount of light spread over a greater area.

Radiance

Radiance is a word used to describe how much energy is released from a light source. The rule is that the greater the radiance, the brighter the light source.

Example
You walk into a dark room and turn on the light. If you are looking at the light bulb, you see the amount of radiance it is producing. You are not necessarily interested in how well it is lighting the room! A low wattage (the amount of electricity flowing through it) light bulb will be less bright and have less radiance than a high wattage light bulb that will be brighter and have a greater radiance. 

Illuminance

Illuminance is a word used to describe the result of light from a source **onto an object**.

Example
When you walk into a dark room and turn on the light, the room is illuminated. You see the effects of the light in the room.
Illuminance is the intensity or degree to which something is illuminated. Below we have images of the same room experiencing differing amounts of illumination.  

---

[10] Solid State Lighting, 2009, online image, viewed 11 November 2011, http://solidstatelighting.files.wordpress.com/2009/03/

Luminance

Luminance is a word used to describe the amount of light *leaving a surface* in a particular direction and can be thought of as the measured brightness of a surface as seen by the eye.

Example

You look at two walls. One is painted black, and one is painted white. Next, you turn on a light 50 feet away from them. Which wall will be easier to see? Which wall will reflect the most light? The white one because it has a better luminance compared to the black wall. We often refer to this as reflected light.

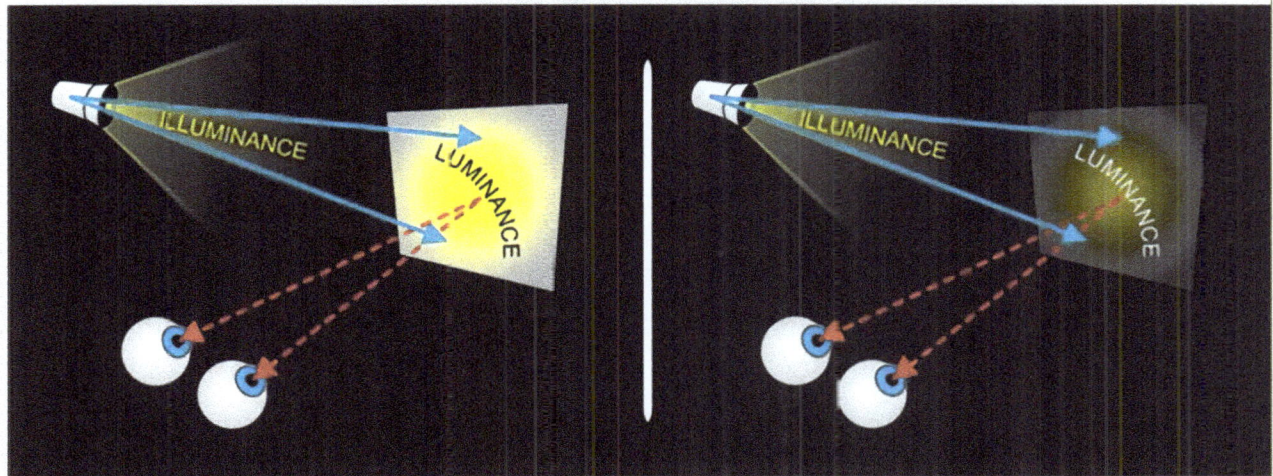

White sand at night will have a better luminance than dark green trees. An area of water may have better luminance when compared to grass, etc.

Example

Different surfaces can have different luminance - this is referred to as albedo (more about that later). The images below show Illustrated below are two rooms with exactly the same lighting (illuminance), but a different floor surface and thus have different luminance.

Example

The most obvious object that has luminance when viewed from the earth is the moon. The moon is *illuminated* by the sun, but because the moon's greyish surface has good *luminance*, it can redirect the sun's light onto the earth and thereby providing *illumination* at night to the earth.

Summary of Light Terminology

Candlepower	Candlepower is a rating of **light output at the source**, using English measurements based on a spermaceti candle.
Foot-candle	Foot-candle is a measurement of the **amount of light at a distance of 1 foot from a light source**.
Lumen	Lumen is how much **light is measured over a 1-foot square area at 1 foot from the light source**. A **Lumen** is the standard measurement in comparing **NVD photocathodes**.
LUX	LUX is how much **light is measured over a 1-metre square area at 1 metre from the light source**.
Radiance	**Radiance** is how **bright** the light is.
Illuminance	Illuminance is the **effect the light source has on an object**.
Luminance	Luminance refers to **the object's ability to reflect light**.

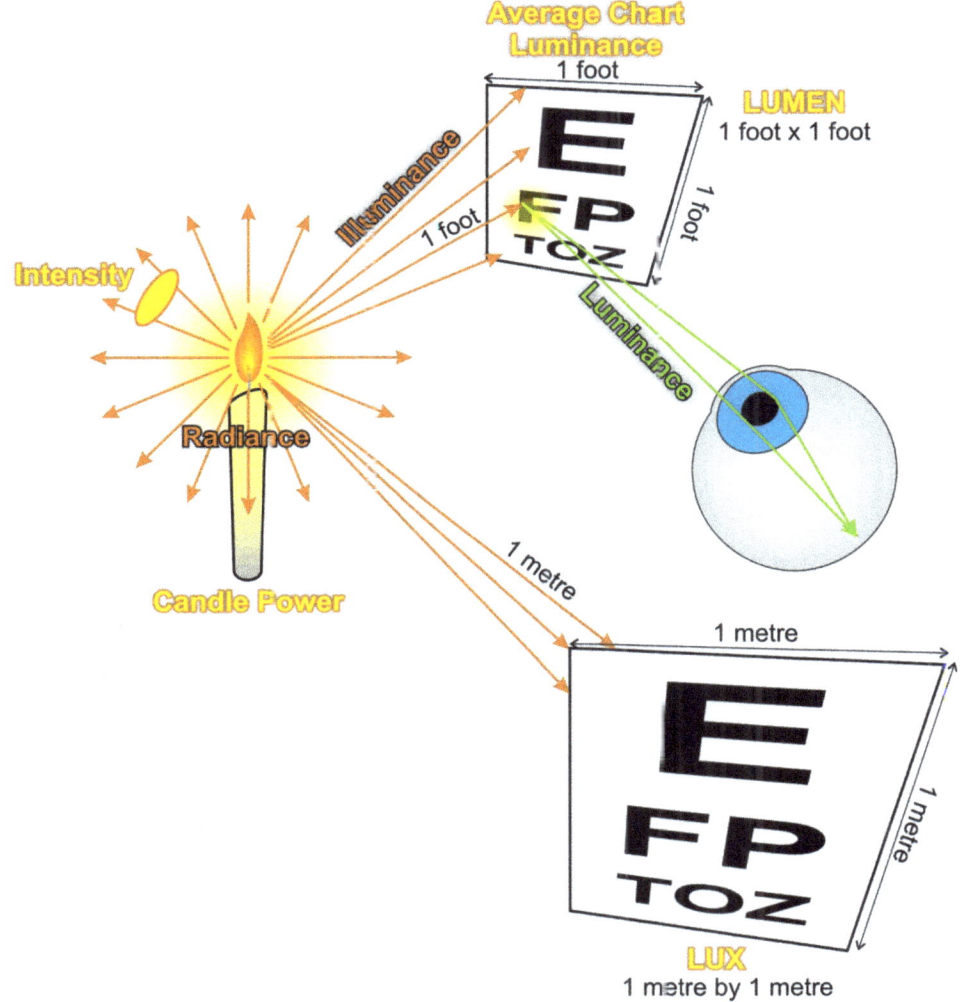

What is a Laser

*L*ight *A*mplification by *S*timulated *E*mission of *R*adiation or **LASER** is an artificial means of creating a concentrated beam of light. A LASER is not found in nature.

Normal light, as we know, is made up of many different wavelengths or colours of light that make up our visual spectrum and if we combine all of these wavelengths, we get white light.

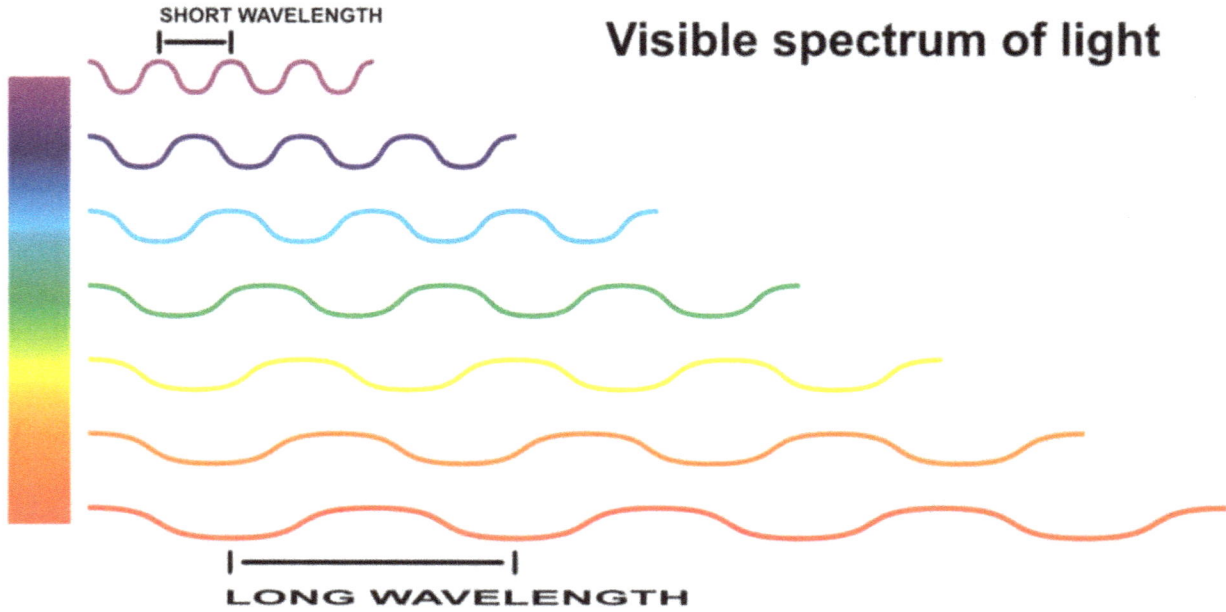

Because white light is made up of 7 differing wavelengths, each wavelength will go in its own direction and have a different effect on objects which is why we have colour.

Laser light has three distinct properties that differentiate it from white light. First, it contains only one wavelength or colour; therefore, lasers are **monochromatic** (meaning one colour). Secondly, all wavelengths making up the one colour are in phase. They are all moving together, referred to as being **coherent**. Thirdly, unlike normal white light that spreads out from its source, the waves emitted from a laser light will all travel in the same direction, exactly parallel. This means laser light can be a very narrow and concentrated beam of light. This is referred to as being **collimated**.

Figure 15 White light torch [11]

Figure 16 Laser pointer [12]

---

11 Air fans (2019), online image, viewed 16 February 2022, https://commons.wikimedia.org/wiki/File:Torcia_a_batterie_3B.jpg [Creative Commons 4.0]

12 Lasers- Risks & Benefits (8169993658) viewed 16 February 2022, https://commons.wikimedia.org/wiki/File:Lasers-_Risks_%26_Benefits_(8169993658).jpg [public domain]

Night Vision Goggles *for Helicopter Pilots*

Lasers are commonly used as pointers, rangefinders, designators, dazzers, or designated weaponry and can threaten night operations because they can interfere with the NVD and damage the eye. To be protected from a laser, proper training in using lasers around NVDs is required. Additionally, a filter may be fitted to the objective (outer) lens to protect the tube, or the user may wear special glasses, or technology within the intensifier tube may be installed to counter and guard against malicious use of the laser..

Laser Classification System

As an aviator, you should have some knowledge of lasers and the advantages and, more importantly, the dangers they can impose on a person wearing NVGs.

Lasers have been divided into various classes based on wavelength, power output and their related ability to produce damage when exposed to a person. Class 1 Lasers produce no hazard during normal use. Class 4 Lasers can cause a severe hazard for the eyes and skin.

Each class of laser is defined by the acceptable Accessible Emission Limit (AEL), which is a maximum power (in watts) or energy (in joules) that can be emitted by a laser within a specified wavelength range and over a stated exposure time, before damage to eyes or skin will occur. It is the manufacturer's responsibility to provide the correct classification of a laser and equip the laser with the appropriate warning labels and safety measures.

Laser Class Levels and Hazards

There are currently two laser classification systems; one is managed by the FDA (Food and Drug Administration) of the United States, and the other is the International Standard (European based), referred to as IEC60825. Unfortunately, the two systems are not entirely harmonious, but either is acceptable, and both will clearly state the Class of a particular laser.

Table 1 Laser class levels and hazards [13]

Class FDA	Class IEC	Laser Product Hazard	Product Examples
I	1, 1M	Considered non-hazardous. Hazard increases if viewed with optical aids, including magnifiers, binoculars, or telescopes.	■ laser printers ■ CD players ■ DVD players
IIa, II	2, 2M	Hazard increases when viewed directly for long periods of time. Hazard increases if viewed with optical aids.	■ bar code scanners
IIIa	3R	Depending on power and beam area, it can be momentarily hazardous when directly viewed or staring directly at the beam with an unaided eye. Risk of injury increases when viewed with optical aids.	■ laser pointers
IIIb	3B	Immediate skin hazard from direct beam and immediate eye hazard when viewed directly.	■ laser light show projectors ■ industrial lasers ■ research lasers
IV	4	Immediate skin and eye hazards from exposure to either the direct or reflected beam; may also present a fire hazard.	■ laser light show projectors ■ industrial lasers ■ research lasers ■ medical device lasers for eye surgery or skin treatments

---

13 US Food & Drug Administration (2021), viewed 16 February 2022 https://www.fda.gov/radiation-emitting-products/home-business-and-entertaiNMent-products/laser-products-and-instruments

Laser Warning and Classification Labels

Below are examples of laser warning and classification labels: [14]

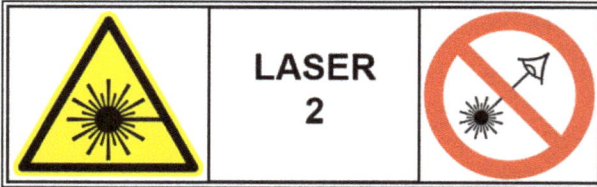

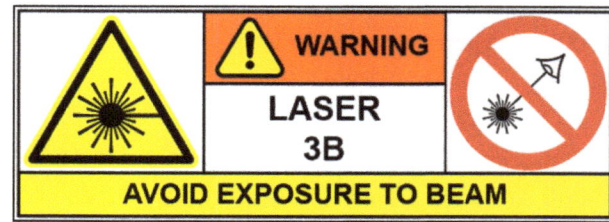

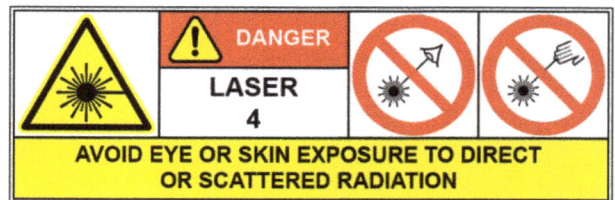

Laser Type and Wavelength

There is an increasingly diverse range of lasers and uses for lasers. The following table describes some commonly used laser types, including their spectrum and wavelength.

Laser Type	Spectrum	Wavelength (nm)
Argon fluoride	UV	193
Krypton fluoride	UV	248
Xenon chloride	UV	308
Nitrogen	UV	337
Argon	Blue Green	488 514
Helium neon	Green	543
Helium neon	Red	633
Rhodamine 6G dye	(Red / Orange / Yellow)	570-650 (tuneable)
Ruby ($CrAlO_3$)	Red	694
Nd:Yag	Near IR	1,064
Carbon dioxide	FAR IR	10,600

---

14 Queensland Health (2020), viewed 16 February 2022, https://www.health.qld.gov.au/system-governance/licences/radiation-licensing/legislation/laser-ipl-labels/laser

Components of the NVG

The information contained in this chapter is based primarily on the type of NVG that is used and available at Becker Helicopters. We do not intend to promote any one brand of NVG over another.

Through our experience working in a civil environment (outside of the Military), we have found there are political and government restrictions or some of the NVG equipment. This is particularly relevant to equipment originating from the United States (US) with ITAR (International Trade in Arms Restrictions) managed through the US State Department. Although the technology is no longer new or cutting edge, there are still historical security issues to consider and manage.

Throughout this chapter, we will focus primarily on the NL-94-AU NVGs that do not originate out of the US, but will also refer to the ITT F4949 NVGs that originate out of the US.

Components

The night vision goggles (NVGs) for aviators is made up of several components, including:

- the binocular housing
- the battery pack
- the mounting system, and most importantly
- the intensifier tube.

There are currently multiple NVG manufacturers and models from around the world. Countries like Russia and China make their own and are typically unavailable to western countries. European and US manufactured NVGs are what we currently use in the west, with the two most common examples of Night Vision Goggles used in Australia being the:

- NL-94-AU supplied by Point Trading, and
- ITT F4949 supplied by ITT.

Both are shown below, attached to helmets.

Figure 17 NL-94-AU on a Gallet Helmet

Figure 18 ITT F4949 on an Alpha Helmet

Figure 19 The NL-94-AU NVG system (unattached)

Binocular Housings

Unlike regular binoculars that magnify an image to bring it closer to the viewer, the NVG binocular housing does not provide any image magnification, referred to as a 1x1 magnification.

Instead, they are constructed to house the image intensifier tube and allow for the attachment of the:

- objective lens, and
- the eyepiece, which houses the dioptric lens.

Night vision devices can come in many shapes and sizes. Below are three common configurations.

Monocular NVG

1 x Objective lens to 1 x Eyepiece

This configuration has one eyepiece, one intensifier tube and one objective lens. Only one eye will use this configuration at a time.

Biocular NVG

1 x Objective lens to 2 x Eyepiece

This configuration has two eyepieces, but through mirrors, they both see information from only one intensifier tube and one objective lens. Both eyes will be able to view the same image.

Binocular NVG (Aviation Standard)

2 x Eyepiece to 2 x Objective lens

This configuration has two eyepieces, two intensifier tubes and two objective lenses. Each eye will see an independent image from two separate systems.

Night Vision Goggles *for Helicopter Pilots*

Aviation night vision goggles currently in use only come in a standard binocular configuration. There is current research and experimentation with multiple tubes and colours, but these are not approved and not available.

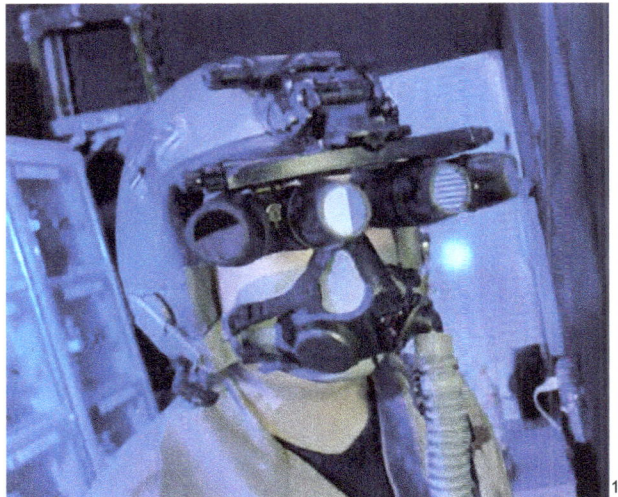

Lenses

Within the NVG, there are two primary sets of lenses; they are the:

- objective lens (front of the goggle), and
- the dioptric lens (closest to the eye).

A lens is a transparent (can see through it) piece of glass, crystal or plastic with at least one curved surface. Interestingly, the word lens comes from the Latin word for "Lentil", a type of seed used in cooking.

We can only assume that the most common form of lens, the "convex lens", physically looks like a lentil seed and hence the name.

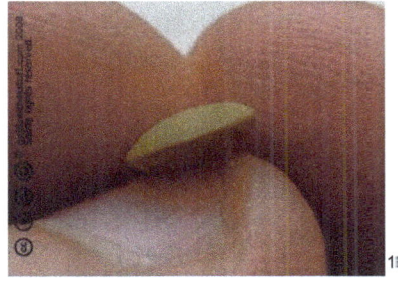

A lens works by refraction; it bends light as it passes through the lens, changing its direction. An image viewed through a lens appears to be bigger (closer) or smaller (further away).

There are two basic types of lenses; they are the:

- Convex lens, and
- Concave lens.

---

15 Salimbeti.com, online image, viewed 23 July 2013, www.salimbeti.com/aviation/helmets7.htm

16 Explain That Stuff.com, online image, viewed 11 November 2011, www.explainthatstuff.com/lenses.html

Convex Lens

A convex lens, sometimes called a positive lens, has a curved surface that bulges outwards in the centre. When light passes through a convex lens, it makes the parallel rays of light passing through it bend (refract) inwards to converge and meet at a single point just beyond the lens. We call this the focal point.

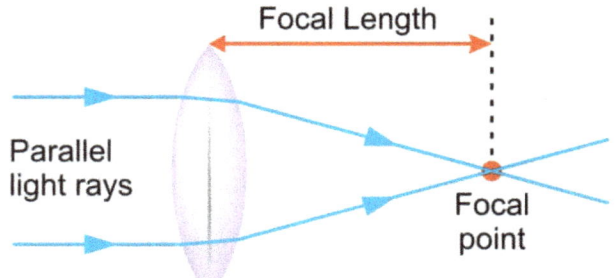

Refraction by convex Lens

Convex lenses are commonly used in telescopes, microscopes, and binoculars and bring images closer.

The distance from the centre of the lens to the focal point is known as the lens's focal length and is a measurement of the power of the lens; the longer or bigger the focal length, the more powerful the lens.

Focal length is described in standard units of measurement such as centimetres, millimetres, or inches.

In special optical devices, it can be measured in units called diopters. The diopter measurement of a lens is the reciprocal of the focal length in meters that is one divided by the focal length.

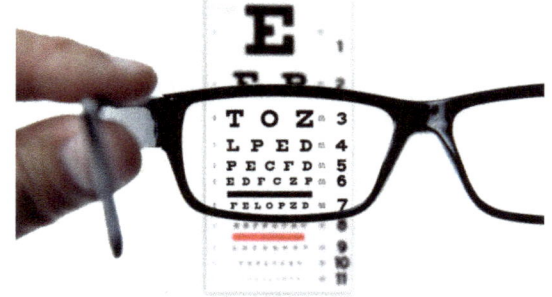

For example:
1 divided by 1 meter = 1 diopter.
1 divided by 0.5 of a meter = 2 diopters.
1 divided by 0.33 meters = 3 diopters
and so on.

If you wear glasses and go to an optician for your prescription, they will typically state the strength of the corrective lenses you need in diopters.

Convex Lens Image Inversion

A key characteristic of an image viewed through a convex lens is that it will invert the image 180 degrees.

Convex Lens

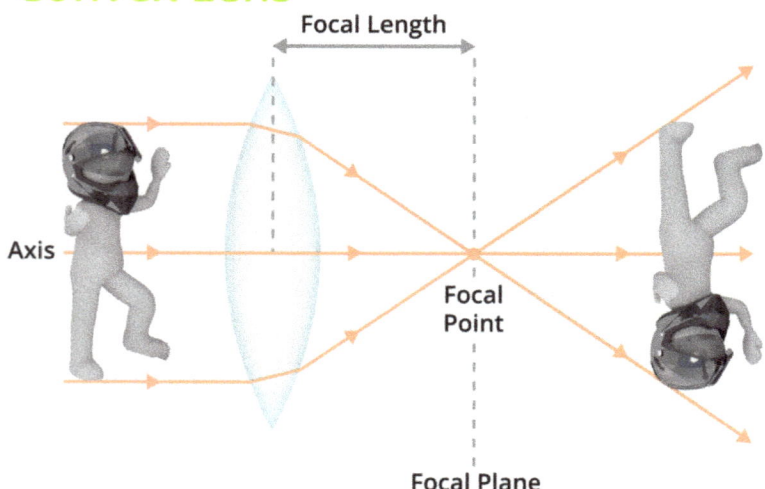

As the light reaches the focal plane, it will cross over and be viewed out the other side as an inverted image.

Night Vision Goggles *for Helicopter Pilots*

In NVGs, all images reaching the photocathode are inverted through the objective lens, which will require correction before it reaches the eye of the viewer. This can be done by using another lens in the eyepiece, or more advanced technology using fibre-optic inverters will do the same job more efficiently with fewer errors.

It is a misnomer (un-truth) that all images will be inverted if viewed through any lens as some lenses (concave and planar) allow light to travel straight through or enlarge the image with no inversion. Glasses or spectacles don't enlarge or invert; they simply correct focus.

Concave Lens

A concave lens, sometimes called a diverging lens, has outer surfaces that bend in towards the middle. When light passes through a concave lens, it makes the parallel rays of light passing through it bend (refract) outwards so that they diverge away from the centre of the lens.

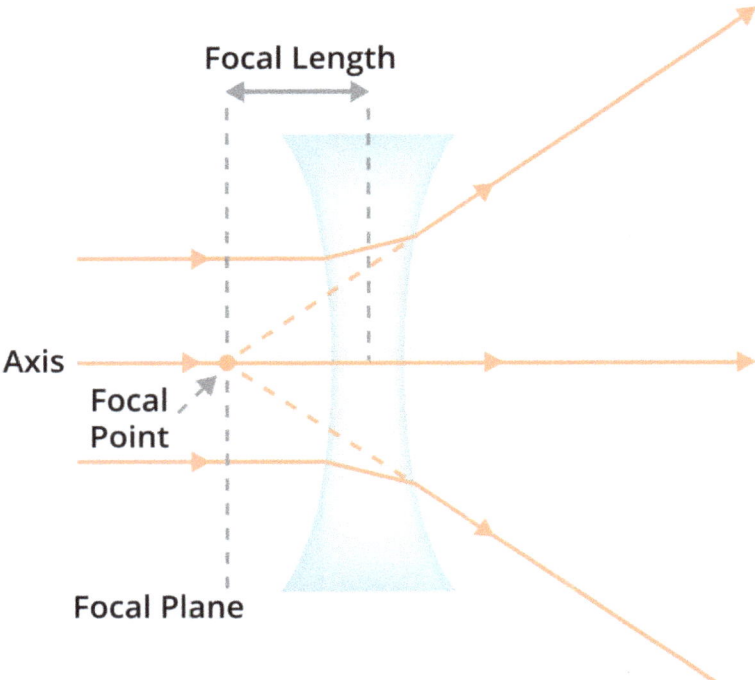

Concave lenses are commonly used in projector screens to spread the image over a distance and make the image seem bigger than it is.

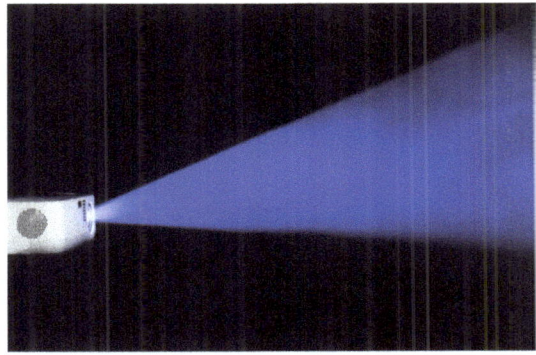

Planar Lens

A planar lens does not have any curvature; it is a flat surface. When light passes through a planar lens, it allows the parallel rays of light passing through it to go straight through without bending; however, these lenses are often used as filters, so their surface may be coated, which will affect the light differently. Usually, filters will stop some light, filtering out the undesired wavelengths.

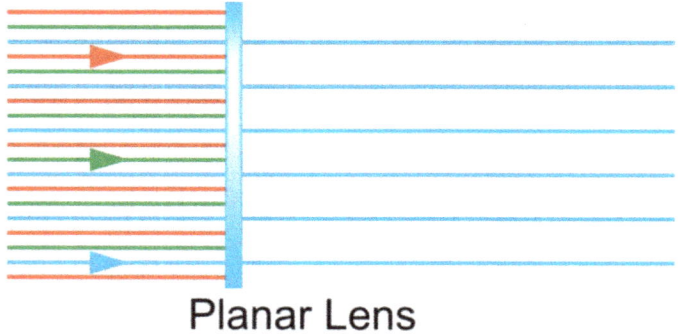

Planar Lens

Compound Lens

A compound lens is when two or more simpler lenses (convex, concave or planar) are combined to form a new lens. This allows the manufacturer to refract light in more complex ways so that images may be manipulated from their source to the medium we want to view it. Below is an example of various lens shapes and their names.

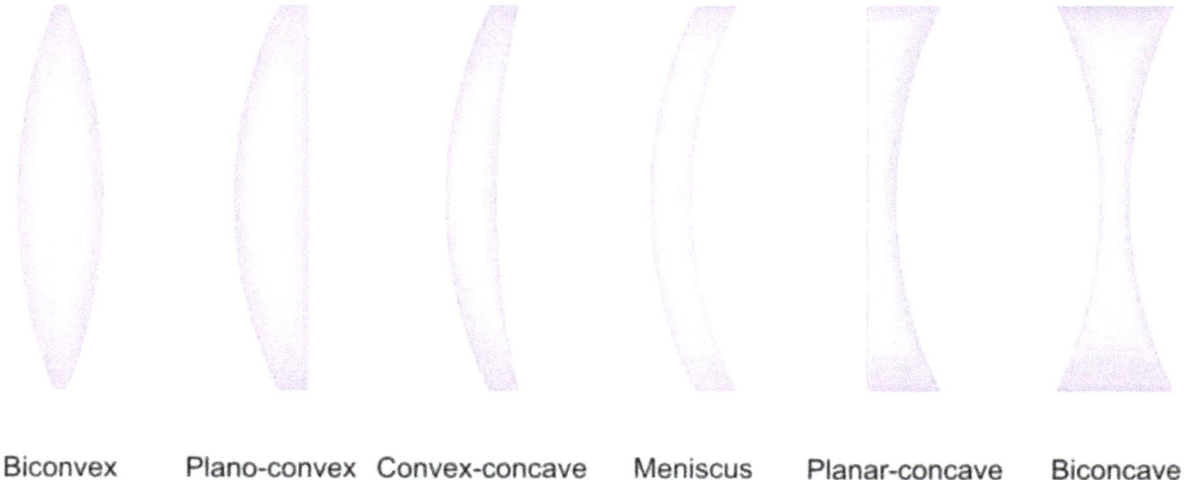

Biconvex   Plano-convex   Convex-concave   Meniscus   Planar-concave   Biconcave

NVG Objective Focal Adjustment

Light (photons) will first arrive at the objective lens at the front of the NVG. This is a convex optical glass lens that focuses the incoming photons onto the photocathode of an intensifier tube.

The user can **adjust the objective lens by turning the focus ring** (objective focal adjustment) clockwise or anticlockwise within a limited range of movement to get the best focal adjustment for the distance of the object.

When using aviation NVG, we always focus to infinity because we are more interested in viewing what is outside the cockpit rather than what is inside the cockpit.

This can be done by using:

- a Hoffmann 20/20 Focus Box,
- a Focus lane using a USAF 1951 calibration chart, or
- by simply looking through the NVG and focusing on an object greater than 150 feet (45 meters) away.

It is possible to focus the NVG for close work, such as viewing the cockpit instruments, but this is not practical or necessary as we can view the instruments without the aid of the NVG by looking under the goggles when we need to.

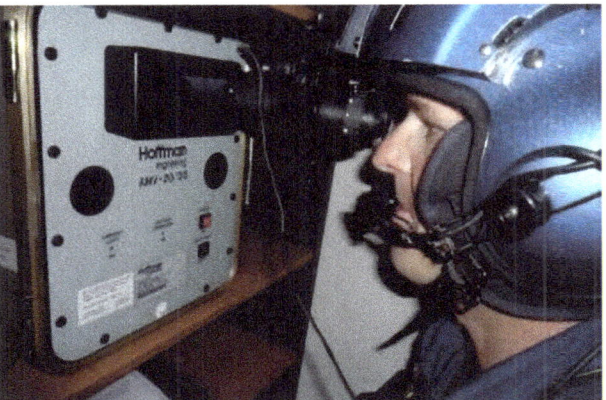

Figure 20 Hoffmann 20/20 focus box

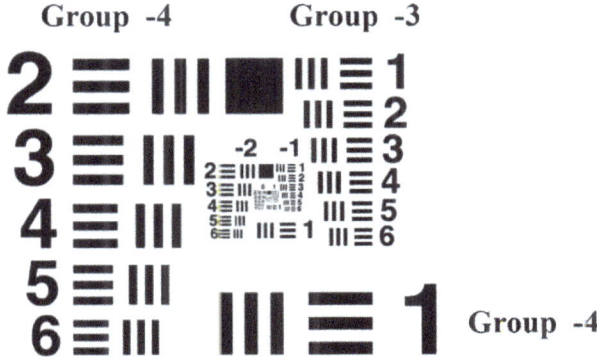

Figure 21 USAF 1951 calibration chart

Note: Any distance that you focus on over 33m away is officially classified as infinity.

NVG Filters

Depending on the type of cockpit lighting installed in the aircraft, and depending on the type of image intensifier tube installed in the binocular housing, it may be necessary to have a filter placed in front of the objective lens to filter out specific light waves that are not compatible to the intensifier tube.

Filters can be a piece of glass or a thin film or coating attached to or moulded into the objective lens. It can even be an electromagnetic filter created as electricity flows through a conductive material such as used in the Ion Barrier filter (explained later).

Filters are an advantage as they protect the intensifier tube and allow them to do their job when being used in a cockpit that may have light sources that could affect the performance of the NVG. However, they are a disadvantage because they will now reduce the number of photons (amount of light) that can pass through the objective lens to the photocathode. This will reduce the number of electrons that enter the microchannel plate (MCP) and, therefore, reduce the intensity of the image seen by the pilot. It is better not to have a filter and, instead, modify the cockpit lighting to match the NVG.

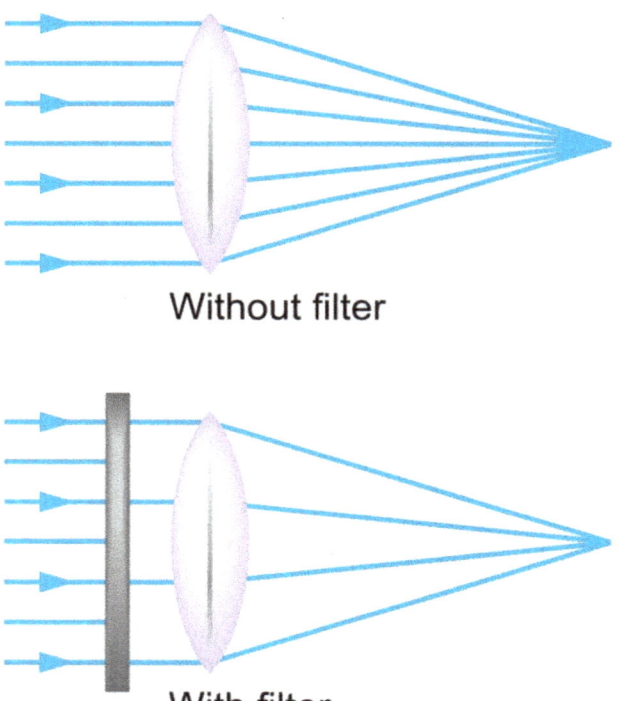

Light Intensity Filter (LIF)

A Light Intensity Filter (LIF) is an optical filter attached to the outside of the objective lens designed to protect NVGs from laser damage. If someone shines a laser into the NVGs, then the intensity of the laser may damage the intensifier tube and, in turn, damage your eye. If a LIF is fitted, it will filter out the damaging laser light. However, it will also reduce the number of good photons passing through the objective lens and onto the MCP. The LIF, therefore, can reduce the overall efficiency (gain) of the NVGs. All US manufactured NVGs supplied from OMNIBUS III onwards have LIF protection. European NVGs with autogating technology do not have LIF protection because it is unnecessary as the autogating feature provides the protection.

Figure 22 Green Laser Dazzler [17]

Figure 22 is an example of a green laser dazzler. Without LIF protection, these dazzlers can cause serious injury and even blindness if viewed through an NVD.

Class A and B Cockpits

It is important that cockpit lighting is compatible with (and does not interfere with) NVG use. Currently, two types of cockpit lighting are used to configure an aircraft for NVG use. They are:

- NVIS Green A, and
- NVIS Green B

These two configurations are more commonly called Class A or Class B cockpit lighting and are used for all primary and secondary lighting components, including radios, instruments, warning and caution lights, map lights, etc.

Because the lighting of individual radios, instruments, warning and caution lights etc., within the cockpit can be different, this can lead to conflicting incandescent lamps or LEDs (light-emitting diodes) interfering with the NVG. This is because they may be individually emitting significant infrared light, which can cause conflicts with NVG functionality within the cockpit. This can best be seen when the goggles experience a bloom (a halo-like glow around the instruments and warning lights), create ghosting images (infrared reflections from the cockpit surfaces, especially onto the windows), or the loss of goggle sensitivity due to activation of the automatic gain control due to higher levels of infrared (more about these later).

Below is an image as seen through a set of night vision goggles. Both images are of the same cockpit using the same NVGs, but the image on the left has the standard lighting supplied by the aircraft manufacturer, and the image on the right uses the modified NVG lighting installed aftermarket.

Figure 23 Non-filtered lighting

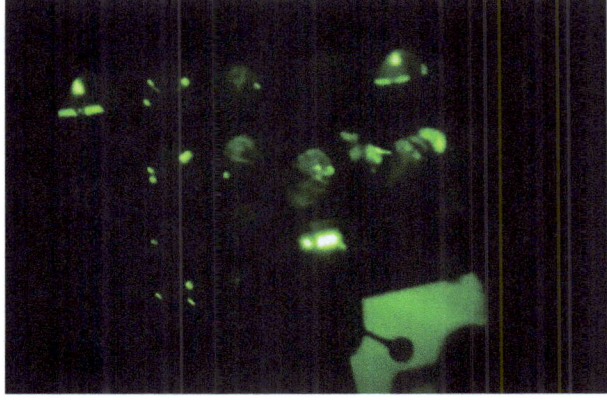

Figure 24 Modified and/or Filtered lighting

---

17 Armorcorpus.com, online image, viewed 11 November 2011, armorcorpus.com/1214518899.jpg

Class A and B Filters

Class A cockpits require a minus blue filter that will reduce 50% of the light wavelengths in the 625 nm spectrum, and Class B cockpits require a minus blue filter that reduces 50% of the light wavelengths in the 650 nm spectrum.

In real terms, Class B filters allow less of the visual red spectrum to pass through the objective lens, which means that Class B NVGs are compatible with red and orange cockpit lighting, whereas NVGs with Class A filters cannot be used with red and orange cockpit lighting.

Modified Class B Filters

There is also a Modified Class B filter. This filter incorporates a "notch" (a small beak in the allowable light) filter in the green spectrum that allows a small percentage of light into the image intensification process. This allows modified Class B filtered NVG operators to view fixed Heads Up Display (HUD) symbology through the NVG without the HUD light energy adversely affecting NVG performance.

Current NVG Requirements

Current US manufactured NVGs require a "minus blue" filter as part of their standard configuration. Fortunately, there are several different NVG manufacturers, so not all NVGs suffer from this problem. However, because ITT (US manufactured) goggles are seen as the industry standard, other goggle manufacturers (Europe manufactured) have been forced to place these minus blue filters on their objective lenses by the Civil Aviation Authorities in various countries, even though they are not required.

With the NL-94-AU, you will find the letter **B** stamped on the outer ring of the objective lens. This indicates that it has a minus blue filter coating on the objective lens. If there is no letter **B** on the outer ring, the NVG does not have a minus blue filter.

In reality, NVGs should be independently evaluated based on their overall performance within a specific cockpit configuration of lighting and, where possible, filters should be avoided.

NVG Eyepiece and Dioptric Focus Lens

Some of us wear glasses (corrective lenses), and others do not. Each of us may have varying focal lengths to which our eye is naturally attuned.

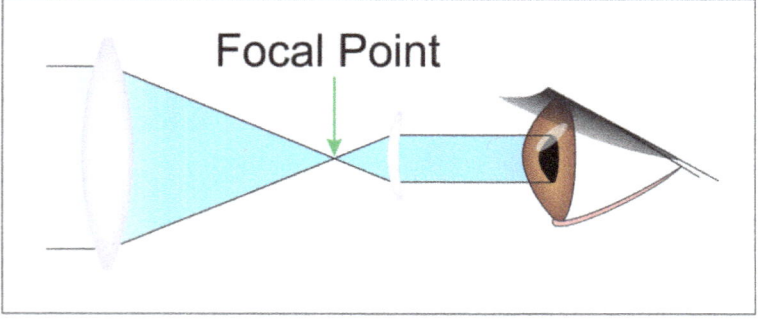

Night Vision Goggles *for Helicopter Pilots*

The eyepiece is the housing unit for the dioptric focus lens, which allows the user to adjust the optical eyepiece to accommodate each individual's optic variation. Most aviation NVG systems provide a +2 to -6 diopter range.

The eyepiece is located closest to the eye and has a small ring that can be rotated clockwise or anticlockwise, allowing the image to come into sharp focus and allowing for any variation between users.

You may have heard the terms long-sighted and short-sighted. A short-sighted person can focus on objects that are close but not objects that are a distance away. A long-sighted person can focus on objects that are a distance away but not close objects.

If the dioptric lens is focused correctly and you are short-sighted, you will not have to wear glasses to see through the NVG as the dioptric setting will adjust for your short-sightedness. If you usually wear glasses to see close images because you are long-sighted, you may have to focus the NVG with your glasses on so that you can still view the instruments from under the goggles through your glasses.

If you suffer from other vision problems such as astigmatism, etc., you will have to experiment with the combination of NVGs and glasses for your particular case.

Intensifier Tube

The intensifier tube is the powerhouse of the NVG; it is why it works.

It has undergone several evolutions of technological advancement (generational and performance changes) and is the primary device in converting very low visible light (such as at night) and infrared radiation into an image that we can see.

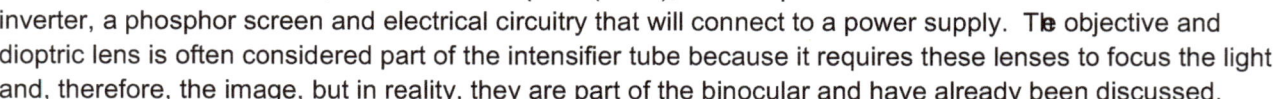

The image intensifier tube comprises a photocathode, a vacuum chamber, an ion barrier film, a microchannel plate (MCP), a fibre optic inverter, a phosphor screen and electrical circuitry that will connect to a power supply. The objective and dioptric lens is often considered part of the intensifier tube because it requires these lenses to focus the light and, therefore, the image, but in reality, they are part of the binocular and have already been discussed.

Depending on the manufacturer's design, the intensifier may have some or all of these components.

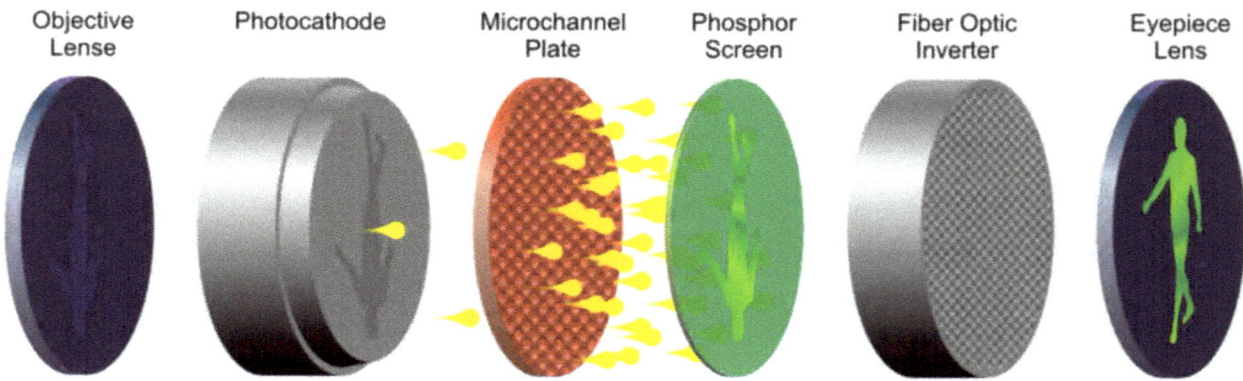

The intensifier tube is a charged device converting photons into electrons and then back into photons again. To do this, it is essential that one side of the intensifier tube is negatively charged and the other is positively charged to ensure the electrons move in a constant direction. Before moving on to each component, it is important to understand what the term "gain" means.

Gain

The role of the intensifier tube is to amplify the light from the small amount entering it into a brighter image exiting it. The difference between what light goes into the tube and what comes out after going through the intensifier tube is called **"gain"** (also called brightness gain or luminance gain). The word gain is used because it refers to how much light is **gained** by using the intensifier tube.

There are two gain measurements used in NVDs: Tube Gain and System Gain.

Tube Gain

Tube gain is measured as the light output divided by the light input. It does not consider the light having to go through filters or lenses; instead, it is a pure measurement of the effectiveness of a particular intensifier tube and is usually seen in values of tens of thousands.

Be careful when reading specification sheets for various tubes, as they sometimes do not use the same calculation to get the result.

In its purest sense, a tube gain calculation should represent the following:

- Light input in lumens x (photosensitivity – ion barrier loss) x MCP amplification x (± phosphor screen) x (± fibre optic inverter) = light output seen by the viewer
- Light output divided by light input equals tube gain

System Gain

System gain is measured as the light output divided by the light input, and it takes into account the light having to go through filters and lenses etc.; it is a comparison of light going in compared to what the user sees. In other words, it measures the gain of the entire optical system. System gain is usually seen in the thousands.

In any night vision device, the tube gain is reduced by the system's lenses and is affected by the quality of the optics or any filters; therefore, **system gain is a more accurate measurement of performance to the user**.

In its purest sense, a system gain calculation should represent the following:

Light input in lumens x (±filters) x (±objective lens) x (photosensitivity – ion barrier loss) x MCP amplification x (± phosphor screen) x (± fibre optic inverter) x (±dioptric lens) = light output seen by the viewer

Light output divided by light input equals system gain.

MTTF (Mean Time To Failure)

The Mean Time To Failure (MTTF) value, expressed in hours, gives an idea of how long a tube typically should last. It's a reasonably common comparison point that takes many factors into account. The first is that tubes are constantly degrading. This means that the tube will slowly produce less gain over time than when it was new. When the tube gain reaches 50% of its "new" gain level, the tube is considered to have failed, so primarily this reflects this point in a tube's life.

Additional considerations for the tube lifespan are the environment that the tube is being used in and the general level of illumination present in that environment, including bright moonlight and exposure to both artificial lighting and use during dusk/dawn periods, as exposure to brighter light reduces a tube's life significantly.

Also, an MTTF only includes operational hours. It is considered that turning a tube on or off does not contribute to reducing overall lifespan, so many civilians tend to turn their Night Vision equipment on only when they need to, to make the most of the tube's life. Military users tend to keep equipment on for longer periods of time, typically, the entire time while it is being used, with batteries being the primary concern, not tube life.

Typical examples of tube life are:

- First Generation: 1000 hrs
- Second Generation: 2000 to 2500 hrs
- Third Generation: 10,000 to 15,000 hrs.

Many recent high-end second-generation tubes now have MTTFs approaching 15,000 operational hours.

Photocathode

The photocathode is the light-sensitive input surface of a photomultiplier or image intensifier tube used in the NVG. It is made up of a clear window, usually made of glass or quartz, with a coating of a material or a combination of materials such as caesium, rubidium, potassium or gallium arsenide applied to the inside of the glass that is adjacent to the evacuated (vacuum) tube.

Light (photons) from the objective lens will strike the photocathode and be transformed into electrons out the other side. This is achieved by a process called collisional ionization.

To explain: You can probably remember from your High School chemistry or physics lessons that atoms consist of three subatomic particles: a nucleus consisting of positively charged protons and neutrally charged neutrons, and orbiting around this nucleus are negatively charged electrons.

Atoms are electrically neutral when the number of negatively charged electrons orbiting the nucleus equals the number of positively charged protons within the nucleus. When the number of electrons is greater than or less than the number of protons in the nucleus, atoms are not electrically neutral and carry a net negative or positive charge. They are then termed *ions* and are chemically reactive, tending to combine with other ions of the opposite net charge.

When a photon of light strikes a photocathode, an ionizing particle and a negative electron is released. The negative electron will then travel through the intensifier tube towards the positively charged anode (the phosphor screen) on the other side.

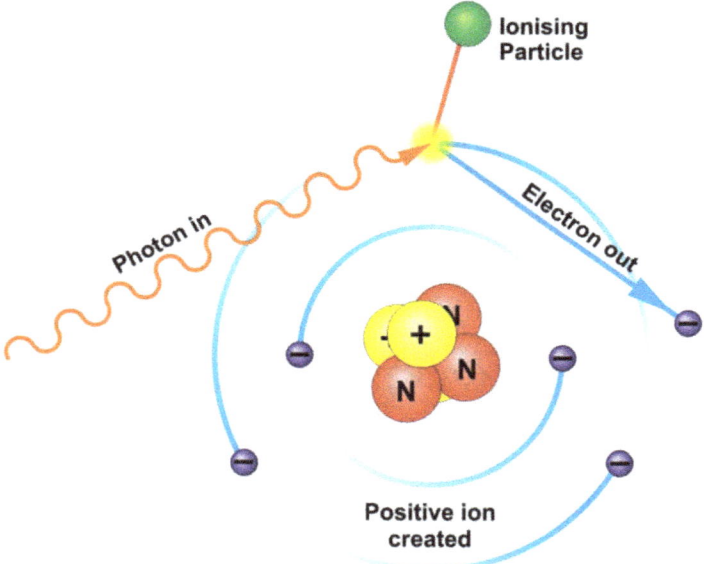

Night Vision Goggles *for Helicopter Pilots*

In early generation intensifier tubes, the photocathode was not very effective as the materials used were not highly photosensitive, resulting in most photons either being reflected off or passing straight through the photocathode without producing electrons. To remedy this, the photocathode was attached to a photomultiplier using 5000-volt bursts between oppositely charged electrodes, the photomultiplier would generate more electrons from the single-photon.

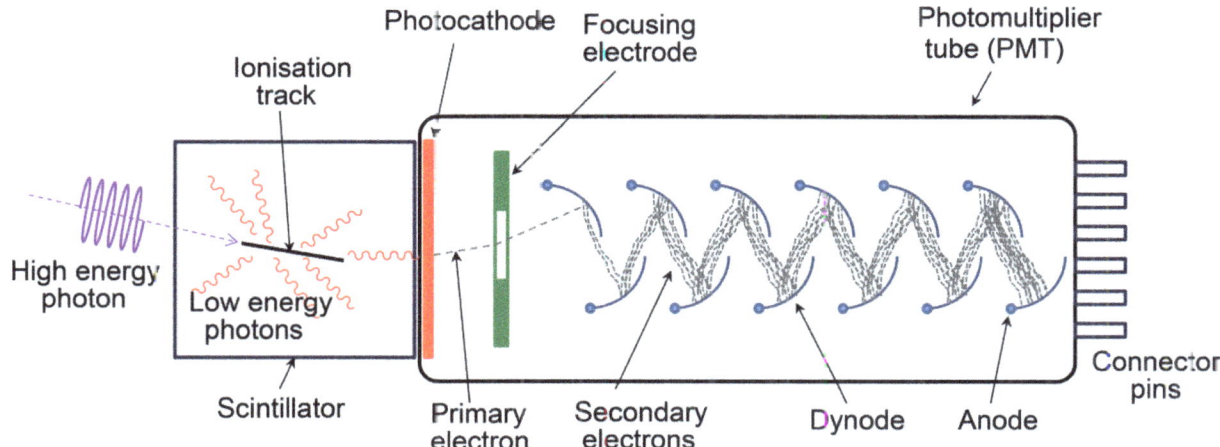

Figure 25 Diagram of photomultiplier [18]

The significant disadvantage was the acceleration of the electrons in the photomultiplier would result in the electrons being diverted from their linear path as they had to bounce around the various dynodes to generate more electrons resulting in the output image becoming distorted.

Geometric Distortion

Geometric distortion, commonly referred to as the "fisheye" effect, is inherent in all Generation I tubes but has been eliminated in Generation II and above, so it should not be an issue in NVGs used by pilots today. In pre-Generation II tubes, as the electrons are diverted from their linear path through the photomultiplier, the result is a very focused image in the middle and a fuzzy bending image towards the edges. There are two possible geometric distortions; the image could either bend out towards the edge, known as barrel distortion or bend in, known as pincushion distortion.

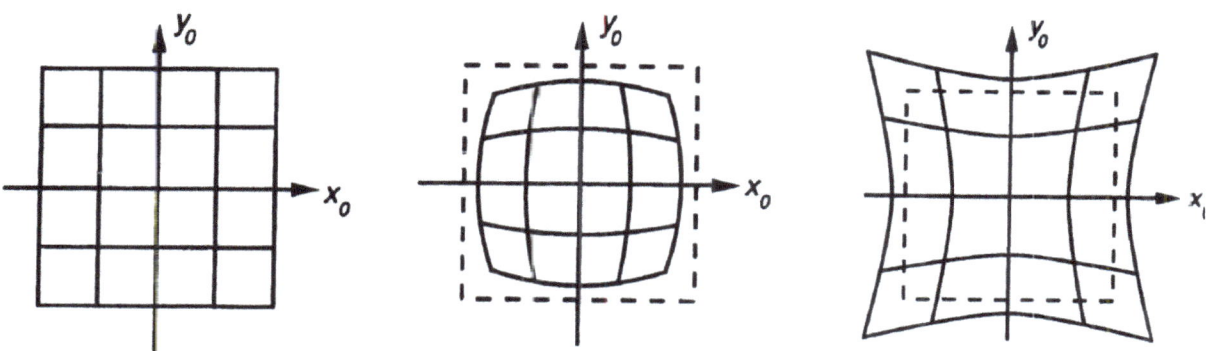

Figure 26 Perfect Image - No distortion   Figure 27 Bending out - barrel distortion   Figure 28 Bending in - Pincushion distortion

---

18 Qwerty123uiop (2013), Wikipedia.org, online image, Schematic of a photomultiplier tube coupled to a scintillator, https://en.wikipedia.org/wiki/Photomultiplier_tube#/media/File:PhotoMultiplierTubeAndScintillator.svg, viewed 22 February 2022

Below we are viewing the same set of straight window blinds, but the image on the left shows curved lines, with the image being very sharp in the centre but fuzzy towards the edges. This is a classic case of pincushion geometric distortion. The image on the right shows the same image using different generation NVGs, and in this case, there is no geometric distortion.

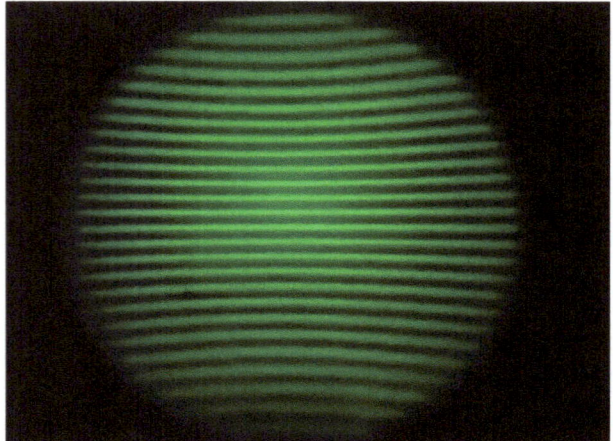

Figure 29 Generation I intensifier tube [19]

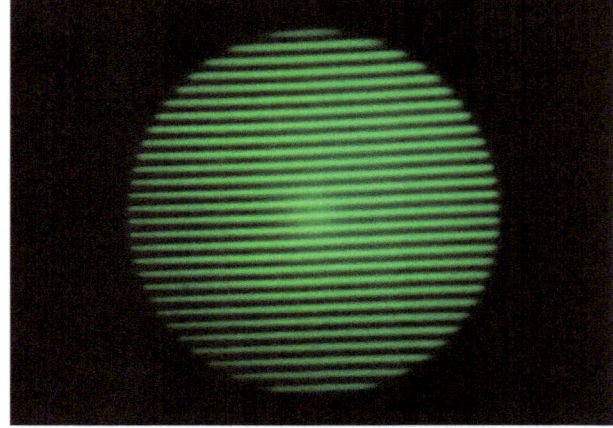

Figure 30 Generation III intensifier tube [20]

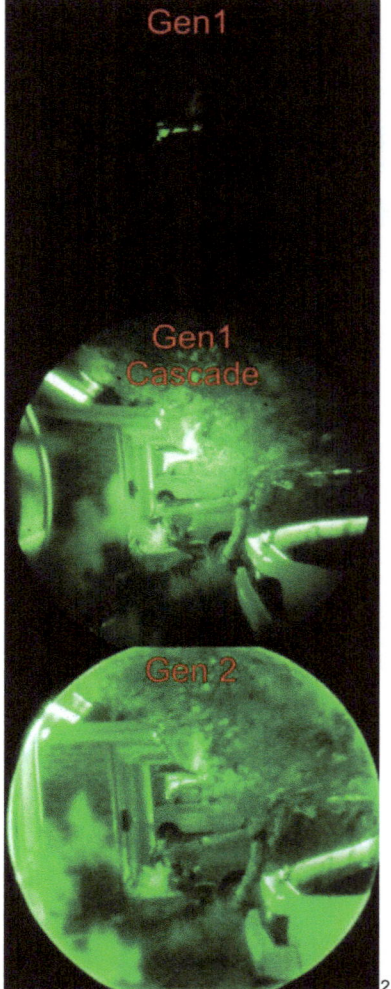

The image on the right shows an image using different generations of intensifier tube. The top image is a Generation I intensifier tube with no photomultiplier. The middle image clearly shows the geometric distortion as the image is intensified through the photomultiplier. The bottom image shows a clear image using a Generation II intensifier utilising an MCP instead of a photomultiplier.

In later generation tubes, the photomultiplier was limited in the number of dynodes the electrons passed through or removed and replaced with an MCP (more about that shortly) to increase the number of electrons. Another disadvantage of using electricity to generate more electrons was the heat generated and the ion particle by-products.

Making a Photocathode for NVG

For industrial purposes, a photocathode can be made of silicone, copper, gold or similar based material, but these will not allow visible light through; instead, they convert photons to an electrical current (electrons).

To make a photocathode for an NVD, you must first create a shaped piece of glass or quartz to use as a platform for the photocathode material. Then a wafer of photosensitive material is placed over the glass and heated until it melts and bonds with the glass. As it is cooling, it is placed in a press that firmly bonds the material to the glass; then, it is ground and polished to a finish.

The wafer of photosensitive material usually starts as a fine powder processed to form a solid sheet.

---

[19] Nightvisionforums.com, online image, viewed 11 November 2001, //www.nightvisionforums.com/phpBB3/viewtopic.php?f=1&t=1924&start=0

[20] Nightvisionforums.com, online image, viewed 11 November 2011, ://www.nightvisionforums.com/phpBB3/viewtopic.php?f=1&t=1924&start=0

[21] BlackIce.com.au, online image, viewed 11 November 2011, general.blackice.com.au/pics/newpics/cascade4/3way-compare.jpg

Photosensitivity

Photosensitivity is also referred to as photocathode sensitivity or photoresponse. Photosensitivity is the ability of the photocathode material to produce an electrical response when subjected to light (photons).

Microamp (also called a microampere) per lumen (uA/lm) are the units used to measure the photocathode's sensitivity. If you remember, a lumen relates to foot-candles and how much light a spermaceti candle produces within a one-foot radius, and a microamp is a millionth of an amp, so in its direct translation, uA/lm refers to the number of a millionth of an amp produced per lumen of light. It is a measurement that describes the number of electrons released by the photocathode. In general, the higher the value, the better the ability to produce more electrons and, therefore (in theory), a better image. However, even though the photocathode can be more efficient, to determine the quality of the viewer's output image, the entire system must be used and evaluated, as filters, ion barrier films, phosphor screens, mirrors, etc., all affect the resulting image.

Generational Change

As stated previously, the photocathode used in NVGs has gone through several generational and performance changes over the years. Some of these changes have been to do with the materials used to make the photocathode.

Early photocathodes were made of a silver-oxygen-cesium combination referred to as S1. This material has a photosensitivity of around 60 microamps per lumen (uA/lm) and a quantum efficiency (an accurate measurement of the material's electrical sensitivity to light) of 1% in the ultraviolet spectrum and 0.5% in the infrared spectrum. S1 photocathodes were used in Generation 0 NVG.

In 1956 the S20 photocathode, made with a sodium-potassium-antimony-cesium material, was discovered by accident but allowed photocathodes with a sensitivity of 150-200 uA/lm to be introduced into Generation I NVGs.

Generation II NVGs still used the same multi-alkali photocathodes as Generation I NVGs. However, using thicker layers of the same material allows the new S25 photocathode to have a sensitivity of 230 uA/lm and higher quantum efficiencies.

Generation III NVG introduced a new photosensitive material called gallium arsenide. This material increased the sensitivity to 800-900 uA/lm. Although the sensitivity of this material is high, a thin film of aluminium oxide (referred to as the ion barrier film) is required to protect the photocathode from the positive ions and gases produced by the MCP (a similar problem as the photomultiplier). This thin ion barrier film reduces the flow of electrons from moving through the remainder of the photocathode by up to 50%. This potentially reduces the efficiency that may have been gained by the new gallium arsenide photocathode by 50% and, therefore, reduces the real sensitivity output of the Generation III tube to 400-450 uA/lm. These are the photocathodes used in the ITT F4949 NVG.

Technology developed outside of the United States focused on further developing the Generation II tubes by improving the multi-alkali photocathodes to more than double their previous sensitivity while also improving the MCP technology, so there was no need to have the thin ion barrier film. This brought the sensitivity of these photocathodes to a genuine 700uA/lm and was called "Super Second Generation". These are the photocathodes used in the NL-94-AU NVG.

Note from the author: The uA/lm numbers given above are approximations only based on literature available when writing this book. Each manufacturer will have to state their intensifier tube's performance based on the technology used to manufacture their tube. What is important to note here is Super Generation II and Standard Generation III are almost identical in their output performance. In other words, the image seen by the viewer in either tube under the same conditions is practically identical.

Vacuum Chamber

All the image intensifier tube components are brought together into a laboratory and placed into an evacuation (vacuum) chamber. An evacuation chamber is a container with the entire atmosphere sucked out, so there are no air, dust or water particles. It is just like the atmosphere (or lack of it) you would experience in space, except it is artificially created in a laboratory.

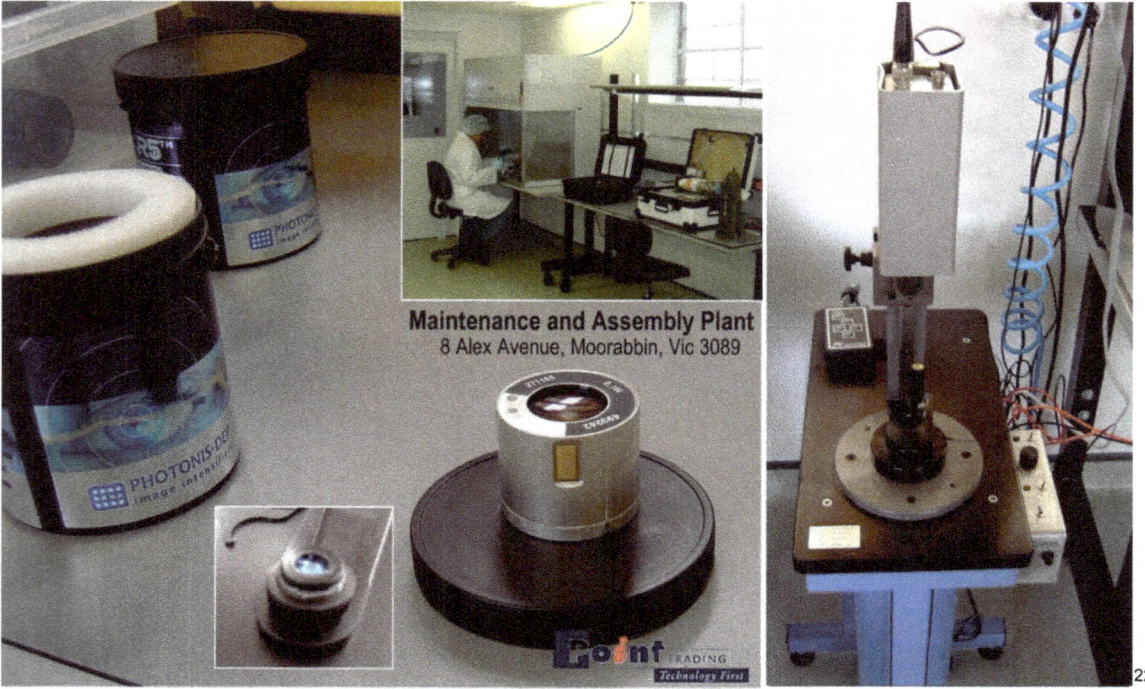

The intensifier tube must be assembled in an evacuated chamber so that once the electrons leave the photocathode and travel towards the MCP, they do not interact with any other atoms or particles that could divert their path, cause resistance, alter their state or slow them down. If an intensifier tube leaks, then its performance will drastically reduce.

Microchannel Plate

The microchannel plate (MCP) acts similarly to a photomultiplier in that it will multiply the number of electrons that enter it. For every electron that goes in, there will be 30,000 or more coming out (and technology is improving that number every year).

The big difference is the electrons in the MCP will not be diverted from their linear path as they bounce and multiply along each of the channels. This results in a clear, detailed output image for the viewer without distortion.

There are several different MCP designs depending on the manufacturers' requirements and desired outcome. In general, they can be described as consisting of a metal-coated glass disc with millions of tiny channels (tubes) that have an electrifying current that will allow the electrons to multiply each time they strike a channel wall (the NL-94-AU has 6 million channels).

An Assembly of MCPs can consist of single, double or triple plates. The number of MCPs adjacent to one another will depend on the application for which the MCP is required. For example, typical image intensifier tubes for low-level light used in NVG contain only a single MCP, whereas more advanced ion detectors have two or double MCPs, sometimes referred to as the Chevron or V-stack. A three-plate (also known as the Z-stack) MCP Detector is used to detect (count) and image single particles.

---

22 Point Trading Group, online image, viewed 11 November 2011, www.pointtrading.com/index.php?page=corporate-gallery

Night Vision Goggles *for Helicopter Pilots*

In Figure 31, you will note that the channels are not parallel with the incoming electron. Each channel is set at approximately a 5-degree angle to prevent the electron from going straight through without hitting the channel walls and which promotes the cascading (multiplying) effect of the electron each time they strike the walls.

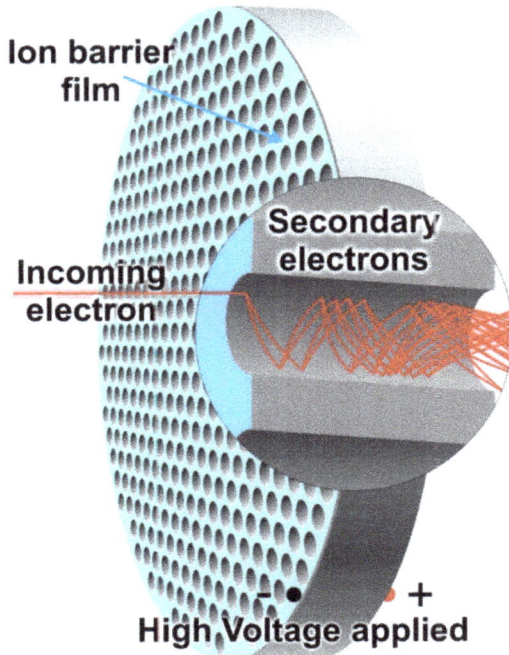

Figure 31 Microcannel plate illustration

Another MCP design currently used in some late generation NVGs is the parabolic or curved MCP. Curved microchannels improve the number of electrons produced (gain) while reducing the ion particle feedback to the photocathode. This allows the removal of the Ion Barrier film (with obvious advantages discussed later). The disadvantage was some distortion of the image, but because this distortion is known, technology, such as using a fibre optic inverter, can resolve the image seen by the end-user.

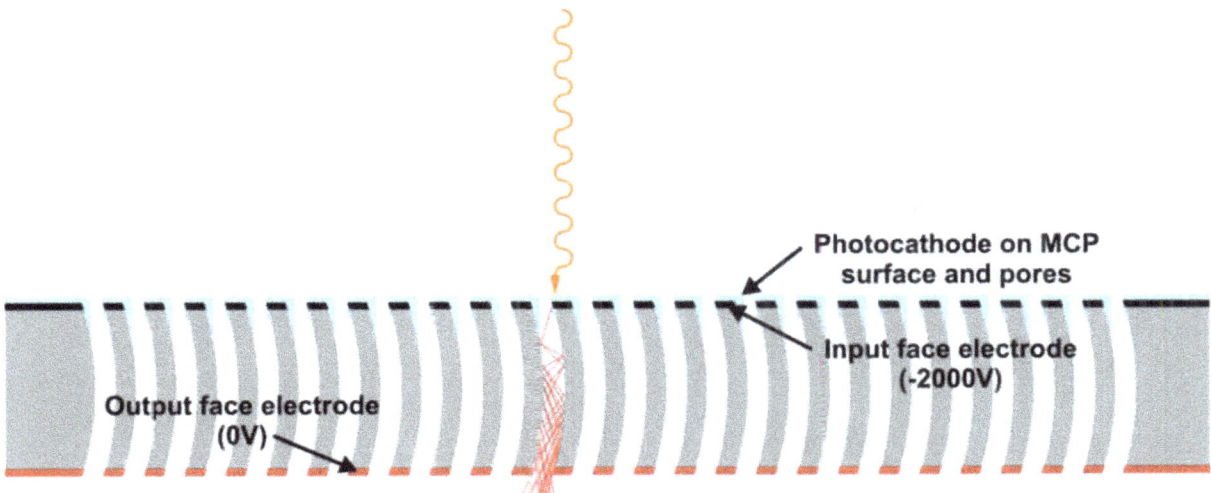

Figure 32 MCP with curved channels

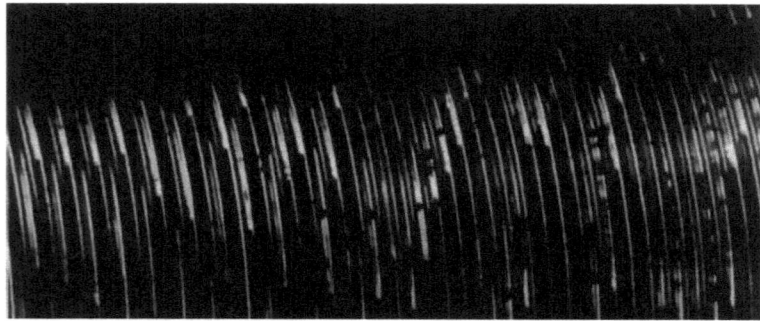

Figure 33 Cross-sectional magnified image of an MCP with curved channels

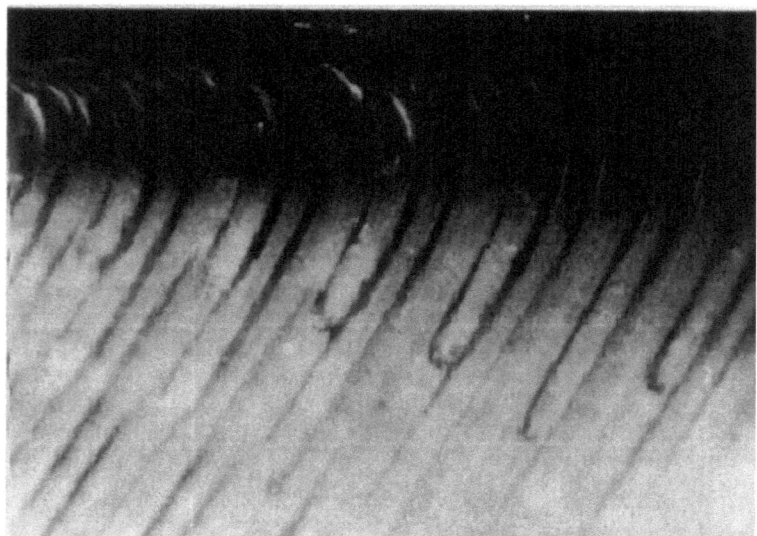

Figure 34 Cross-sectional magnified image of an MCP with "coma" shaped channels [23]

Currently, the NL-94-AU does not have an ion barrier film, but the ITT F4949 does. Filmless intensifier tubes out of the US are still restricted by the US Military and not available to civilian users outside the US.

---

[23] Boutot, JP, Eschard, G, Polaert, R, and Duchenois, V, A Microchannel Plate with Curved Channels: An Improvement in Gain, Relative Variance, and Ion Noise for Channel Plate Tubes, Laboratiroes d'Electronique et de Physique Appliquee, Paris, in Morgan, BL (ed.), Photo-Electronic Image Devices, e-book, Google Books, viewed 12 July 2013,
https://books.google.com.au/books/content?id=bG1xAj9w5TgC&pg=PA104&img=1&zoom=3&hl=en&sig=ACfU3U2h-G-PrlRBmxEc9WgCwFtHeXcR7Q&w=1280

Night Vision Goggles *for Helicopter Pilots*

Making a Microchannel Plate

To make an MCP, a thin hollow length (called a billet) of lead oxide is held in shape by inserting a rod of etchable (able to be carved) glass. This length of lead and glass is then pulled through a heated oven which produces a "first draw" fibre of approximately 1mm in diameter. These first draw fibres (which look like straws) are then stacked together in a hexagonally shaped container called a boule. The entire boule is then drawn through another vacuum sealed oven where all the first draw multi-fibres are fused together to form a length of multi-fibre hexagonal-shaped lead and glass referred to as the "second draw".

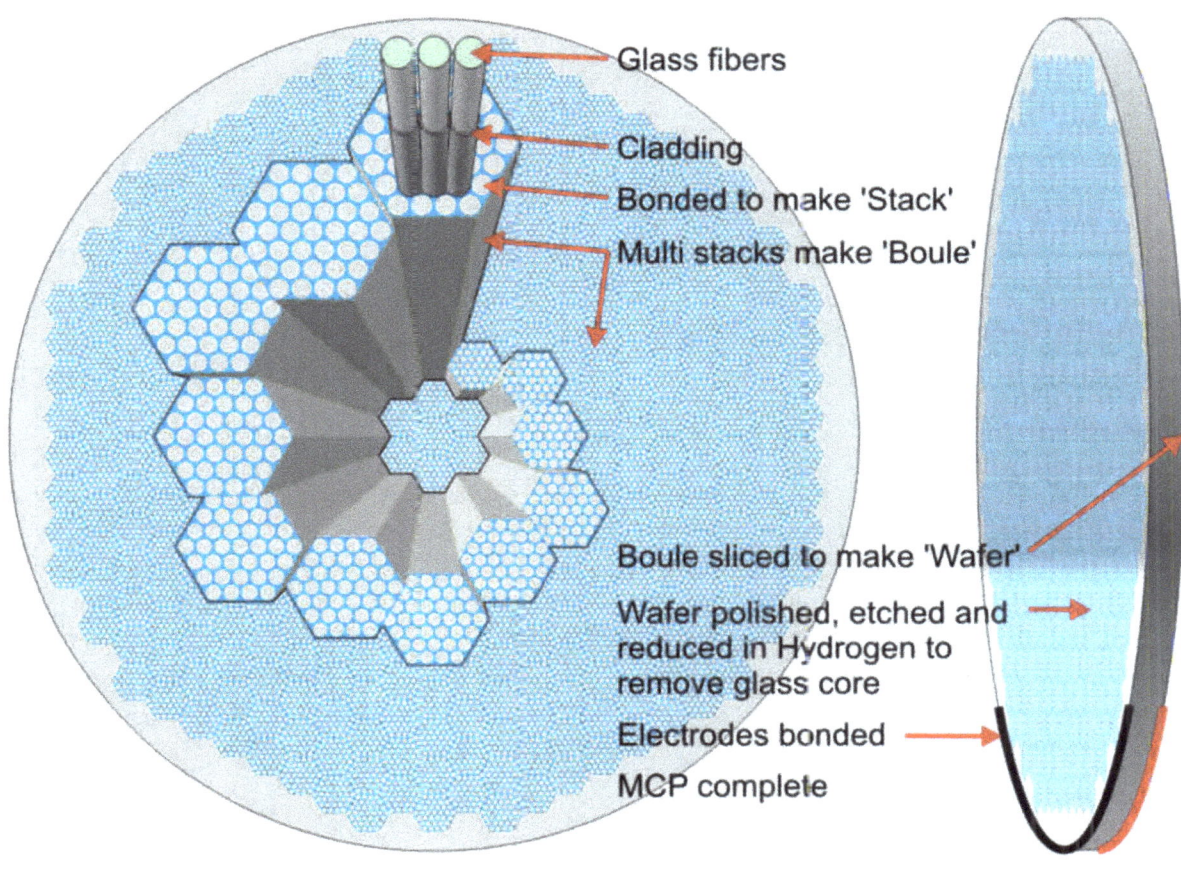

Once these small individual boules are formed, they are stacked together to create an even larger array of boules where an acid is used to etch (hollow or carve) out the glass.

Finally, the etched microchannel plate is then fired in a hydrogen oven to produce a semiconducting surface layer with the desired resistance and secondary electron yield and referred to as the "third draw". Once cooled, it is then sliced at an angle (a bit like slicing bread) into wafer-thin slices typically only 2mm thick, and each slice is then polished to the required thickness and shape.

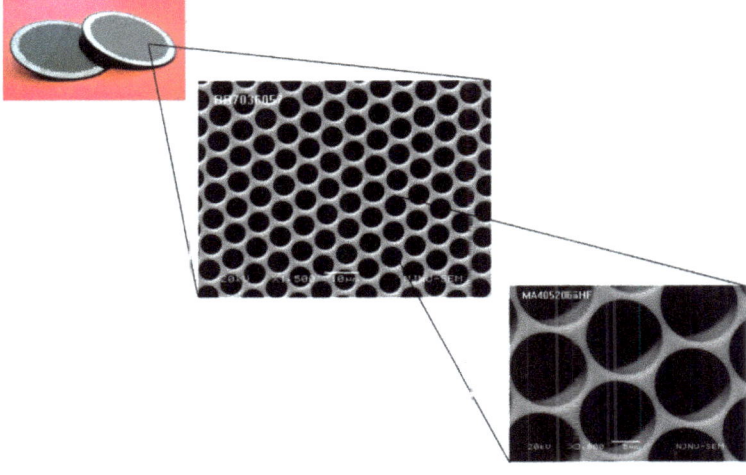

Getting the size and spacing of each channel is critical to have a clear, crisp image. The diameter of a human hair is approximately 60-80 microns (that is 0.060-0.080 mm); the diameter of a channel can be accurately manufactured down to 25 microns (0.025 mm). In Figure 35 (supplied by Photonis, the manufacturer of the intensifier tube in the NL-94-AU), the channels are 12.5 microns in diameter and spaced 15 microns apart.

Figure 35 MCP channels [24]

Ion Barrier Film

Historically, Philips Electronics Research laboratories in Redhill, England, first created the MCP technology. They also had a laboratory in Eindhoven in the Netherlands that experimented with and developed varying resistivities (varying voltage) to optimise plate performance in second-generation NVG intensifier tubes. Philips was bought out by Photonis almost 40 years ago and was an independent Company until 2005, when three major companies (Photonis, DEP and Burle) joined together.

MCPs are very difficult and expensive to manufacture, so the Europeans held on tightly to their patented technology. This saw a divergence in the NVG technologies as the Europeans, and the Americans (ITT) focused on differing technologies to obtain better night vision.

The Americans (ITT) advanced the photocathode to achieve high photosensitivity using gallium arsenide. The main disadvantage of this was the electrostatic fields established within the intensifier tube that would transport the negative electrons from the photocathode to the MCP also allowed positive ions present within the MCP to be transported back towards the photocathode. Since the gallium arsenide photocathode was producing a lot more electrons, there were more positive ions coming back, called ion particle feedback.

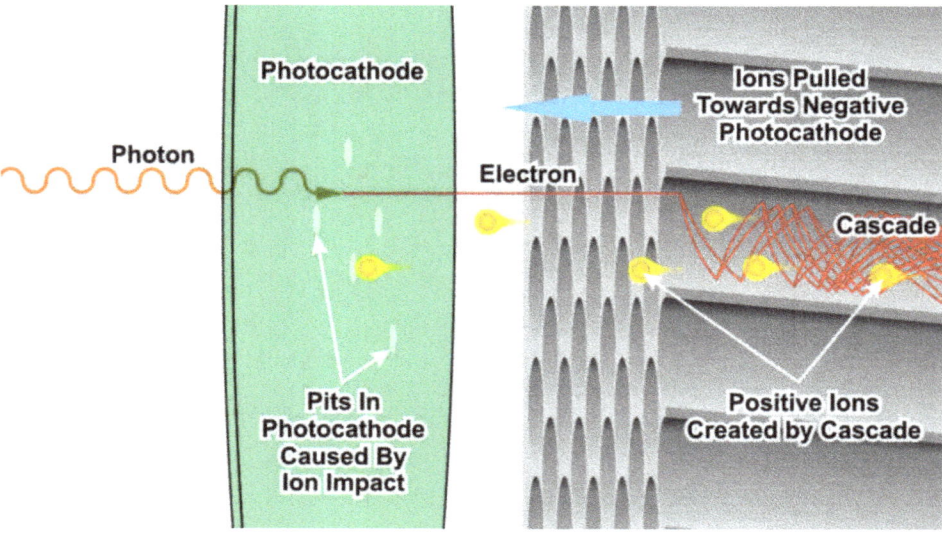

Figure 36 Ion particle feedback illustration

---

24 HRC, online image, viewed 11 November 2011, www.harvard.edu/HRC/mcp/mcp.html

Positive ions can be reasonably large and are capable of causing physical and chemical damage to the photocathode. This reduces the image intensifier's life from 10,000 hours down to 10-100 hours, which was not acceptable and defeated the purpose of using gallium arsenide on the photocathode.

Example	
Consider a car driving in a sandstorm. The sand represents the positive ions striking the glass window, and we all know how much damage and how difficult it is to see when that happens.	

To fix this problem, these intensifier tubes included a thin ion barrier film formed on the face of the MCP that prevented the positive ions from reaching the photocathode. The ion barrier film consists of a thin coating of Aluminium Oxide (Al^2O^3) or, depending on the manufacturer, Silicon Dioxide (SiO^2), forming a protective photochemical layer on the front end of the MCP. It is not a physical lens or filter that is often used in diagrams to depict the ion barrier film (but it does the job in a similar manner) but is instead an electrically charged barrier (imagine it as being a force field). When electricity is applied to the MCP to allow the cascading effect of electrons, the electricity reacts with the Aluminium oxide activating the barrier. This prevents positive ions from passing through and returning to damage the photocathode.

In any text regarding NVG technology, it will be stated that the ion barrier film is there to increase tube life, and this would be correct, but it does have some serious drawbacks.

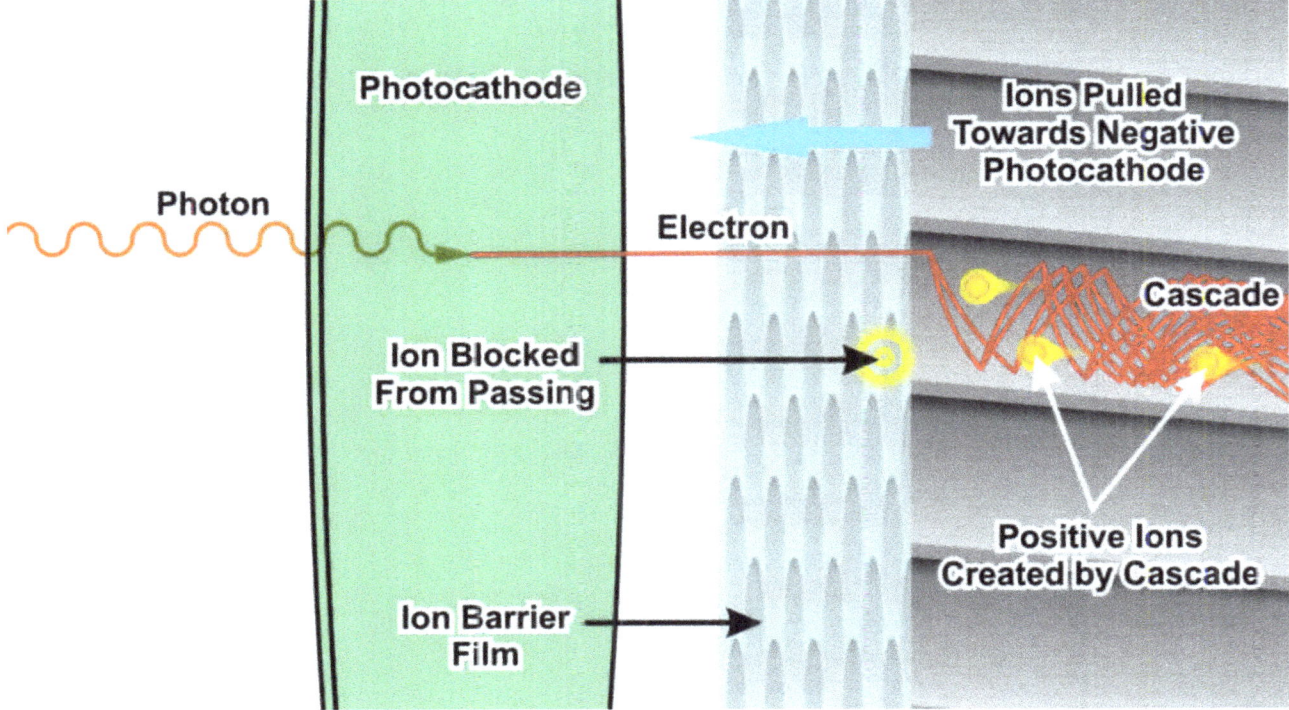

Below is a significantly magnified image of the Aluminium Oxide coating on the face of the MCP.

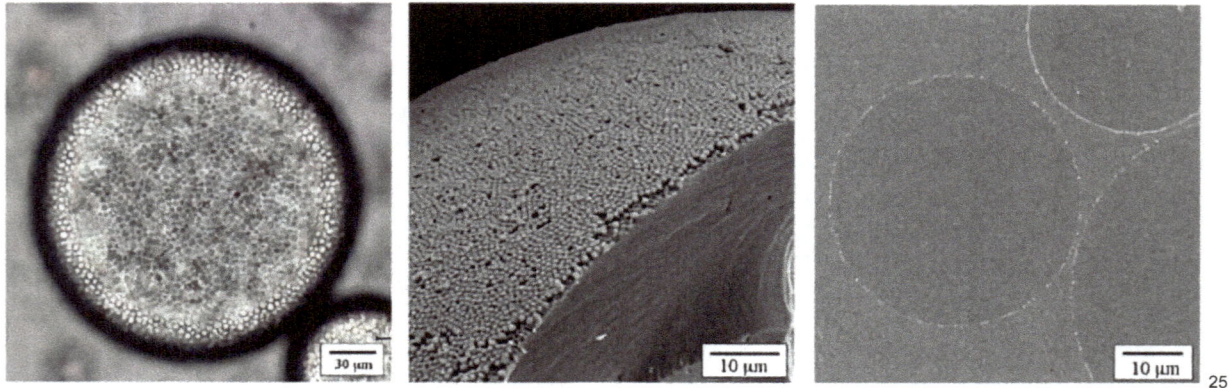

The main drawbacks or disadvantages of having an ion barrier film include:

1. The electrons from the photocathode are now restricted in making their way to the MCP. In effect, the ion barrier film reduces the number of electrons by 50%. This brings the actual photosensitivity result of the gallium arsenide photocathode down from 1800 uA/lm to 900 uA/lm in actual performance.
2. A "halo" (or shadow) around the edge of the image can be created because some electrons striking the ion barrier film do not penetrate it, instead impacting at another location.
3. A higher voltage is required between the photocathode and the MCP to overcome the electron barrier established by the ion barrier film.

Figure 37 Early generation with ion barrier film   Figure 38 Later generation without ion barrier [26]

The Europeans and now later Generation III plus intensifier tubes out of the United States have been able to do away with the ion barrier film by advancing technology in the MCP by using curved or parabolic channels and increasing the efficiencies of the multi-alkali photocathode in the Generation II tubes.

---

25 Kumamoto University, online image, viewed 11 November 2011, www.chem.kumamoto-u.ac.jp/~ihara/research/MCP2008m.jpg

26 ATN, online image, viewed 11 November 2011, www.atncorp.com/night_vision_images/info_pages/gen_4.png

Phosphor Screen

As the electrons leave the MCP, they need to be turned back into photons of light in the visible spectrum so that the human eye can see them. To do this, the electrons have to pass through a lens covered in a phosphor material called a phosphor screen.

Figure 39 White Phosphor Screen

Figure 40 Green Phosphor Screen

When the electrons strike the phosphor screen, the atoms that make up the phosphor material absorb the electrons and become excited. This simply means the phosphor atom becomes energised. When atoms become energised, they will always try to return to the same state they were originally in before they were energised. This is referred to as its ground state.

As the phosphor atoms return to their ground state, they have to release the energy which they absorbed when taking on the electron in the first place. They do this by releasing a photon. This whole process will take less than $100,000^{th}$ of a second.

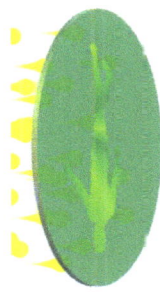

So as electrons hit the phosphor screen, we can see this as visible light. The intensities and image shape are replicated by the phosphor screen dependent on the number and velocity of electrons striking the phosphor screen.

What are Phosphors?

Typically, when you imagine a "phosphor", most of us think of a green liquid that glows in the dark. Although this may be an example of a substance exhibiting phosphorescence, we are more interested in substances that exhibit fluorescence. (Yes, this is confusing.)

A phosphor is a substance that exhibits luminescence. Luminescence is light that can be created by chemical reactions, electrical energy, subatomic motions, or stress on a crystal at low temperatures (in other words, heat is not involved in creating the light energy that would make it incandescent!). This can include materials that can exhibit either phosphorescence or fluorescence.

Once excited by electrons, **Phosphorescent** materials will luminess and slowly (possibly over seconds, minutes, hours, days, weeks, months or years) as the material returns to its ground state.

Fluorescent materials, once excited by electrons, will luminess and rapidly (within a fraction of a nanosecond) decay in their brightness as the material returns to its ground state.

Phosphorescent materials are commonly used in radar screens and glow in the dark toys, whereas fluorescent materials are used in cathode ray tubes (TV screens) sensors and the phosphor screens used in intensifier tubes in NVGs.

Figure 41 Phosphorescent materials – Glow in the dark toy [27]

Figure 42 Fluorescent materials – Green phosphor screen [28]

For high screen refresh rate applications (like the moving images we see when looking through NVGs), the decay time (the time it takes to go from full brightness to only 10% brightness after being excited by an electron) of the phosphor has to be short to prevent crosstalk (a shadow of the old image) between subsequent images.

The phosphors used in cathode ray tubes and, therefore, NVGs were first classified into a category around 1940 and were designated by the letter **P** followed by a number. The number refers to the phosphor's decay characteristics. In NVGs, the P46 and P48 phosphors with a decay time of only 160 nanoseconds are commonly used.

Contrary to popular belief, phosphor does not have to be green; in fact, any fluorescent colour is really a phosphor. Green is the preferred phosphor used for NVG because it is the colour that has the most variation in shades that the human eye can naturally see. Green is easy on the human eye and will minimise the effects of fatigue and eye strain.

New developments have been made with white phosphor screens so that some newer NVGs show an image in a greyscale similar to a black and white TV. Chemically, phosphors are transition metal compounds commonly referred to as rare earth minerals or compounds and can be found within the periodic table of elements. Despite the name, they are not as rare as they sound. In fact, they occur in reasonable amounts within the earth's crust. What makes them rare is they are economically hard to extract.

---

27 Weiku.com, online image, viewed 30 July 2013, www.weiku.com/products/11427582/glow_in_the_dark_toy.html

28 Night Vision Guys.com, online image, viewed 11 November 2011, www.nightvisionguys.com/media/catalog/product/cache/1/image/800x600/9df78eab33525d08d6e5fb8d27136e95/4/2/4228-1.jpg

Night Vision Goggles *for Helicopter Pilots*

PERIODIC TABLE OF THE ELEMENTS

[Periodic table image with elements organized by Group (1-18) and Period (1-7), including lanthanides (58-71) and actinides (90-103). Legend shows Metals (Alkali, Alkaline earth, Transition, Lanthanide, Actinide, Other), Metalloids, and Nonmetals (Other, Halogen, Noble gas).]

[29]

One property of transition metals is the formation of highly coloured ions in solution. Figure 43 shows just a few colours associated with transition metal ions. There have been thousands of phosphor fluorescent colours that have been created.

Figure 43 Some colours of transition metal ions [30]

---

[29] Sandbh, Taxonomic Periodic Table with halogens, online image, viewed 24 March 2021, https://commons.wikimedia.org/wiki/File:Taxonomic_PT_with_halogens.jpg (Creative Commons 4.0)

[30] Randolph College, online image, viewed 11 November 2011, www.randolphcollege.edu/Images/academics/chemistry/fluoresce_small.jpg

Making a Phosphor Screen

To make a phosphor screen for an intensifier tube in an NVG, you first create the phosphor material, usually refined down to a powder. Then on a shaped piece of glass, quartz or fibre optic plate (to use as a platform), the phosphor material is layered over the inside surface (the vacuum side) of the output window. This layering may be done by growing a crystalline structure, dusting or spraying the powder, water laminating, using electrolysis or some other method. The idea is to get a uniform, even layer over the entire disc.

On top of this, a thin layer of aluminium film is applied to increase light efficiency by up to 100% since light created at the phosphor is reflected back at the aluminium layer. It is then baked in an oven so the materials will all bond together to form the screen.

The phosphor screen in an intensifier tube will receive electrons from the MCP, but they will not be able to pierce the aluminium layer unless an electron acceleration energy (electrical current) of approximately 3 kV is applied to the phosphor screen. For this to happen, an extra layer of aluminium is layered around the outside of the disc in a ring approximately 1.3 mm wide. This allows for electrical contact with the phosphor screen when placed inside the intensifier tube housing.

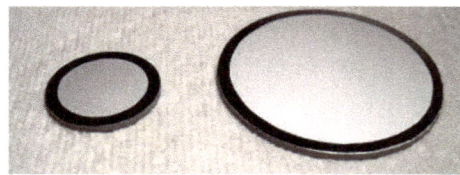

Figure 44 Phosphor screen [31]

As the new photons leave the phosphor screen, they will be focused on the eyepiece for the viewer to see the image clearly.

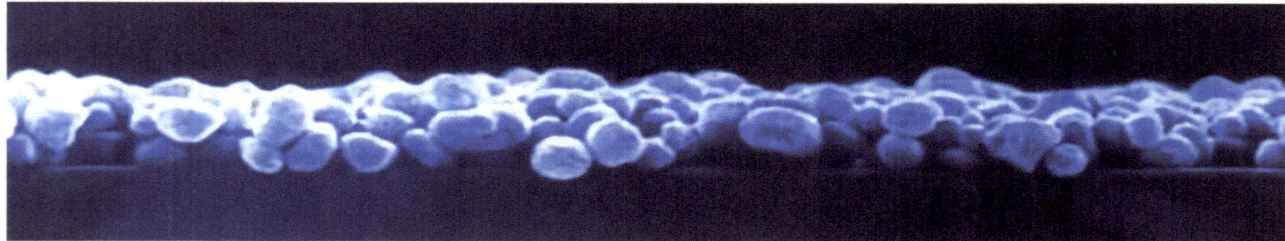

Figure 45 Example of a 2-micron thick P43 phosphor screen magnified to show the phosphorus particles [32]

Fibre Optic Inverter

As previously stated, as the image comes in through the objective lens, it will be inverted. This means the image will remain inverted through its entire passage through the intensifier tube. For the viewer to see the image the right way up, something has to rotate it 180 degrees. In early generation NVGs, this was done optically in the eyepiece using various lenses. Not only does that make the NVG longer and heavier, but as we know, each time light goes through a lens, it will lose some of its quality. So, if lenses could be done away with, the result would be a better image. With the advent of fibre optics in the 1960s, using that technology in an intensifier tube didn't take long.

What is Fibre Optics?

Figure 46 Fibre optic strands [33]

Fibre optic lines are strands of glass, about the size of a human hair, that are optically pure (meaning there are no contaminants in the strands). They are used to transmit light signals.

---

[31] Beam Imaging Solutions Inc, online image, viewed 11 November 2011, www.beamimaging.com/Images/screen-R2(350).jpg

[32] Beam Imaging Solutions Inc, online image, viewed 11 November 2011, www.beamimaging.com/pscreen.html?gclid=CJavudvapaMCFQYdbgodj3c52w

[33] Getus.com, online image, viewed 11 November 2011, www.getus.com/images/cable/Fiber_optic_bundle.jpg

To understand how light can travel through fibre optic cabling, which is twisting and turning, it is helpful to apply an analogy.

Imagine standing at the entrance to a long tunnel, and you shine a torch down that tunnel; someone at the other end can see the light because it can go in a straight line. Now let's put a bend in that same tunnel. When you shine your light, it will go straight, but it will not go around the corner, and the person at the other end will not see it.

To solve this problem, you could place a mirror just at the right place on the curve in the tunnel, and the light will reflect off it and continue to the other end so the person standing there can now see it. If there was more than one bend, you could repeat this as many times as required to get the light to the other end of the tunnel. This is the same process used to move light through a fibre optic cable, but instead of using mirrors, the light will continuously reflect off the interior glass fibre within itself.

This process is known as total internal reflection. To create a fibre optic inverter, instead of the light going around corners, the cable has a 180-degree twist so that whatever image went in at the front of the inverter will be inverted 180 degrees on the output side.

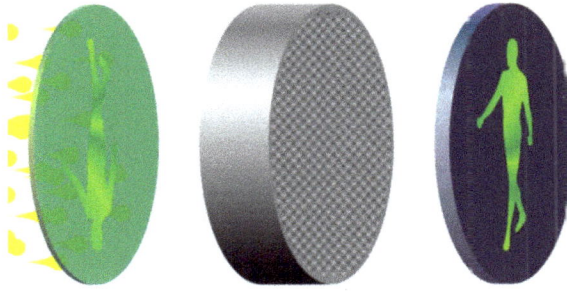

Another advantage of a fibre optic inverter is that it is made of glass. Therefore, instead of requiring a separate phosphor screen before the inverter, the phosphor screen is manufactured on the actual face of the inverter. Again, this does away with another lens and allows for a better overall image. Using a fibre optic inverter instead of the traditional lens arrangement in the eyepiece improved the resulting image by over 60%.

Distortion

Because the fibre optic bundle is a manufactured component, it may suffer from some errors or imperfections during the manufacturing process. This can lead to the image being distorted as seen by the viewer. There are two types of distortion associated with fibre optic inverters: *S-Distortion* and *Sheer Distortion*.

Figure 47 Phosphor screen on face plate [34]

S Distortion

S Distortion results from imperfections in the twisting process during the manufacturing of the inverter. It is usually tiny and difficult to detect with the unaided eye. Late Generation II and Generation III tubes have nearly no perceptible S-Distortion.

---

34 Tradenote.net, online image, viewed 11 November 2011, www.tradenote.net/images/users/000/426/230/products_images/642730.jpg

Sheer Distortion

Sheer Distortion can occur in any image tube that uses the surface of the fibre optic bundles for the layering of the phosphor screen. It appears as a break in a straight line as though the line were sheered. This is due to imperfection in the layering of the phosphor onto the fibre optic bundle.

 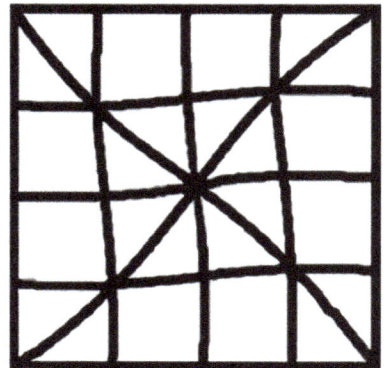 

Figure 48 Perfect Image   Figure 49 S-Distortion   Figure 50 Sheer Distortion

Russian tubes do not use fibre optic inverters; instead, they use optical lenses that do not suffer from this type of distortion.

Electrical Supply

At the very beginning, we stated that the intensifier tube is a charged or electrical device. Without applying electricity at various positions within the intensifier tube, the result would be a blank screen with nothing to view because our amplifier (the intensifier tube) needs electricity to work.

The photocathode, the MCP, and the phosphor screen can all receive an electrical current at some point depending on the manufacturer, the design and generation or performance category of the intensifier tube.

Anode and Cathode

The terms anode and cathode are words to describe positive and negative terminals. For example, the positive terminal on a car battery is the **anode,** and the negative terminal on the car battery is the **cathode**.

In an image intensifier tube, the photocathode is the negative terminal, and the phosphor screen is the positive anode; therefore, negative electrons leaving the photocathode will be drawn towards the positive anode (good), but positive ions created in the MCP will be drawn back towards the negative cathode (bad).

Figure 51 Car battery terminals

Voltages generated within the intensifier tube will vary according to their design, but, in general, the photocathode will be a negative terminal, and the phosphor screen will be a positive terminal at low voltages varying between -200 and positive 10,000 volts. The MCP can receive very high voltages across the channels to promote the electron cascade. Surprisingly this can be anywhere between 0 volts at the entry to 50,000 volts at the exit.

Additionally, those intensifier tubes with ion barrier films need an electrical current to accelerate the electrons from the photocathode through the ion barrier film into the MCP.

Figure 52 shows a straightforward schematic with some voltage examples. These examples do not represent any specific intensifier tube but give the reader some idea of the variance in voltages that may be utilised.

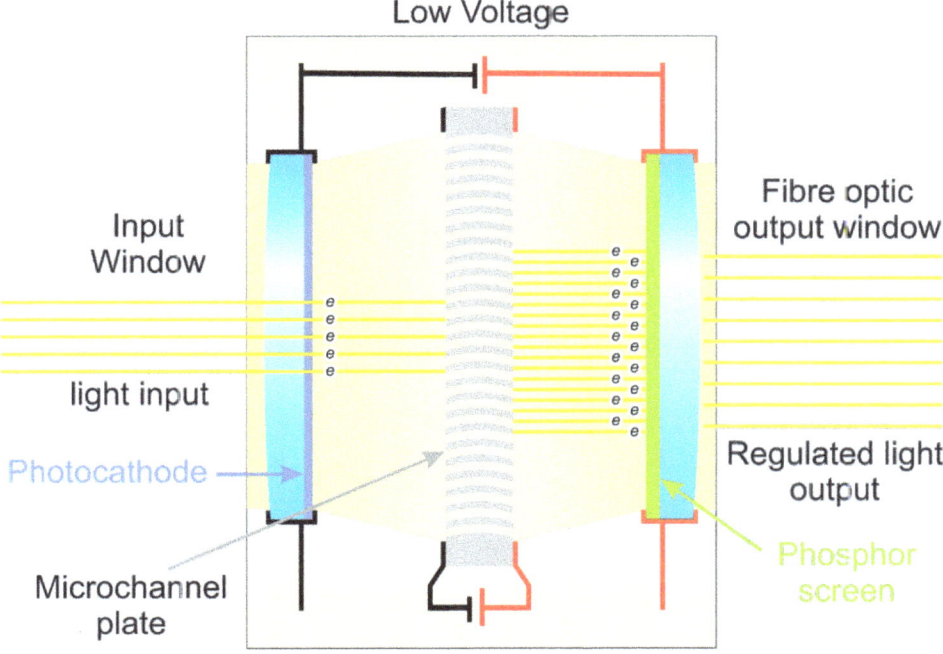

Figure 52 Schematic of intensifier tube voltages (example)

Controlling the Amount of Light

From your reading now, it would become evident that the intensifier tube can receive too much light and that this can cause too many electrons to be created, resulting in the output image having very bright spots or the entire image being a very bright green screen which in turn can lead to the tubes "burning" out internally.

This was a big problem with the early generation goggles, and indeed, movies always depict the person wearing the NVGs having a torch shone in their face and the goggles "blooming" out and blinding the user allowing the good guy to either win or get caught. The two most common terms used when experiencing bright light are "Blooming" and "Halo Effect".

Blooming

Blooming is where parts, or all, of the image, is too bright and the intensifier tube overloads. This may cause the entire image to "bloom", or it may only mean small parts of the image "bloom". The two images below show examples of blooming.

Figure 53 Entire tube starting to bloom out [35]

Figure 54 Localised light too bright for the tube [36]

---

35 War Is Boring.com, online image, viewed 11 November 2011, warsboring.com/wp-content/uploads/2008/08/nvg.jpg

36 Marine Gouge.com, online image, viewed 11 November 2011, marinegouge.com/~marin43/mediawiki-1.13.3/images/3/3c/Nvgvies.jpg

Halo Effect

The halo effect is still considered blooming; the main difference is around the bright source of light, the viewer will see a "halo" as a secondary bloom to the primary light source. Figure 54 is a good example of blooming spots with a halo.

In the military, this exposure to bright light was also a significant problem as flashes from explosions or weapons or transiting from dark to daylight or darkness to brightly lit rooms would result in the same blooming out.

Because of these problems, procedures and training were very important in controlling the use of "white" light in the cockpit and around the aircraft at night. Pilots, crew members and passengers all had to adhere to strict protocols and procedures on the use of light that may affect the NVG. This concern is still seen today and is part of the reasoning behind the content typically found in helicopter operators' opeations manuals in preventing incompatible light from being used while utilising NVG in an aircraft and why any new device must first be tested and approved before it can be used in the aircraft.

Manufacturers also recognise this as a problem and have devised ways to counter the effects of bright light by creating a Bright Source Protection (BSP) and Automatic Brightness Control (ABC) system.

Bright Source Protection (BSP)

Bright-Source Protection (BSP) was initially devised for Generation I intensifier tubes that utilised photomultipliers. It is an electronic function that reduces the voltage to the photocathode when the night vision device is exposed to bright light sources that would otherwise overload the intensifier tube and cause it damage.

It works by either reducing or totally cutting off the electrical power circuit to the photocathode and therefore restricts the light (photons) that may enter the photomultiplier. Designed to protect the image tube from damage and enhance its life, the significant disadvantage was the coarseness of its design so that when the voltage was reduced, the image resolution to the viewer was very poor, or in the worst-case scenario, the voltage would be completely turned off when a bright source was encountered, and the viewer would see nothing. Once the bright light source had gone, it would still take 1-2 minutes for the NVD to resume its normal operation.

Automatic Brightness Control (ABC)

Instead of varying the voltage at the photocathode, in later Generation II intensifier tubes and above, the designers could now adjust the voltage at the MCP. This allowed the voltage to be varied with greater control to keep the image intensifier's brightness within its optimal limits and therefore protect the tube and prolong its life. More importantly, it allowed an image to be seen even under bright conditions without turning it off.

Initially, this was done through an Auto Gain electrical circuit, with later generations moving onto an Auto Gating electrical circuit. To explain these, it is helpful to use an analogy we use every day.

Consider you are in a dark room. No lights, eyes open. Someone walks into the room and turns on a very bright light. What is your body's automatic reaction?

First, you shut your eyes. This is equivalent to the bright source protection where you switch off the power so no light can get through. This is not very efficient because if it is an enemy who has turned on the light, you can no longer see them. So the next thing you do is put up your hand to shield yourself from the bright light, then slowly open your eyes, knowing that your pupils will constrict to reduce the amount of light into the eye and that you will only open your eyes slightly to reduce the amount of light that can come in (you will be squinting).

You then move your hand a small amount to look past your hand to see who has turned on the light. If it is still too bright, you move your hand in front of your face then away from your face rapidly to see who it is while keeping your eyes open but squinting.

In this instance, you are using both autogain and autogating principles.

Autogain

Remember that Gain (specifically tube gain) is the difference between the amounts of light that goes into the tube compared to what comes out at the other end after being amplified. Because this amplification relies on electricity, if the designer of the tube can control the amount of electricity based on the amount of light coming in at the source, then it is possible to control the amount of amplification so that a bright image does not create too bright an image that the viewer cannot see or that will shut the tube down.

This "varying" the voltage up or down at the MCP is called "Autogain". In effect, the tube will automatically control the amount of "gain" through the tube based on the intensity of the input light source. There is nothing that the user can do to control the "autogain" because it is all controlled automatically through the electrical circuitry within the tube.

An easier way to understand this is to look at a typical light dimmer switch used in a home or office. You turn the light on with a switch but can vary the brightness of the light by moving the dimmer switch to allow more or less electricity to flow through to the light bulbs.

Within the intensifier tube, in general terms, the brighter the light source, the lower the voltage allowed to flow through the MCP and the fewer the number of electrons created to amplify the image as seen by the viewer.

The dimmer the light source (dark night), the greater the voltage allowed to flow through the MCP and the greater the number of electrons created to amplify the image as seen by the viewer.

The photocathode may still have bright source protection when the autogain cannot cope, but this is much less likely to be utilised for regular night operations.

Tubes with autogain still may not have full day-night-day capability, but they can handle brighter light sources without shutting down. However, a bright light source will still have a larger halo or blooming effect as it takes time for the autogain to work (half a second). This can be obvious as you look through the goggles from a dark area to a very bright area; the image will bloom then adjust.

Figure 55 Initial view

Figure 56 One second later

Mike Becker

Autogating

Autogating is a clever way of making technology work better than nature. Instead of varying the voltage up or down at the MCP (autogain), autogating will completely turn the electricity on and off at the photocathode, but it will do this at such a high speed (measured in nano-seconds which is a billionth of a second) that the viewer will not notice. In effect, the light is gated or shut off at the entrance to the tube.

Example

Try looking at a very bright light. It is tough and possibly painful to do. Now open and close your eyes very quickly (blinking). If you cycle through quickly enough, you can see the light by "gating" your intensifier tube – the eye. You are turning the light source on and off, the same principle used in autogating intensifier tubes.

| Open | Closed | Open | Closed |

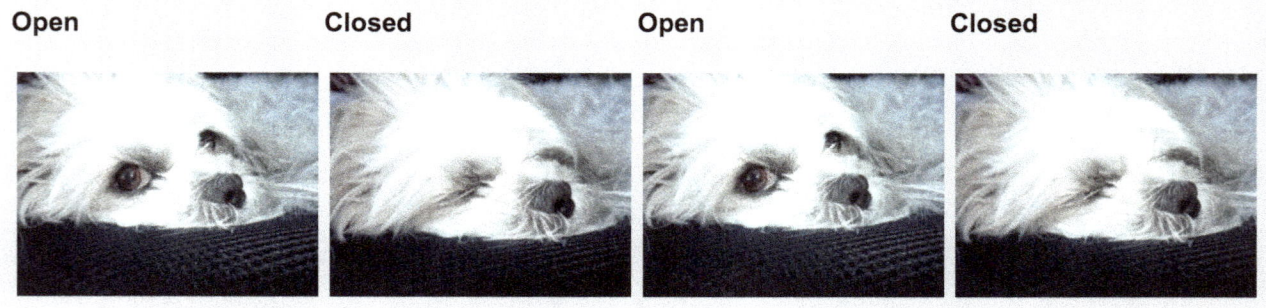

Autogated tubes will also have some autogain functionality where voltage can still be varied at the MCP, but this will work independently. Additionally, the autogating circuit is also the bright source protection (BSP) so that autogated tubes can genuinely function in day-night-day operations without completely shutting down in bright light.

In general terms, the brighter the light source, the faster the cycle rate of the electricity being turned on and off at the photocathode. This reduces the electrons flowing through to the MCP and thereby controls the image seen by the viewer.

The dimmer the light source (dark night), the slower the cycle rate of the electricity being turned on and off at the photocathode. This allows more electrons to flow through to the MCP, controlling the image seen by the viewer. If there is an instant bright light on a very dark night, the autogating circuit will react at the speed of light to adjust.

One of the significant advantages of an autogated tube is its ability to handle white light and unexpected bright light sources.

Autogating technology is relatively new and was first patented by Photonis in Europe and was trademarked by Photonis as IRIS™ technology. This has allowed the technology to be retrofitted to any generation of intensifier tube; however, you will find that most American manufactured tubes, which did not have access to the autogating technology until recently, still only utilise autogain and the BSP. The autogating feature in American tubes is restricted to Military use only and is not currently offered for sale. The ITT F4949 intensifier tubes approved in Australia have autogain and BSP.

The NL-94-AU tubes approved in Australia have autogated tubes with autogain at the MCP, making them more effective in bright light situations (Day-Night-Day).

Operational Defects

An operational defect is a flaw in the reliability of the image intensifier and is an indication of a pending failure. The failure can be caused by problems with the photocathode, microchannel plate, phosphor screen, fibre optic inverter, or lenses.

Some of these defects are acceptable, allowing the user to continue to use the NVGs while flying. Some are unacceptable, rendering the NVGs unserviceable. Acceptable defects could be conditional, meaning that a minor defect is acceptable, but a more significant defect may be unacceptable, and the user can make this determination.

Unacceptable Defects

Unacceptable defects mean that once the user has identified one of the issues below, the NVG device cannot be used until it has been serviced.

- Shading
- Edge Glow
- Emission Points
- Flashing, flickering or intermittent operation

Shading

Each monocular should present a full circle when being looked through by the user. Dark shading that is in high contrast with a distinct line of demarcation around one or more of the edges will make the image look slightly elliptical, referred to as "edge shading". This defect starts on the edges and moves its way in towards the centre until eventually there is no image. Typically, the shading is very dark, and images cannot be seen through it.

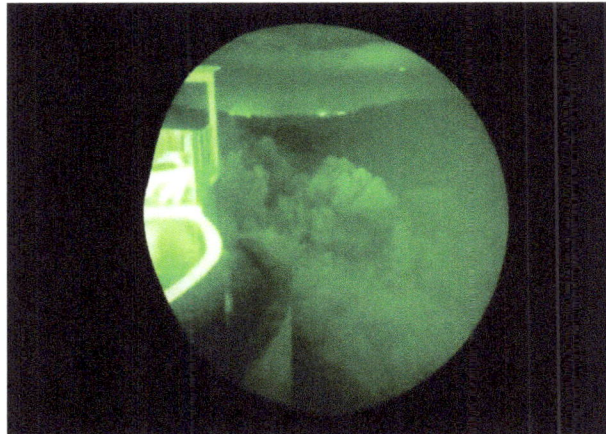

Figure 57 Example of edge shading

Edge shading is an indication that the photocathode is dying. This can be caused by the vacuum seal of the intensifier unit being defective or damaged.

Edge Glow

Edge glow is a very bright, sometimes sparkling, area around the outer portion of the viewing area. Edge glow can be caused by a bright light source just outside the field of view or by a defective phosphor screen that permits feedback to the photocathode.

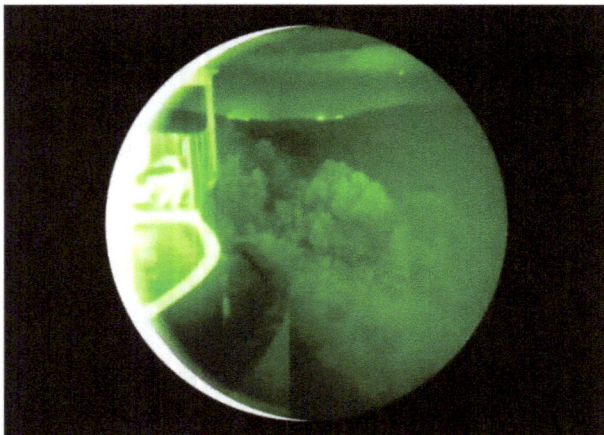

Figure 58 Example of edge glow

To check that what you are seeing is an edge glow and not just a bright light source outside your field of view, block out all light by cupping your hand over the end of the objective lens. If you can still see an edge glow through the tube you are covering, you have an edge glow.

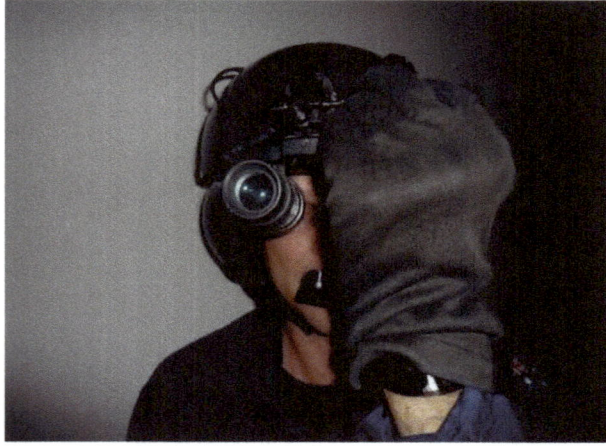

Emission Points

Emission points is a steady or fluctuating pinpoint of bright light in the image area which does not go away when all the light is blocked from the objective lens of that tube when you cup your hand over it. The position of an emission point within the image area does not move.

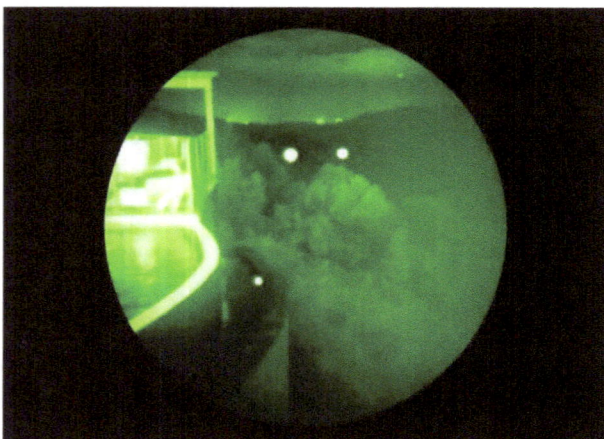

Figure 59 Example of Emission Points

Night Vision Goggles *for Helicopter Pilots*

Flashing, Flickering or Intermittent Operation

The image may flicker or flash intermittently in either or both of the intensifier tubes. The odd one or two flickers is not necessarily a problem. If it is consistently doing this, you may have a power supply issue – i.e. low voltage, loose wires, unsecured battery cap, loose plugs, dirty contacts, corrosion, etc.

A changing light source due to head movement may also cause flickering. To confirm, you should be able to look at a consistent image in one direction with a stable lght source and not see flickering or flashing.

Acceptable Defects

Acceptable defects mean that once the user has identified one of the issues below, the NVG can still be used based on the opinion and comfort level of the user. This is also referred to as being a conditional defect.

Bright Spots

Bright spots are signal-induced blemishes in the image area caused by a flaw in the film on the MCP. A bright spot is small and can be an irregular shape that may appear to flicker or be constant. Bright spots usually go away when all the light is blocked out and therefore do not necessarily make the NVG unserviceable.

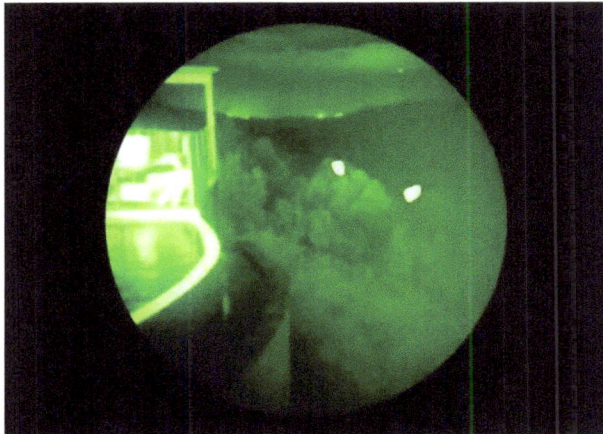

Figure 60   Example of bright spots

The difference between an emission point and a bright spot is an emission point will remain bright no matter the brightness of the image being viewed, whereas a bright spot will tend to fade and can even disappear under bright light but become visible again in low light. Additionally, a bright spot will go away if you cup your hand over the objective lens and take away all the light, whereas an emission point will remain.

Black Spots

A black spot can be caused by either cosmetic (manufacturing) blemishes in the intensifier tube or dirt caught between the lenses. For this reason, a black spot does not affect the performance or reliability of the NVD, and some numbers of black spots of varying sizes are inherent in the manufacturing process. If the black spot is dirt on the outside of the lens, then the user can clean the lens surface before use. If the dirt is on the inside of the lens, then this is usually remedied at its next service.

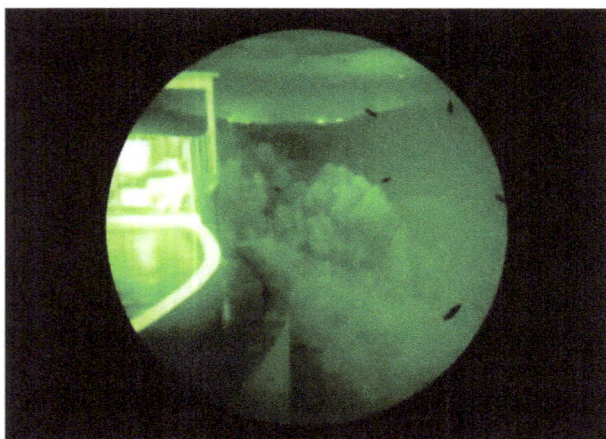

Figure 61 Example of black spots

Fixed Pattern Noise (FPN)

Fixed pattern noise relates to the structures of the MCP and the fibre optic inverter that can be seen on the NVG image under certain lighting conditions. There is no real issue wth this, except it can be distracting. The NVG remains serviceable, and both chicken wire and honeycomb can be controlled by reducing the bright light source.

Chicken Wire

A consistent hexagonal pattern of thin dark lines that resemble "chicken wire" located either in parts or throughout the whole image area. This is usually more prevalent in high light conditions. What you are seeing are the individual boules that make up the fibre optic inverter.

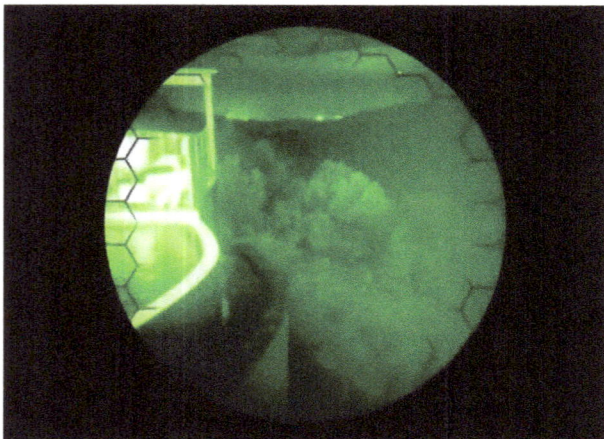

Figure 62 Example of chicken wire

Honeycomb

Honeycomb is a faint hexagonal (honeycomb) pattern throughout the image area that often becomes evident under high light conditions. What you are seeing is the structure of the fibre optic inverter with the edges of the individual boules being internally lit up.

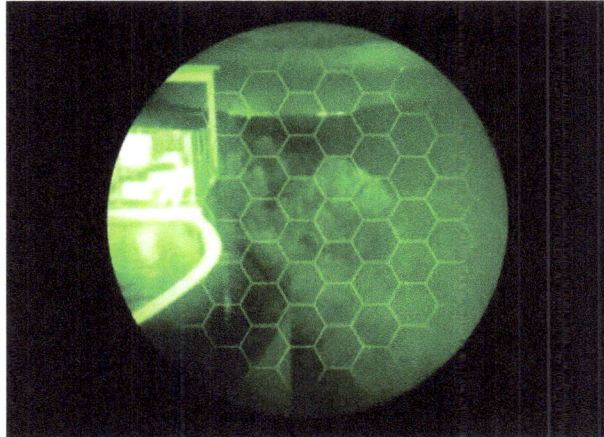

Figure 63 Example of honeycomb

The most common time this will be seen is when close to the ground and the white search light is on. The bright light bouncing back from the ground makes the honeycomb very obvious.

Scintillation

At low light levels, the resolution of the image is limited by internal noise that prevents a clear build-up of the image and effectively reduces image contrast. Internal noise is caused by the electrically charged particles being generated within the intensifier tube itself.

> **Example**
>
> Consider listening to a radio that is not tuned to a particular station. What you hear is static or electrical noise. The same can be said for a television that has lost the station signal. The sparkling or scintillating image on the screen is the visual manifestation of electrical noise.
>
> Now think of the electrical noise that may be created by the internal circuitry of the intensifier tube. In high light conditions, this will not be noticeable because the image will be stronger than any electrical noise, but in very low light conditions where the intensifier has very little or no light to work with, then the user will start to see a sparkling effect we call scintillation or sometimes referred to as video noise.
>
> In the image on the right, look carefully at the top, you can see how it looks like it is sparkling.
>
>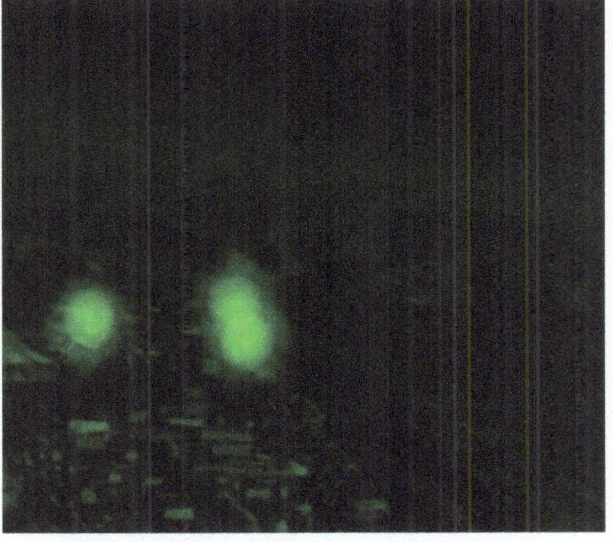

Scintillation is a normal characteristic of image intensifier tubes with MCPs and is not a cause for rendering the NVG unserviceable. If you are experiencing scintillation, then it is simply getting too dark to use the NVGs. The best remedy is to provide more light, and this can be done by turning on a landing light or finding a light source.

Each design of the intensifier tube may suffer more or less from scintillation and, therefore, in the datasheet of the individual tube the manufacturer can allocate a number known as the signal to noise ratio or SNR so that the intensifier tubes can be compared. The SNR and the resolution of the intensifier tube, can combine to give a tube a figure of merit (FOM).

Signal to Noise Ratio (SNR)

The signal to noise ratio measures the light signal reaching the eye divided by the perceived noise generated within the intensifier tube as seen by the eye. A tube's SNR will determine the low light resolution of the intensifier tube. Therefore, the higher the SNR, the better the ability of the tube to resolve objects with good contrast under low light conditions. Because the SNR is directly related to phosphor efficiency and MCP operating voltage, it is the single best indicator of individual image intensifier performance.

Resolution

Resolution refers to the ability of the image intensifier to distinguish between objects that are close together. It relates to the number and size of the lines or pixels that go into making up an image. The smaller the lines or pixels and the greater the number, the better the resolution of the image. The larger the lines or pixels and the smaller the number, the poorer the resolution of the image.

The two examples below are of the same image. The image on the left (Figure 64) has a low resolution with few lines and large pixels. It is hard to make out what the image actually is. The image on the right (Figure 65) has a higher resolution with more lines and smaller pixels. You are now able to see that you are looking at an image of grapes on a vine.

Figure 64 Low resolution image

Figure 65 High resolution image

Image intensifier resolution is measured in line pairs per millimetre (lp/mm), while system resolution is measured in cycles per milliradian (cy/mr). For any particular night vision intensifier tube, the resolution will remain a constant, however, the system resolution can be affected by adjusting the objective or eyepiece lens or by adding filters, splitters, magnification or other additional equipment to the system. It is not uncommon for the resolution in the centre of the image to be better than the resolution at the edge of the image.

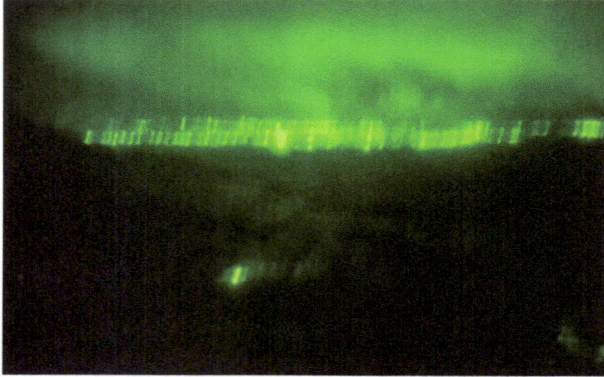
Figure 66 Adjusted objective lens

Figure 67 Focused objective lens

Figure of Merit (FOM)

The figure of merit is obtained by multiplying the intensifier's tube resolution by the signal to noise ratio. It is a number used to compare the performance of individual intensifier tubes.

For more information on the FOM, go to The Generation Game chapter.

Power Supply

As we know, the NVGs are powered independently of the aircraft's electrical system. This means that they require their own internal power source and can function even if the aircraft has a total electrical failure.

This is achieved by having an external power pack that connects via the mounting system to the intensifier tubes. As a redundancy, the power pack will have an alternate supply and a low battery power indicator as part of the system. Each manufacturer may have varying shapes and sizes for power packs. All of the images here will relate to the NL-94-AL.

Battery Compartment

The power pack consists of two battery compartments, each able to accept two AA size batteries that are housed within a small cradle.

The cradles will slide into the battery compartments and be locked in place with the compartment cap. Each compartment is labelled "PRIMARY" (on the left) and "SECONDARY" (on the right) as this indicates which batteries are to be used as the primary source of power and which batteries are used as the alternative emergency backup or secondary source of power. Each operator will have a battery usage plan in order to control the life of the power pack, and they will explain the use of primary vs secondary batteries within the Company Operations Manual or Standard Operating Procedures.

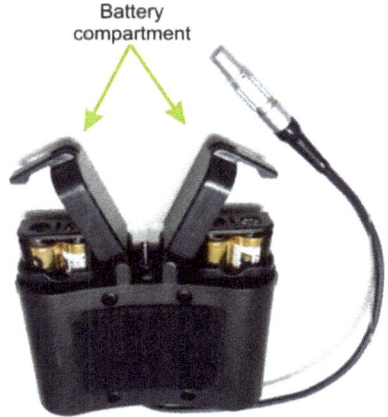

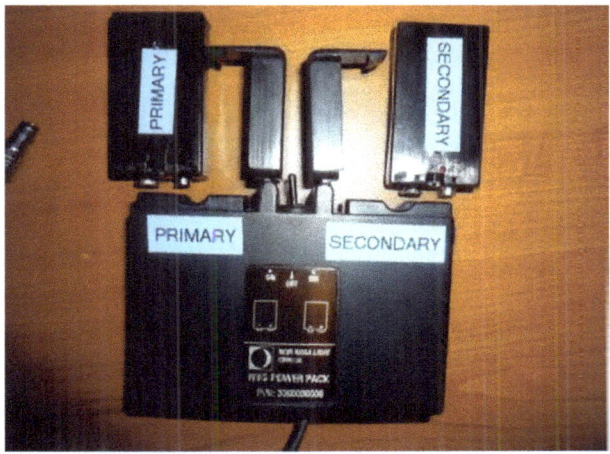

The power pack is usually attached to the back of the helmet with velcro or another attaching mechanism for two reasons:

- The connector cable is short, so there is minimal voltage loss from the battery pack to the NVG.
- The power pack provides ballast so that the extra weight produced by the NVGs at the front of the helmet can be balanced by the weight of the batteries at the back. Most times, the power pack by itself is not sufficient, so there is an additional ballast bag or piece of lead that is added to achieve the right centre of balance for each individual pilot.

The connector cable is not directly attached to the goggles. Instead, it is connected to the NVG mounting system. This allows the NVG device itself able to be quickly released and disconnected without having to go through the procedure of unplugging cables.

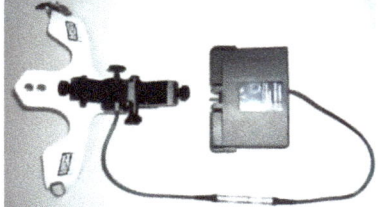

The power pack will have a three-way power switch that allows either primary or secondary batteries to be turned ON or both of them OFF. The switch will work in a natural function in that if it is:

- pushed to the left, the primary batteries will be ON
- placed in the CENTRE, both will be OFF
- pushed to the right, the secondary batteries will be ON.

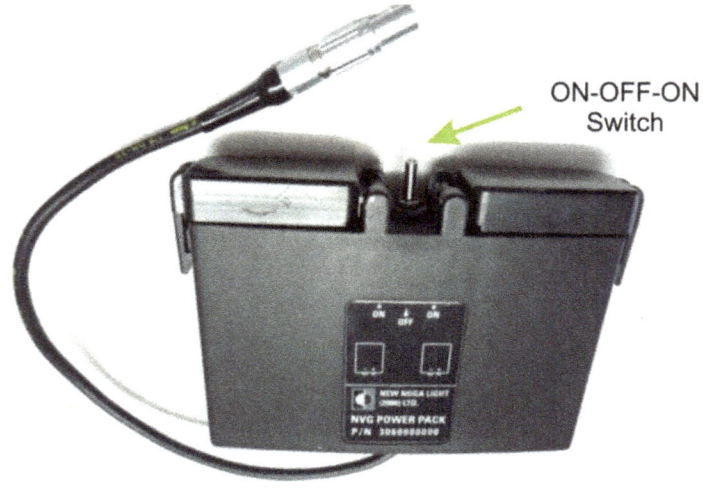

ON-OFF-ON Switch

An example of a power pack circuit is as follows:

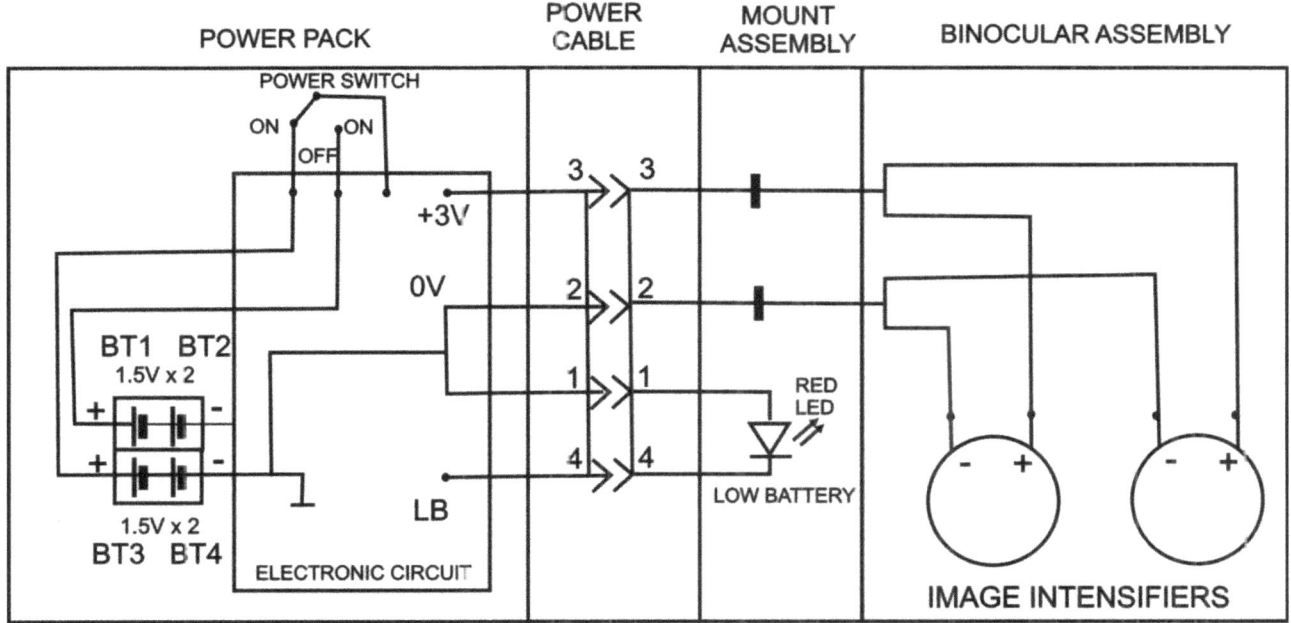

Battery Usage Plan

It is important that the correct batteries are used in NVG power packs. Currently, the only batteries able to be used are 1.5 volt AA alkaline or lithium batteries that are equivalent to or better than those specified by the manufacturer in the NVG operator's handbook.

It is also worth noting here that lithium batteries were initially not able to be used in NVG because they were considered to be a dangerous good prone to overheating and difficult to dispose of. As they have improved in their reliability, they are now included as an approved battery source in most NVG.

Rechargeable batteries must not be used. Interestingly the NVG will work the same with rechargeable batteries, but there are several very important reasons against not using them, including:

- It is more challenging to manage the re-use and re-charge of rechargeable batteries
- As rechargeable batteries age, they do not have a reliable voltage life.

A typical 1.5-volt alkaline or lithium battery can last up to 25 hours when powering a set of aviation NVG. In most helicopters, the total fuel endurance is usually just over 3 hours, so 25 hours of primary battery use plus 25 hours of secondary backup battery life is more than sufficient. However, each Company should have a battery life plan so that multiple users of the NVG can track the life and use of the batteries within the pack. The following information, taken from an Operations Manual, is an example of how to manage battery life.

- During the pre-flight inspection of the NVGs, the operator must inspect and confirm the current battery usage details. This can be accomplished by reviewing the NVG usage log and determining that the primary batteries have less than 20 hours of use.
- If they have less than 20 hours of use, then they may be used for this flight.
- If they have in excess of 20 hours of use, then they are to be discarded, and the secondary batteries can be transferred over to the primary side and a new set of secondary batteries installed.
- The batteries used as the secondary batteries (i.e. the right-side battery pack) MUST be new prior to commencing NVG flight operations.
- The primary batteries (i.e. the left battery pack) do not have to be new prior to commencing the flight.
- During the conduct of the flight(s), the crew are required to operate from the left set of batteries. The right set of batteries should only be used if there is a problem with the left side or they are no longer capable of being used.
- Two containers for AA batteries are kept in the NVG storage room. One container will be labelled Primary batteries and consists of batteries that have been used previously. The second container will be labelled Secondary batteries and consists of only unused or new batteries.

- If during a flight the secondary set of batteries are used at any period, or are suspected of having been used, they are to be returned to the Primary battery container after the flight is completed, and new batteries shall be placed in the secondary compartment
- Batteries from the primary container may be used for NVGs on the primary side only or for use in crew torches and equipment.
- If in any doubt as to battery life, install new batteries in both sides prior to the flight

Electrical Circuit Within the Intensifier Tube

The electrical circuit within the intensifier tube regulates the direct current (DC) voltage from the batteries as required by the intensifier tube. It also monitors the output voltage of the batteries that are being used and can activate a low battery indicator.

The high voltage power supply built into the intensifier tube converts the 3 volts (2 x 1.5 volts from each battery) from the battery pack to the required voltages to the photocathode, MCP and phosphor screen to provide optimal conditions for the image intensifier.

The internal circuitry within the intensifier tube will be responsible for the brightness control (autogain or autogating) as well as the bright source protection.

Low Battery Indicator

Low battery indicators may vary depending on the manufacturer; however, they are becoming more standardised, so the following is typical.

Low-Battery Indicator

If the battery voltage in the compartment that is being used drops below 2.1 volts, then a red low battery indicator light located at the base of the mount assembly will start blinking, indicating approximately 30 minutes of operating time remaining.

To test this on the ground before flight, the entire system has to be connected, then whichever compartment the switch is set to shall have its compartment cap popped open. This will instantly drop the voltage to below 2.1 volts, and the light should start to blink. If this test fails on the ground, then the NVGs are rendered unserviceable and shall be sent in for service.

If the low battery light activates in flight, the user should immediately switch to the secondary battery source (using the ON-OFF-ON switch) and notify the other crew members that they are operating on secondary power.

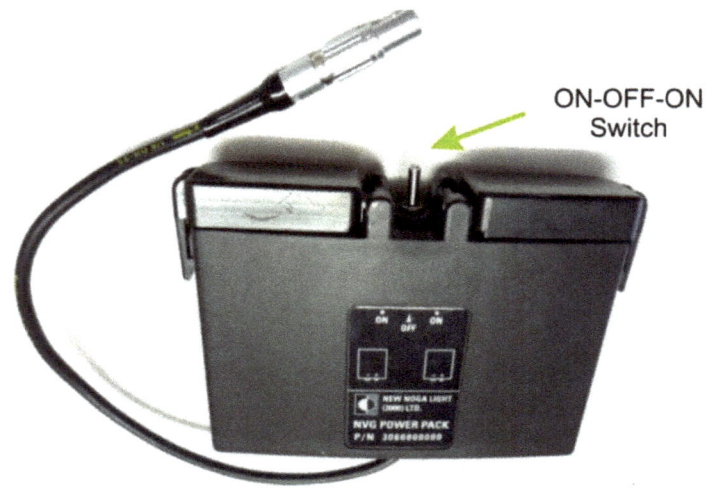

ON-OFF-ON Switch

Night Vision Goggles *for Helicopter Pilots*

Mounting System

The mounting system for a set of NVGs onto a crewmember's helmet must have several key elements. It needs to be able to be easily attached to the helmet, connected to the power pack, attached to the binocular housing, adjusted to each individual's unique needs, and finally, it needs to have a breakaway ability in the event of an emergency to protect the wearer's neck.

Helmet Mounting

There are many ways a mount may attach to a helmet. In most cases, this revolves around a bracket and mounting screws or plugs that are either an additional attachment or are built into the manufacture of the helmet. Below are examples of the helmet attaching points provided on helmets from Gentex and Gallet.

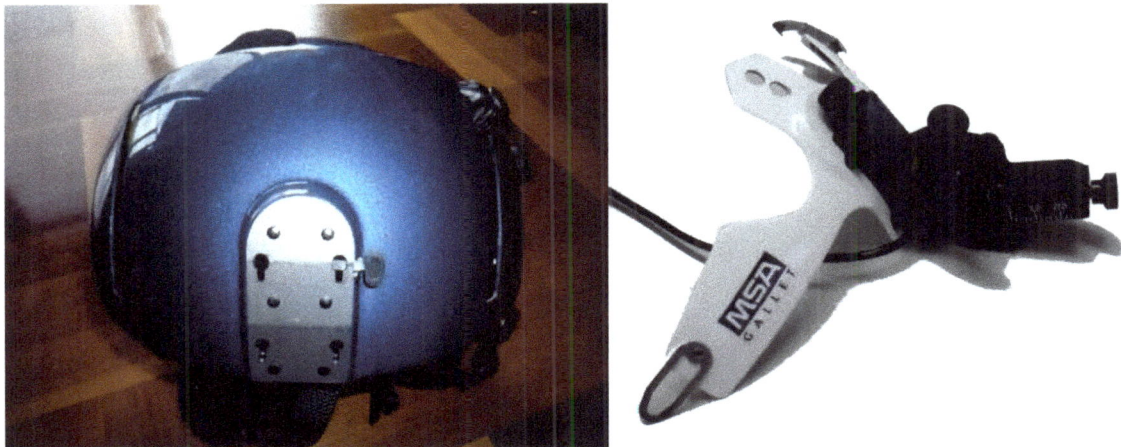

Figure 68 Gentex attachment Figure 69 Gallet attachment

As part of the helmet mounting process and prior to using the helmet, make sure the helmet attachment points are secure and not oversized, as there is nothing worse than a loose mount.

Mount Assembly

The NVG mount assembly will attach to the helmet and consists of a:

- locking pin so that the binocular housing can be moved in and out of place so that the user can choose to either be goggled up or de-goggled,
- vertical adjustment for moving the binoculars up and down,
- fore and aft adjustment to adjust the Field of View (FOV) and bring the eyepiece closer or further away, and
- tilt adjustment to change the angle or tilt of the binoculars relative to the eye line.

Additionally, the binocular housing has part of the mounting system attached to it, allowing an eye span distance adjustment that can accommodate eyes that are wider or closer together.

The mount assembly will also have a spring-loaded attachment system so the binocular housing can attach to the mount but automatically break away in an emergency and allow electrical contact from the battery pack.

There are various mount assemblies made of various materials depending on the manufacturer's design. This book concentrates mainly on the NL-94-AU as an example.

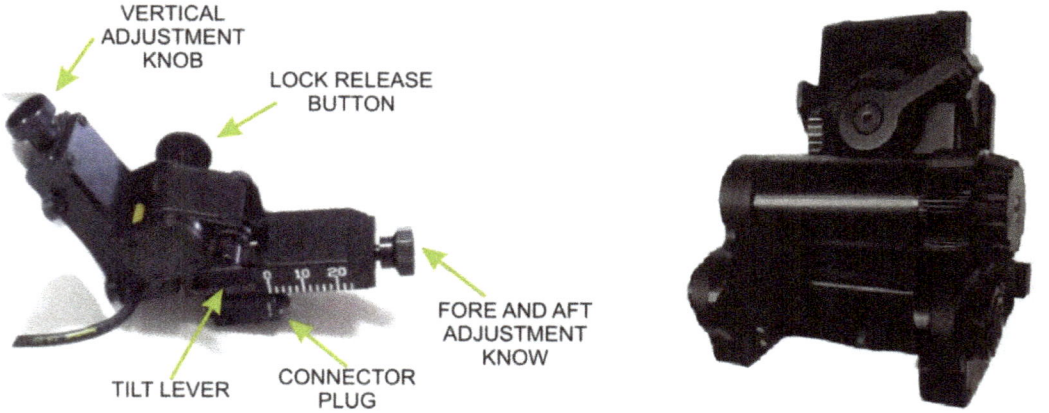

Figure 70 Mount assembly NL-94-AU

Figure 71 Mount assembly ITT F4949

Locking Pin

When pressed, the locking pin will release, allowing the user to rotate the binocular housing up out of the way where it can then be locked in place for unaided use or rotated down in front of the user's face where it can then be locked in place and adjusted with the other adjustments for night aided (NVG) flight.

1. Press Lock-Release Button

2. Rotate the binocular up.

Vertical Adjustment

The vertical adjustment knob allows the user to move the binocular housing up or down on a screw adjustment so that the user's eyes are correctly aligned with the eyepiece.

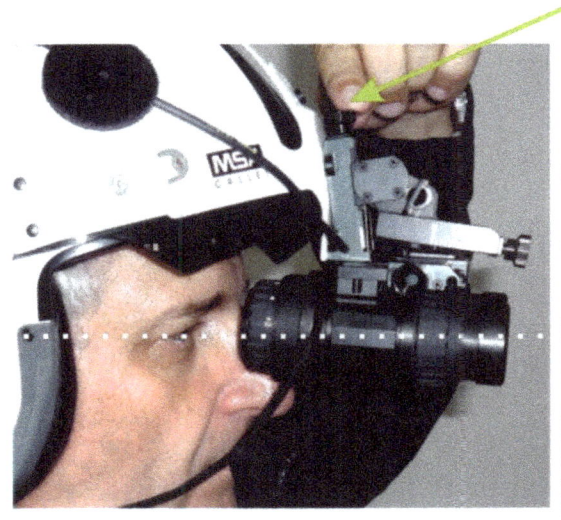

Vertical Adjustment Knob

Adjust the binocular up and down

Tilt Adjustment Lever

The tilt lever has a very small degree of movement where the user can rotate it a quarter of a turn either way to adjust the tilt of the binocular housing to accommodate the angle that the NVG are on any individual's helmet.

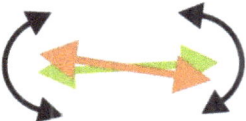

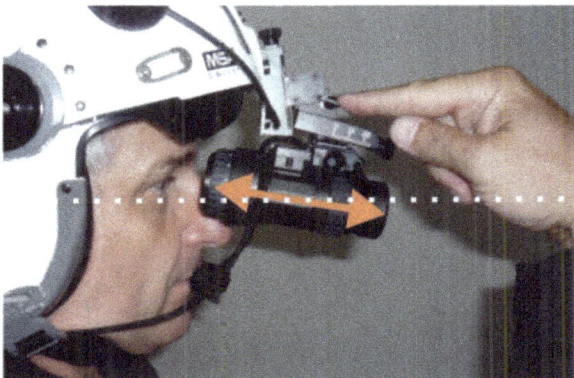

If the upper or lower edges of the image are blurred, or the image is not circular with the top or bottom portion of the image missing, then adjust the tilt lever until this is corrected. Sometimes it is a combination of vertical and tilt adjustment to get the desired result.

Fore and Aft Adjustment Knob

The fore and aft adjustment knob is important to get right because there are several elements you are trying to accommodate including obtaining the:

1. maximum field of view (FOV)
2. best visibility of instruments and navaids by viewing them with your eyes under the NVGs.

If the NVGs are too far away from the face, you can decrease the FOV and therefore decrease what you can see.

If the NVGs are too close to your face, then you will not be able to see your instruments and navaids under the goggles.

It sometimes takes some experimentation to get the right balance of distance to ensure you can continue to see what you need to see.

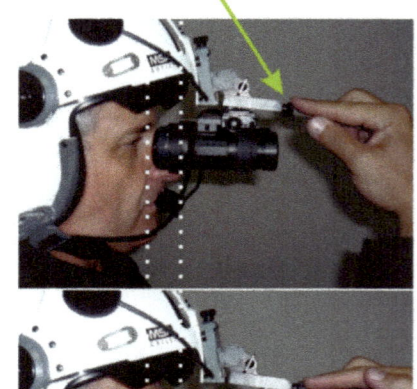

Fore-and-Aft Adjustment Knob

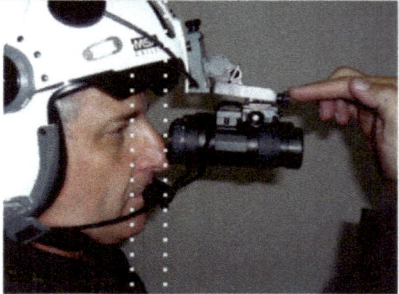

Adjust distance from eye.

Eye Span Distance Adjustment Knob

Often referred to as the **interpupillary adjustment knob** it allows each monocular to be adjusted sideways to accommodate the varying eye span of individual users. It consists of two knobs mounted on the horizontal platform connecting the monocular.

The easiest way to adjust it is to close one eye and adjust the monocular that you can see through until you can see a full circle, then do the same for the other eye. If adjusted correctly, the resultant image, when looking through both tubes, will appear to be one large circle.

Eye-span Adjustment Knobs

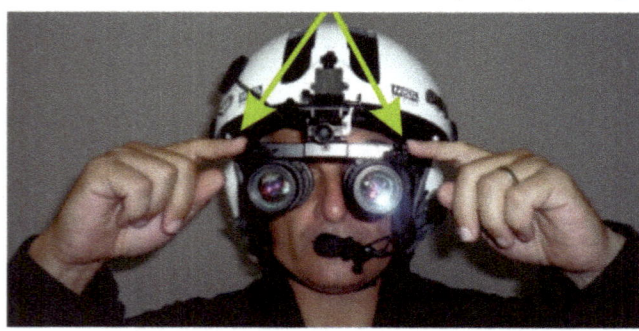
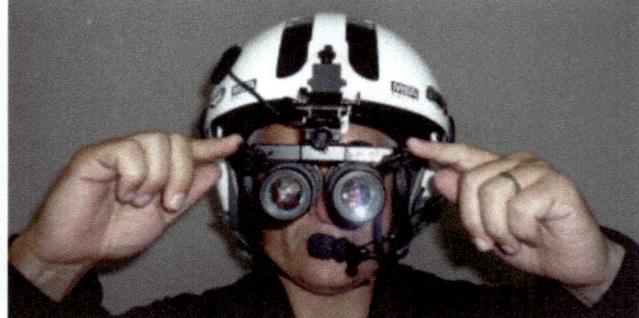

Maximum   Minimum

Breakaway

The bottom of the mount incorporates a low battery LED indicator, a spring-loaded breakaway that also doubles as the electrical connection from the power pack to the NVGs.

For the NVGs to attach to the mount, the user must place the NVGs against the mount and use pressure to snap it into place. This can be awkward the first couple of times because it is usually done while the helmet is on your head, so it has to be done by feel rather than sight.

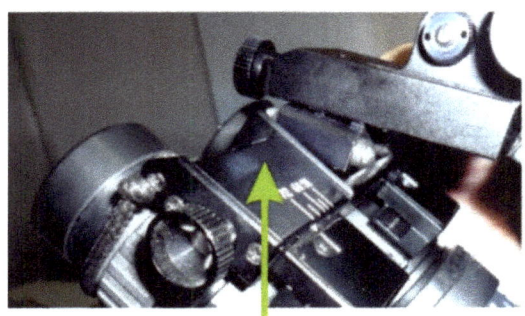

Firstly fit spherical juts into binocular connector socket

Secondly, push the binocular upwards so that the spring-loaded balls snap into the connector socket.

The tensioned springs that snap into place double as the breakaway point in the event of a 10G downward force or more. This system is important and is checked and calibrated at every service because, in a downwards acceleration, the NVGs will break away instead of breaking the user's neck.

Electrical Connection

The electrical connector on the mounting system needs to be able to quickly and easily be connected to the power pack. For safety reasons, it is better that it is not locked in place; however, it also has to be sturdy enough that it does not come loose in flight. It is usually a multiple pin press type connector. Before connecting, check that each connector is clean and that there are no exposed wires.

The electrical connection consists of two brass contacts that will touch once the NVG housing and mount come together. Keep this area clean and clear of corrosion. If the contacts become dirty, then the best way to clean them is by rubbing them with a small eraser (rubber) which is usually supplied as part of the aircrew support equipment within the NVG case.

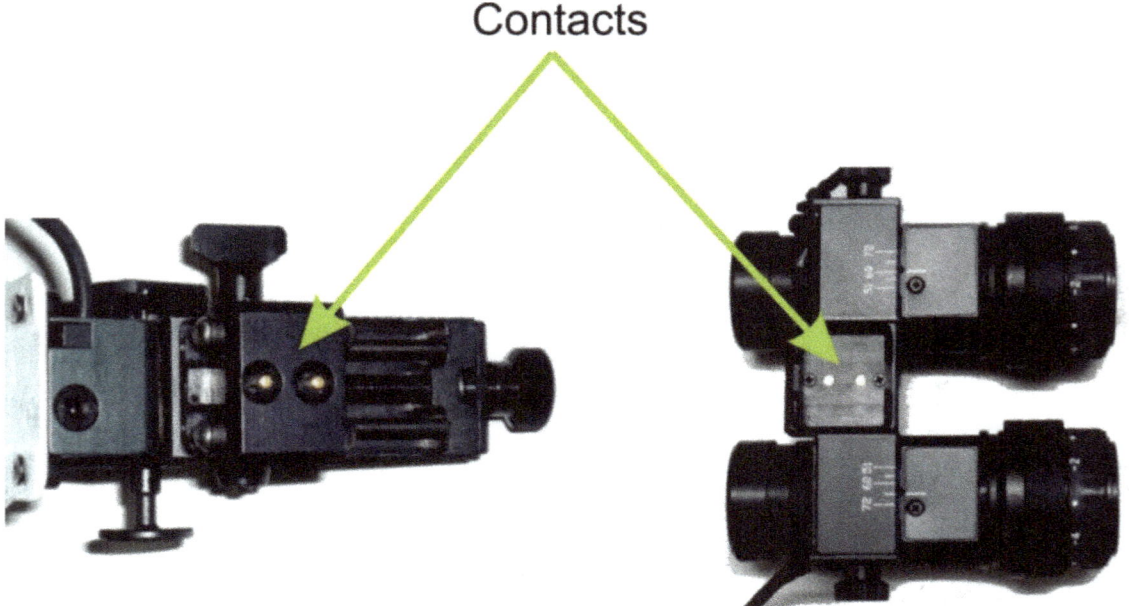

Problems in NVG Adjustment

Because aviation NVGs uses binoculars (2 image intensifier tubes - one for each eye) instead of monoculars (one image intensifier tube for either just one eye or mirrored so the one image can be viewed by both eyes), if there is a disparity between the two images this can cause problems. This disparity could be caused by either:

- an internal variation between the individual intensifier tubes
- the inability to align one tube for one eye compared to the other.

Having a properly adjusted set of binoculars is paramount to best performance.

Tube Alignment

If the user cannot align each monocular housing correctly in the vertical, horizontal, tilt or distance from the face, then the image generated (and being interpreted by the brain) can cause headaches, blurred vision, split images, dual images and distortion.

Collimation

Collimation is how the NVGs take separate pictures from the two monoculars and align them for viewing. Collimation can be seen when using NVGs that are biocular or binocular. When proper collimation does not occur, the user can see an oblong field of view, two separate pictures or shadowing on the edges of the field of view. This will increase eye fatigue and eyestrain and have possible negative physiological effects.

Mechanical problems may also cause improper collimation. First, the intensifier tubes can be off-centre or loose within the housing assembly. Second, the housing assembly may become loose and offset from the visual axis.

A third problem can be a misalignment of the eye span setting (also referred to as the interpupillary distance - or IPD for short). This can occur if the eye span distance is set too far apart. The NVG should be returned for servicing if the user cannot correct the problem by adjusting the mounting settings.

Night Vision Goggles *for Helicopter Pilots*

Optical Image Differences

Optical image differences have to do with varying performances of individual tubes. This is no longer much of a problem in later generation tubes and modern servicing and checking cycles.

If one tube is suffering from a fault of any sort and the other one isn't, this can lead to problems. The bottom line is, if you as the user are not happy with the set of NVGs you are using, then it is up to you to decide to bring it to someone's attention, and either have the problem fixed or be issued with another set of NVGs.

Focus Lane

Proper focusing and testing can identify all of the problems discussed above before a flight. Common methods currently used to focus and adjust NVGs, such as focusing on a small light source, are not sufficient to ensure the NVG tubes are properly adjusted for flight. The NVG eye lane, the USAF 1951 resolution chart, or preferably the Hoffmann box will provide a simple method to adjust and focus the NVGs accurately. The Hoffmann Box system provides a standard to individually assess NVG tube performance and the ability to properly adjust and focus the NVGs. Each tube must be checked individually, and then the two tubes checked together.

Summary

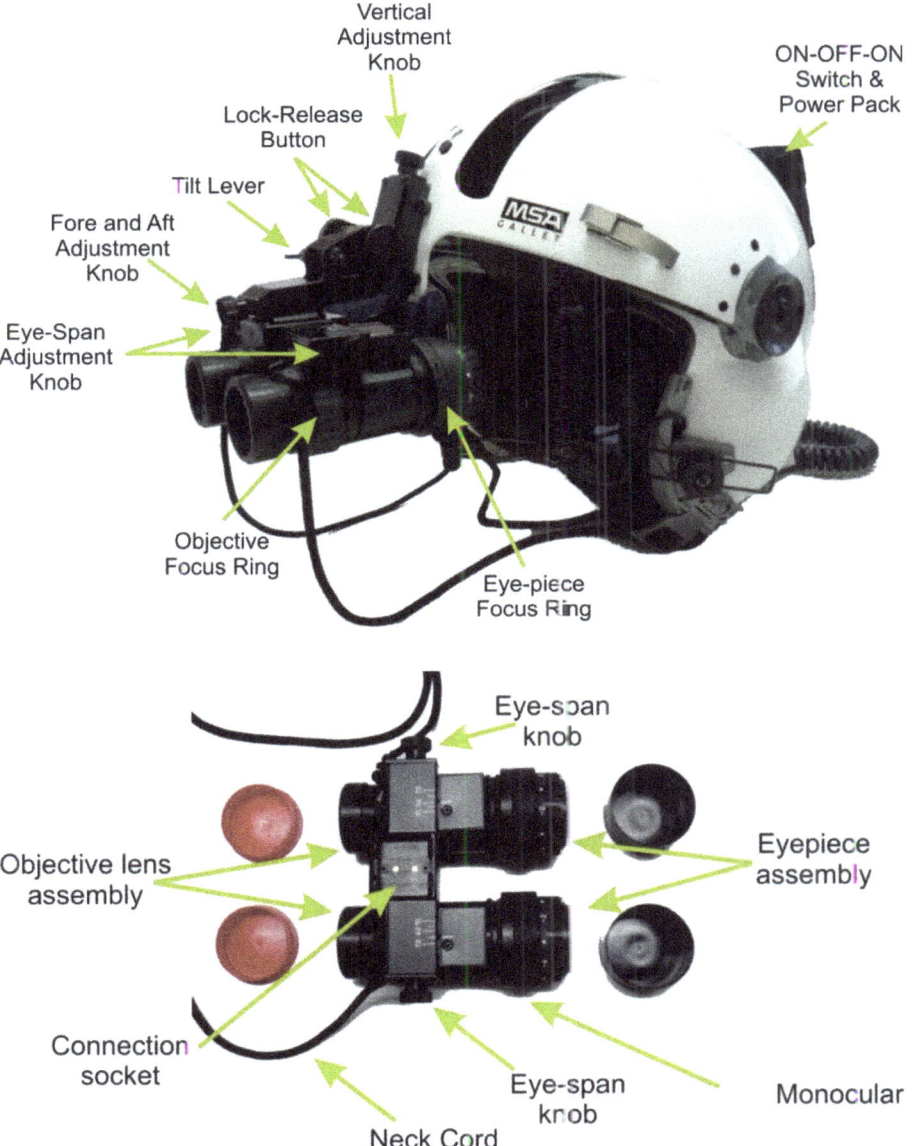

Hoffmann 20/20 Focus Box

To get the best performance from NVGs, they need to be focused properly. In the beginning, this can be difficult to do as the users need to gain experience through practice and use of the goggles to get a good understanding of how to make the fine adjustments necessary for a clear image. Focusing problems with NVGs are the leading cause of eye fatigue and lack of image clarity.

There are three basic methods used to focus the NVGs; which one to use can depend on the budget the operator has available, which can determine the available equipment, the conditions and facilities available on the night, and the amount of time you have to prepare.

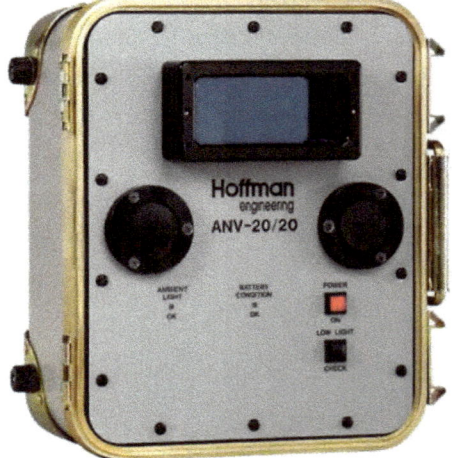

Most military and paramilitary operations can afford to have a portable focus box available. This device has a set of mirrors and a light source that fools the goggles that they are looking into infinity. The big advantage of this focus box is crews can rig their goggles in safety in a very small area prior to getting to the flight line. Any problems or un-serviceabilities can be discovered in the preparation phase. The Focus Box will also have the correct amount of light, enabling checking resolution and contrast in both high and low light conditions. Another big advantage is the focus box is portable.

If a focus box is not available, the next best option is a Focus Lane. Unfortunately, this requires a dedicated area modified to have the right light and a target that is over 150 feet (45 meters) away. Because a 45-metre Focus Lane is not practical, everything has to be scaled down for the same effect. Focus Lanes are not portable; they take up considerable space and may not have the right illumination levels. Unless all operations are from a fixed base, a Focus Lane is not a practical option in a changing aviation environment.

Finally, if neither of the two options above is available, the user can simply focus the NVGs by looking at an object greater than 150 feet (45 meters) away and focusing to the best of their ability. The secret here is to choose something that has vertical and horizontal lines. The big disadvantage is that you cannot control the light, so you cannot test if the NVGs will be working the same under both high and low light conditions.

This chapter will explain how to focus the NVGs using the Hoffmann 20/20 Focus Box.

The Hoffmann box is a portable optical alignment system that allows the accurate adjustment and focus of NVGs prior to use and also allows for a quick check on NVG system resolution (clarity) and dynamic range (ability to observe objects of varying contrast under varying light conditions).

Night Vision Goggles *for Helicopter Pilots*

Controls and Indicators

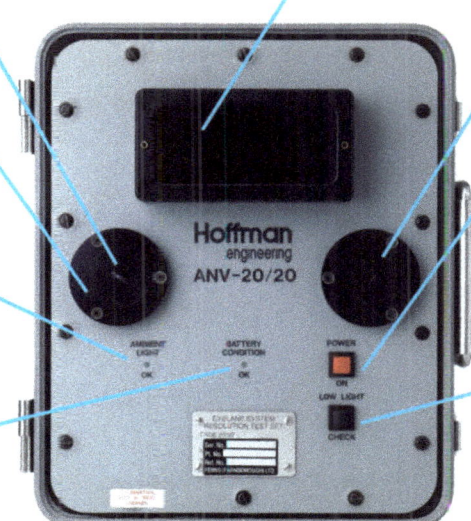

Viewing Port
Target image appears at infinity focus.

Use coin or screwdriver to remove caps

Battery Compartment
2 D-Cells
Load with (+) end up

Battery Compartment
2 D-Cells
Load with (+) end up

Power On switch
Automatic 3-minute timer.
Hold to check status lights.

Ambient light indicator
Check while pressing Power On Switch.

Battery Voltage Indicator
Check while pressing Power On Switch.

Low Light Level switch
Hold to check low light resolution.

The Hoffmann box has the following controls and indicators:

Control / Indicator	Description
POWER ON (red push button)	Pushing the **POWER ON** button starts the interval timer and enables the system status indicator lights. The system will remain on for three minutes after the **POWER ON** button is pushed and automatically turn off. The system indicator lights (**AMBIENT LIGHT OK** and **BATTERY CONDITION OK**) will only display if the **POWER ON** button is held on.
LOW LIGHT CHECK (black push button)	Pushing the **LOW LIGHT CHECK** button reduces the system test level from high-light to low-light while the button is held in. The system will automatically return to the high-light level when the button is released.
AMBIENT LIGHT OK (green LED indicator light)	The **AMBIENT LIGHT OK** indicator will light up when the **POWER ON** button is pressed, and the ambient light in the room is less than 0.1 foot candles (LUMEN). If the light in the room is too bright (because a light is on), this green light will not display.
BATTERY CONDITION OK (green LED indicator light)	The **BATTERY CONDITION OK** indicator will light up when the **POWER ON** button is pressed, and the total voltage provided by the 4 D-Cell batteries is greater than 4.2 volts. Normal total voltage from the 4 D-Cell batteries is 6 volts. If the **BATTERY CONDITION OK** indicator does not come on when the **POWER ON** button is pressed, then replace the 4 D-Cell batteries before using the focus box to check the goggles.

Control / Indicator	Description
Battery Compartment	The battery compartment covers are provided with rubber O-Ring seals and are threaded. Using a large coin or screwdriver and rotating anticlockwise will open the compartments. The positive (+) end faces UP for all cells.
Air pressure relief valve	The Hofmann box case lid is provided with an air pressure relief valve which can either be a press or a screw-type arrangement. Because the Hoffmann box is a portable unit, it can be sealed and is watertight, which can also mean that the air pressure can vary inside the box compared to outside the box. To equalize the pressure before opening, either press or unscrew the pressure release valve to equalize the air pressure.

Checking NVG System Resolution and Dynamic Range

The resolution is checked by using the multi-bar patterns with four elements in two orientations (vertical and horizontal) for each level of resolution.

The NVG dynamic range (contrast) can be checked by using the eight-step greyscale in conjunction with the two preset high and low light illumination options.

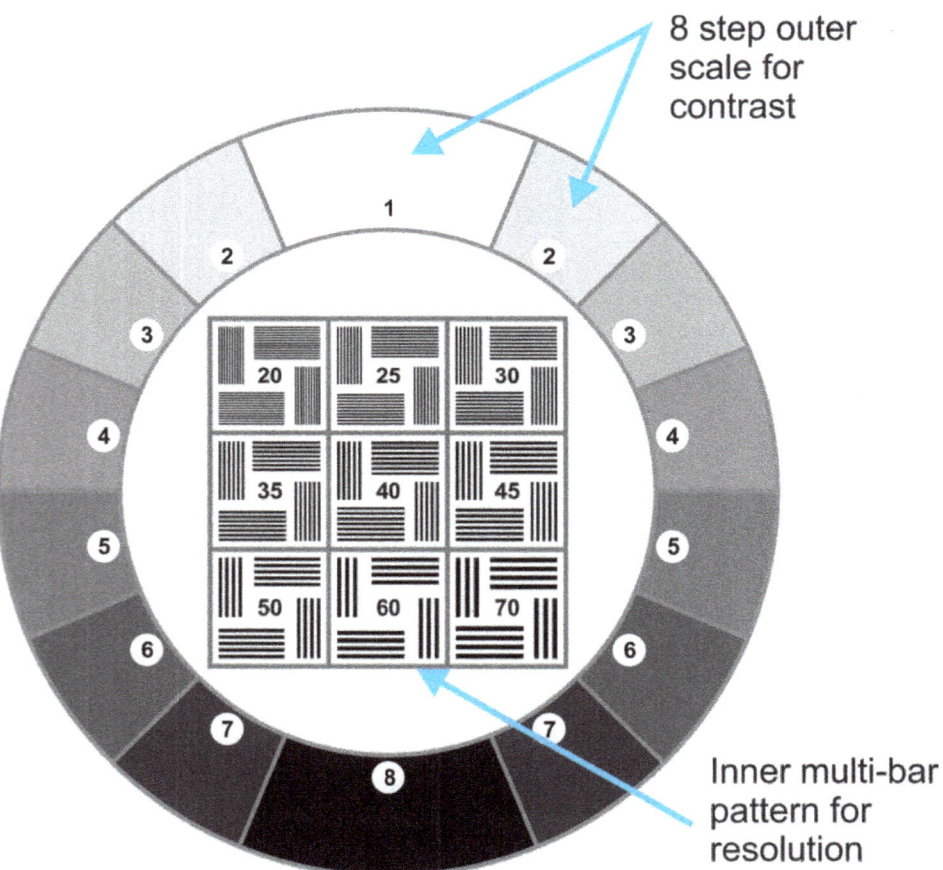

The Resolution Pattern

The resolution pattern in the centre of the image is made up of a series of vertical and horizontal lines in accordance with the standard Snellen resolution fraction.

The Snellen resolution fraction or pattern requires that the thickness of the black lines equals the thickness of the white spaces and that the height and width of each individual block of vertical and horizontal lines is 5 times the thickness of each block of lines and spaces.

In other words, the group of vertical and horizontal lines are not random; they have been specifically and mathematically designed so that they are a measure of visual acuity or resolution (how clear the image is)

A person with 20/20 vision can see the smallest line on a Snellen Chart at 20 ft.

If someone has poor vision and they cannot see the white spaces between the black lines until they get to say, the 40 mark then the visual acuity is deemed to be 20/40. In other words, what a normal person would see at 40 feet, the person with poorer vision can only see at 20 feet.

Because we are now viewing the image through a set of NVGs, they have to be focused and perform to a certain level before going flying.

Minimum Resolution

When looking through the NVGs, we should be able to focus each individual tube to a minimum resolution as specified by the manufacturer.

In the case of the F4949 and NL-94-AU NVGs, **under high light conditions,** the minimum resolution for either and both eyes should be **20/35**.

Under low light conditions, this resolution can be reduced to **20/40**.

These are the minimum resolution standards required before you can go flying with these NVGs. You will find that the F4949s and NL-94-AUs can do much better, usually achieving 20/25 under high light and 20/30 under low light.

Because we have two individual intensifier tubes, we cannot have a discrepancy of **more than one grid** between the goggles.

Example
With the right eye closed, the left tube had a resolution of 20/25 under high light and 20/35 under low light, but when you did the same test on the other tube, you found that you had a high light resolution of 20/35 and a low light of 20/45. One tube is not performing as well as the other one, which could lead to headaches and more significant fatigue so the NVGs should be returned for service and not used on this flight.

Greyscale Outer Ring

The greyscale patterns around the outer edge of the Snellen pattern are used to check the dynamic performance of NVGs. This relates to both the NVG and the user's ability to see the contrast or differences between two objects side by side.

Conditions of low contrast and low light would give the NVGs a low dynamic performance.

Conditions of high contrast and high light would give the NVGs a high dynamic performance.

Looking at the greyscale ring, we see that each number corresponds to a different shade. The brightest step in the scale is at the top, and the darkest is at the bottom. Each progressive step around the pattern is twice as bright as the previous step except for step 8, which is opaque.

The word opaque means not transparent, impenetrable to light, or does not allow light to pass through it. In simple terms, it means black.

Corresponding pattern steps on the left and right sides have equal brightness.

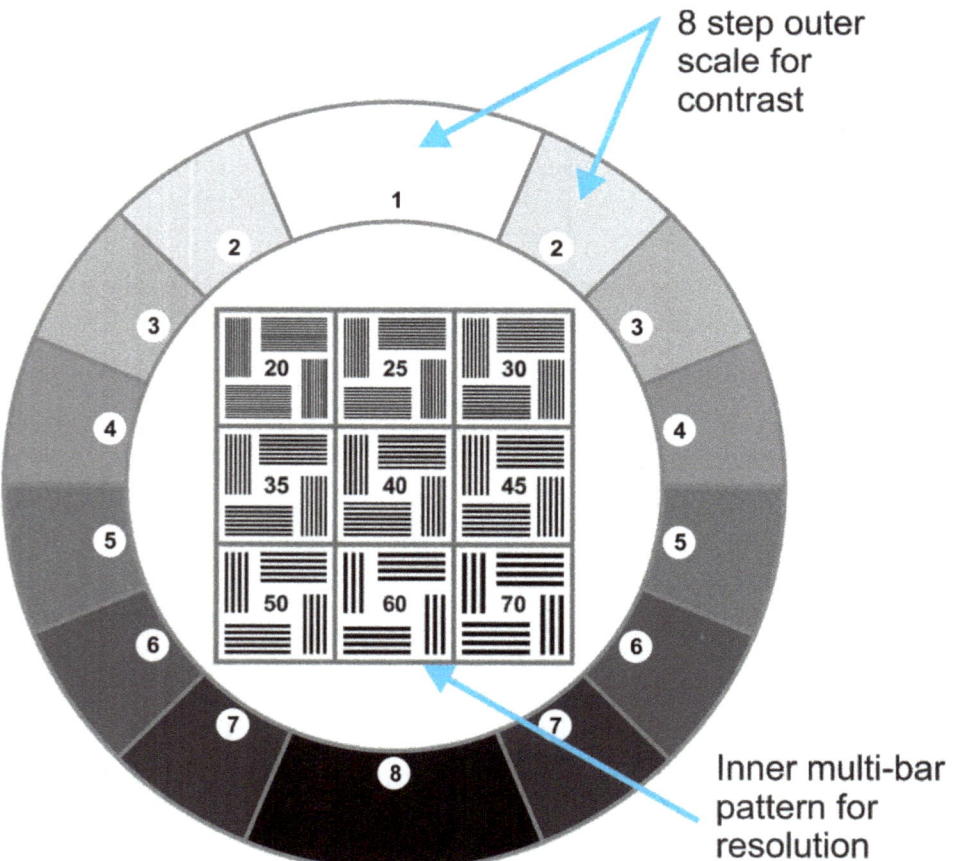

We can now check the dynamic performance of NVGs based on either high light or low light conditions. Each step around the scale then represents a particular luminance level that can be encountered in flight. The table below describes this:

Grey Scale Step	High Light	Low Light
1	Full moon	Starlight +
2	$1/2$ Moon	Starlight
3	$1/4$ Moon	Hazy starlight
4	$1/8$ Moon	Cloudy starlight
5	$1/16$ Moon	Light overcast starlight
6	Starlight +	Medium overcast starlight
7	Starlight	Heavy overcast starlight
8	Opaque	Opaque

Low light levels can be checked by pressing and holding the LOW LIGHT CHECK button. Because performance at low light levels is a test of both the NVGs and the user, total darkness in the room is required, and the user must allow 3-5 minutes to become dark-adapted for the test to be done correctly.

Minimum Greyscale Dynamic Performance

So, what are we looking for?

Under high and low light conditions, you are looking to see where you can see a difference in the shade between the steps. If the steps blend together so that you cannot tell the difference, then this indicates the limit of the dynamic performance (contrast) under those conditions.

Example

With older generation NVGs under high light conditions, you may only have been able to see a difference between steps 1-5, with numbers 6-8 all blending as if they were one shade. This may have deteriorated under low light conditions so that only steps 1-3 were discernible, and all the others blended as if they were the same shade.

With later generation NVGs and particularly the F4949s and NL-94-AU, under both high and low light conditions, the user should be able to see a contrast between all eight steps (1-8).

The NL-94-AU should have a minimum dynamic performance under high light of 1-8 and under low light a minimum dynamic performance of 1-4.

1-8 means you can see the difference in contrast between all of the eight steps. 1-4 means you can see a difference in the steps from 1 to 4, but 5 to 8 are blending as if they are one shade.

Hoffmann 20/20 Focusing Procedure

Step	Action	Desired result
1	Pre-set the objective ring all the way to the left and the dioptic setting to the middle or zero.	The goggles are ready for adjusting for the individual user at a pre-set datum.
2	Fit the NVGs to the helmet and adjust as required for use. Do not turn them on at this time.	Able to flip the goggles down, and they are adjusted horizontally, vertically, tilt and eye span for the individual user.
3	Enter the focus room, turn off the lights, flip the goggles down, and turn the goggles on.	You should be able to see through the goggles. At this point, do not be concerned with focus but fine-tune the adjustments of horizontal, vertical, tilt and eye span so that each eye can individually see a circle and then both eyes will see a single oversized circle. At the same time, you should be able to look under the NVGs to be able to read the NVG log book. If you cannot, then adjust the horizontal until you can.
4	Proceed to the Hoffmann 20/20 focus box, press and hold the POWER ON button.	Looking under your goggles, check that the **AMBIENT LIGHT OK** and the **BATTERY CONDITION OK** indicators are green.
5	Release the POWER ON button.	The Focus Box is now activated and ready for use. It will remain on for 3 minutes at High Light.
6	Position yourself so that the objective lenses of the NVGs are in the viewing port.	You should now be able to see the Snellen target (although it will probably be out of focus).
7	Close or cover one eye and rotate the objective focus ring for the best image clarity.	The horizontal lines of the appropriate grid should come into focus. You should be able to define the difference in the vertical and horizontal lines compared to the vertical and horizontal spaces. The F4949 and NL-94-AU should be able to focus to the 25 grid; however, the minimum acceptable for use is the 35 grid (under high light conditions).
8	Move your hand to adjust the eyepiece dioptric ring. Rotate the ring counterclockwise until the image is sharp and then keep turning until the image becomes slightly blurred. Stop for a second, blink, let the eye relax, and slowly rotate the dioptic ring back clockwise until the image becomes sharp.	The image should now be at its clearest as the dioptric setting allows the individual to adjust the focus to their individual eye.

Step	Action	Desired result
9	Now fine-tune the objective focus ring for the best image clarity on the smallest Snellen number target with any visible structure. Take your time, blink after each adjustment and leave the lens set at the best focus point.	This will help you achieve the best possible focus.
10	Repeat the above process until you are satisfied you have achieved the best clarity.	At worst, you should see the Snellen 35 grid, at best, the 25 or even the 20 Snellen grid.
11	Repeat this process with the opposite eye. If the focus box turns off at any time, press the POWER ON for another three minutes of activation.	You should achieve the same or very similar result to the first eye.
12	Press and hold the LOW LIGHT button.	The amount of light will reduce.
13	Check each eye individually, closing one and then taking note of the smallest resolution pattern that can be resolved, then repeat with both eyes. DO NOT READJUST THE FOCUS IN LOW LIGHT CONFIGURATION	F4949 and NL-94-AU NVGs should have a minimum resolution of 20/40 in low light to be acceptable.
14	Read the greyscale around the outer circle of the Snellen pattern.	This will indicate the dynamic performance of the NVGs. The F4949 and NL-94-AU NVGs should get a score of 1-8; however, the **minimum acceptable is 1-4.**
15	Move away from the focus box, turn the NVGs OFF, then flip them up.	Focusing is completed.
16	Remove the NVGs and note the various settings you have set on your NVGs.	You can record the parameters of horizontal, vertical, tilt and eye span and objective and dioptic focus so that next time you can preset the NVGs prior to attaching them to your helmet, and the focus procedure time will be greatly reduced.
17	Enter the details of the Snellen pattern into the NVG logbook kept in the NVG case.	This allows a progressive record to be kept of individual NVG performance.

NOTES:

1. The eyepiece focusing procedure attempts to achieve the best image resolution with the *least* amount of negative (-) diopter correction.

2. Do not rotate the eyepiece diopter ring clockwise beyond the setting, which brings the image into sharp focus. If the eyepiece focus is adjusted too far clockwise, the eye will initially adapt to the setting but will become fatigued over time. Loss of visual acuity, depth perception and eye strain will result.

3. During flight, *minor* adjustments to vertical height, tilt, eye span and horizontal alignment may be required due to helmet settling and rotation. **Do not change the eyepiece diopter settings during flight.** The setting obtained using the Focus Box should produce the best setting for long term use.

4. The objective lens focus settings obtained using the Hoffmann 20/20 are corrected for infinity focus. If it becomes necessary to refocus the objective lens, then pick a clearly defined object (preferably with good vertical and horizontal lines) that is at least 150 meters away. Avoid lights that are bright enough to cause blooming of the NVG image.
5. DO NOT PERFORM NVG FOCUS IN FULL DAYLIGHT. NEVER LOOK TOWARDS THE SUN WITH THE NVG ON OR WITH THE NVG PROTECTIVE CAPS REMOVED. NEVER LEAVE THE GOGGLES WHERE THE UNPROTECTED LENSES WILL BE EXPOSED TO DIRECT SUNLIGHT.
6. Although the NL-94-AU NVGs have autogating technology and can handle bright light situations to a greater degree than intensifier tubes that do not have autogating, the bright light will reduce the life of the intensifier tube and has the potential to burn out the phosphor screen.

The Generation Game

As technology changes over time, NVGs have undergone various modifications and improvements, resulting in generational changes in how they produce an image. However, different countries treat the name changes differently. Below we will discuss some of the more common generational definitions and how they apply to NVGs.

Omnibus and Generation

During your career using Night Vision Devices (NVDs), you will hear the words Generation and Omnibus and other terms such as ANVIS, AN/PVS and/or AN/AVS, followed by a number. These terms and abbreviations are widely used by the United States (US) and represent how their military forces categorise and identify their NVDs. This has affected how the rest of the world categorises, identifies and compares various NVDs.

It is important to note here that other countries (such as the European Union, Israel, Russia, and China) that have also been developing and using NVDs do not necessarily use the Generation or Omnibus system. Therefore, arguments can develop between Aviation Authorities and Military organisations of various countries when they are trying to compare one NVD to another because they try to compare the various manufacturing processes rather than specifically looking at the individual device's actual performance.

Omnibus

The term **Omnibus** (sometimes referred to as OMNI) translates as "pertaining to or dealing with a variety of topics at one time" (see www.dictionary.net/omnibus).

Every year, the United States Congress will produce documents (called omnibus bills, or bills for short) that appropriate money for all discretionary government spending. Generally, one document is passed for each United States House Committee on Appropriations sub-committee. Ordinarily, each bill is passed separately, one bill for Defence, one for Homeland Security, and so on. Over the years, the committee responsible for Defence in the US has issued several omnibus contracts specifically for Night Vision Devices (NVD's). These contracts allow commercial businesses to compete in an open tender for the services and products described in the omnibus document.

With regards to Night Vision Devices (NVD) there have been several omnibus contracts; a number identifies each one. For example, Omnibus I, Omnibus II, Omnibus III, Omnibus IV and so on.

Each of these Omnibus contracts specifies what the Defence Department is looking for regarding NVD performance, configuration and how they would be used. Based on these Omnibus documents, technology companies create specific equipment that will meet the performance requirements stated in the Omnibus document, and they would offer up the product in an open tender situation. The US Government would then select a successful tender for the product.

Because NVDs were primarily military products, the first company to be awarded a tender would set the benchmark for future comparisons of NVDs.

The first company in America to do this was the International Telephone and Telegraph Company (ITT) which is now a world leader in night vision equipment (visit *www.itt.com/about/history/* to read about their history).

As each new Omnibus contract came out, the performance requirements increased, offering even better equipment. As the equipment evolved, this led to the use of the term *Generation* which identified each new advance in the NVD technology applied to a particular Omnibus contract. At this point in time, NVDs are divided into four basic categories, starting with Generation 0 and finishing with Generation III. Although the US Military has not officially designated generation IV, it is sometimes discussed as the next advance in NVD

Generations

Initially, designers thought that the NVG should be strapped to the user's face to take out any peripheral light; however, as time progressed, it was understood that the user could get a lot of valuable information by looking under or around the NVG; therefore there are two basic NVG designs that apply to aviation.

Full Face Goggles

Full-face goggles (Figure 72) cover the entire face and are no longer used in aviation operations. A pilot using these goggles cannot look under, over or to the side of the goggles but must instead move the head to view the instruments and other peripheral objects. This creates many problems with focusing and ergonomics.

Displaced Goggles

Displaced goggles (Figure 73) have eyepieces that are displaced from the user's eyes so that the user can look through the goggles for night vision, but at the same time can look under, over or around the goggles with unaided vision. With this system, the user could focus the NVGs to infinity for outside viewing while using normal vision to view instruments and objects in the peripherals. Using displaced goggles for aviation is now standard practice.

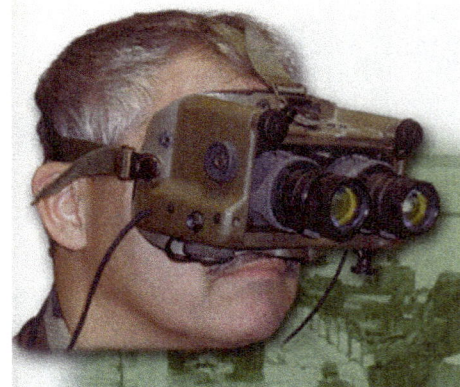

Figure 72 Full-face goggles [37]

Figure 73 Displaced goggles

---

[37] Turpin, T, 2001, 'Night Vision Goggles (NVGs) and NVG Equipment with Market Potential', FAA, pg 35.

Generation 0

The first night vision goggles were developed in 1935 by a German Company called Allgemeine Elektrizitäts-Gesellschaft (AEG) and were introduced to the German army as early as 1939.

By the end of World War II, the German army had equipped approximately 50 Panther tanks, which saw combat on both the Eastern and Western Fronts. The "Vampir" man-portable system for infantrymen was used with Sturmgewehr 44 assault rifles.

Parallel development of night vision systems occurred in the US. The M1 and M3 infrared night sighting devices, also known as the "sniperscope" or "snooperscope", were introduced by the US Army in World War II and were also used in the Korean War to assist snipers.

These devices were **Active IR** systems, using a large infrared light source to illuminate targets. Their image intensifier tubes functioned using an anode and an S-1 photocathode, made primarily of silver, caesium, and oxygen, to accelerate the electrons.

These systems were in use up until the late 1950s.

Figure 74 First night vision goggles ZG 1229 [38]

Generation I

Generation I saw the creation of the "Starlight scopes" used in the 1960s during the Vietnam War and were the first real *passive* systems using a series of three image intensifier tubes to enhance any light allowing the person looking through the scope to see the target.

Figure 75 US M1 infrared night scoping device [39]

They were smaller and more portable when compared to Generation 0 NVDs.

Figure 76 Example of Generation I Night Vision Scopes [40]

Generation I systems can still be used and sold today and provide a sharp image at a low cost which is perfect for boating, observing wildlife or providing security for your home.

Generation I units can make a slight high-pitched whine when switched on, the image can be blurry around the edges (geometric distortion), and it may glow green for some time when it is turned off. It also does not have any bright source protection, so white light can give the typical green overload on the system.

---

38 AchtungPanzer.com, online image, viewed 11 November 2011, www.achtungpanzer.com/images/vampir.jpg

39 US Militia Forum.com, online image, viewed 11 November 2011, www.usmilitariaforum.com/uploads//monthly_01_2010/post-3483-1264665889.jpg

40 GunOwnersResource.com, online image, viewed 11 November 2011, gunownersresource.com/gorole/ images/thumb/b/ba/M16A1_PVS-2.JPEG/180px-M16A1_PVS-2.JPEG

Generation II

The 1970s saw improvements in the intensifier tube by incorporating a **microchannel plate (MCP)** which allowed a dramatic increase in the amount of light able to be amplified, giving a brighter and sharper image and leading to the practical use of a helmet-mounted NVD referred to as a night vision goggle or NVG.

Interestingly the Generation II image resolution was less than that of the Generation I intensifier, but the gain (amplification) was much higher.

Super Generation II

With improvements in the photocathode and refining of the MCP, some Generation II intensifier tubes were outperforming early Generation III tubes.

Figure 77 Example of Generation II NVG [41]

Generation III

The 1980s saw the introduction of a photosensitive chemical called **gallium arsenide applied to the photocathode, which allowed even greater amplification of an image in low light conditions.**

This, along with a thin ion barrier film on the microchannel plate provided much greater tube life extending the meantime to failure (MTTF) of the Generation III tube to 10,000 hours + compared to only 2500 hours for the Generation II tube.

Generation III Plus and Generation III Omnibus "X"

Figure 78 Example of Generation III NVG

Since the first introduction of Generation III intensifier tubes in the 1980s, the Generation III tubes have gone through a continuous improvement process, but there has not been a major leap in technology that has warranted the Generation IV classification, although it did get close.

In the 1990s, some Generation III tubes used by the US Military were supplied with filmless autogating technology, and they were distributed as Generation IV. However, in October 2001, Dr. John Pollard, chief scientist for the Army's Night Vision and Electronic Sensors Directorate (NVESD), announced that the term "Generation IV" was being removed as an identifier of autogated filmless tubes. The move, in effect, tabled indefinitely any plan for ITT to procure a filmless tube, hence sticking with their current 'thin filmed' Generation III Omni VII 'Pinnacle' NVGs.

Generation IV

It would seem that US politics requires that the US purchase each new generation exclusively for their own armed forces only, irrespective of friendly pacts with neighbouring or allied forces. Hence newer generation European type 'Autogated Filmless Tubes', although often referred to as Generation IV type products, are yet to be officially classed as such by the US.

XR5

Gated Filmless technology represents the biggest technological breakthrough in image intensification of the past ten years. By removing the ion barrier film and "gating" the system, the tube now provides substantial increases in target detection range and resolution, particularly at extremely low light levels.

This technology, as used in the XR5 from Photonis-DEP (a European manufacturer), improves night operational effectiveness for military users of NVGs and other NVDs. The filmless MCP provides a higher SNR than Generation III, resulting in better image quality (less scintillation) under low-light conditions.

---

41 ORTEK Ltd, online image, viewed 11 November 2011, www.ortekltd.com/images/NVG2g.jpg

Night Vision Goggles for Helicopter Pilots

The gated power supply improves image resolution under high light conditions, and the reduced halo minimises interference from bright light sources. These improvements also substantially increase the detection range of the systems giving up to a 100% improvement in photoresponse, better performance in extremely low light levels (better S/N and EBI) and at least triple the high light level resolution with a minimum of 36 lp/mm compared to 12 lp/mm in older Generation III.

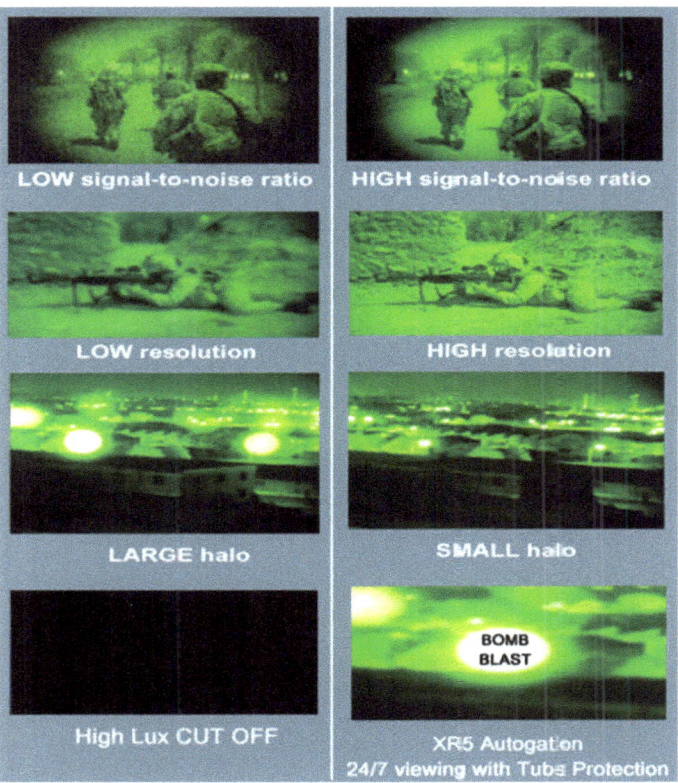

Figure 79 Comparison of ITT Generation III (left) and Photonis XR5 (right)

Comparing US and European Classifications

The Europeans, who have a different system for commissioning and categorising their NVDs, do not have an Omnibus or Generation system. Instead, they will talk about Performance and describe the changes in the technology of each goggle, then give it a specific designator as part of a **Performance Family**.

If we summarise this into categories of NVDs, then anyone coming through the American system may discuss NVDs as meeting an Omnibus Generation specification (for example, Generation III Omnibus VII)

Europeans will simply state how an NVD will perform and give it its own distinct designation. Below is a high-level summary of the two major tube technologies and how they approximately compare to each other:

United States Technology Family (Omnibus and Generation)	European Union Performance Family
🇺🇸	🇪🇺
Generation 0	N/A
Generation I	N/A
Generation II	SuperGEN / SHD3
Generation III	XD4 Autogated
Generation IV (not yet designated in the US)	XR5 Autogated

More Terms

The abbreviations **ANVIS, AN/PVS** and/or **AN/AVS** are simply US assigned military designations for fielded (in use) night vision devices.

AN meaning **A**RMY / **N**AVY and **PVS** meaning **P**assive **V**ision **S**ystem.

ANVIS is the typical designation for military aviation use with **ANVIS** meaning **A**viator **N**ight **Vis**ion or **A**viation **N**ight **V**ision **I**maging **S**ystem.

AN/AVS is another military term meaning **A**RMY-**N**AVY / **A**viator **V**ision **S**ystem.

Example

For example: The latest Omnibus contract released by the US Government is the Generation III Omnibus VII. Manufacturers have offered up a Generation III intensifier tube to meet this contract, and once put to use by the US Military for aviation use, they were given the designation ANVIS 9.

So, when talking to technocrats, you will hear them comparing various NVGs by saying they are Generation III OMNIBUS VII ANVIS 9 or equivalent etc.

Please note here that the Omnibus contract, the Generation of NVGs, and the Military designations and numbers are changing, and the above may not be completely correct at the time of reading this book, but hopefully, you understand the concept.

Figure of Merit (FOM)

Perhaps because the US Military does not necessarily want its technology sold, it has limited the type of technology that can leave its shores and has created a methodology so that manufacturers and distributors only sell a lower version of its technology for export. This methodology is in the form of a number known as the Figure of Merit or FOM.

It is calculated by multiplying the intensifier tube line pair resolution by the signal to noise ratio. These figures will be found on the intensifier tube specification sheets as provided by the manufacturer.

For example: Let's compare the ITT Generation III intensifier tube with the XR5 intensifier tube by Photonis and see which has the better FOM.

Item	ITT F4949	NL-94-AU
System Resolution	1.3 cy/mr	1.3 cy/mr
Luminance gain	5500 FL*	2800 FL*
Field of view	40 degrees	40 degrees
Magnification	1:1	1:1
Spectral transmission	Class A / B	Class A / B
Eyepiece dioptre range	+2 to -6	+2 to -5
Objective focus range	Infinity to 25cm close	Infinity to 30cm close
Exit pupil / eye relief	25mm	25mm
Flip up / flip down	Push button	Push button
Fore and aft adjustment	27mm total	27mm total
Tilt adjustment	10 degrees	10 degrees
Interpupillary adjustment	51 to 72mm	52 to 72mm
Voltage required	2.7 – 3 V DC 50mA nominal. Backup available	2 – 3.7 DC 35mA Backup available
Technology	GEN III image intensifier tubes or equivalent	Photonis XR5 GEN III (IV) with auto-gating
Photosensitivity	1800 uA/lm	700-800 uA/lm (autogated)
Tube resolution	Min 57 Typical 64 lp/mm	Min 64 Typical 70 lp/mm
Signal to noise ratio	21:1	Min 25:1 Typical 28:1

*FL = Foot Lambert, which equals Lumen

The table below clearly shows that the XR5 intensifier tube installed in the NL-94-AU has a higher figure of merit when compared to the intensifier tube in the F4949 manufactured by ITT.

Manufacturer	Tube resolution x Signal to noise	FOM
ITT	64 x 21	= 1344
NL-94-AU	70 x 28	= 1960

All NVDs come with an individual intensifier tube certificate. Due to the chemical manufacturing processes (photocathode, ion barrier film, microchannel plate, fibre optic bundle, phosphor screen), no two tubes can ever be identical, even if manufactured from the same batch of materials.

Instead, each tube will have passed a quality control system within a certain "family" of tubes (Generation II, Generation III and various OMNI requirements) which means they should all have similar performance values plus or minus a given tolerance. This tolerance is so small that the human eye cannot detect it; however, if a tube is rejected, it will be stamped "NOT FOR AVIATION USE" and may then be used for other NVDs that do not require the same high standard, such as infantry, ground observers, civilian use etc.

For this reason, a specification datasheet will have terms next to individual specifications stating *"typical"* (meaning average) and *"minimum"* (meaning the absolute minimum figure required for the tube to pass the quality control system).

Although the figure of merit (FOM) does not appear anywhere on any datasheet, the tube resolution with line pair counts and the signal to noise ratio will be given, so the end-user can work it out.

Why Have a FOM?

The FOM is a very important number. The US Government, through its **International Traffic in Arms Regulations (ITAR),** will not allow the export to anyone outside of the US NVDs with intensifier tubes with a FOM greater than 1600 or any tube that has "gating" technology. This, therefore, limits the performance of the NVDs that can be made available to organisations outside of the US.

All XR5 autogated intensifier tubes from Photonis have a guaranteed average FOM of 1850, with several tubes exceeding values of 2000+. Additionally, European intensifier tubes have no ITAR restrictions; therefore, organisations outside of the US can take advantage and purchase this technology for their operations without restrictions.

Performance-based Not Technology-based

NVDs should be assessed based on their performance, not on the technology with which they achieved that performance. NVDs and NVGs have gone through various technological changes over the past 75+ years. This has led to different ways of categorising them based on their technology rather than their performance. Performance should be the key driver, not technology (although technology is what drives performance and hence the confusion).

The US, through ITAR, restricts the export of their NVD technology to a lower level than that which may be manufactured and sold by European, Asian and Russian manufacturers. The graph below gives an overall summary of NVG performance based on the technology of each Generation.

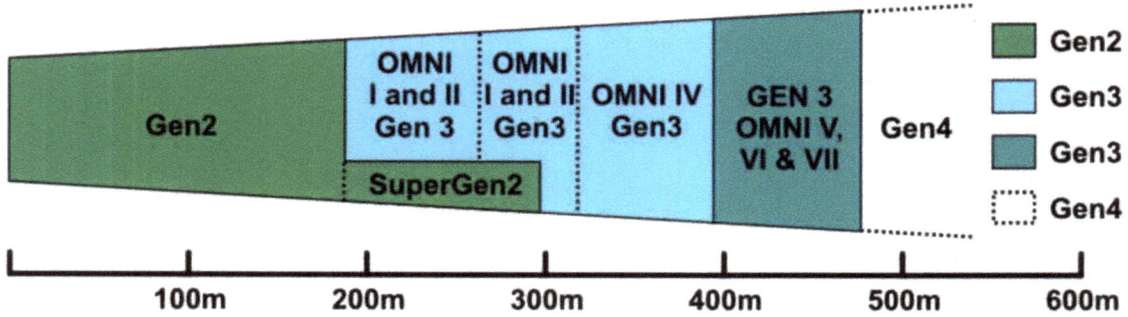

Night Vision Goggles *for Helicopter Pilots*

The information is based on a user of an NVD being able to recognise a human-sized target on the ground using a monocular NVD of that generation. The information is slightly out of date and may not be completely accurate when depicting the Generation III and Generation IV OMNI V, VI and VII, but it gives an indication of expected performance variances.

> **Example**
>
> *For example*: Using a Generation II intensifier tube, you can recognise and identify a human-sized target up to approximately 200 metres away.
>
> Using Generation III OMNI IV intensifier tubes you can identify the same target up to 400 metres away and if using a Generation IV intensifier tube (XR5), you can identify the same target at almost 480 metres away.

One of the most interesting facts is that some Generation II intensifier tubes can outperform some early Generation III intensifier tubes.

Summary

Below is an overall summary of the various Generations of intensifier tubes and their comparative sizes.

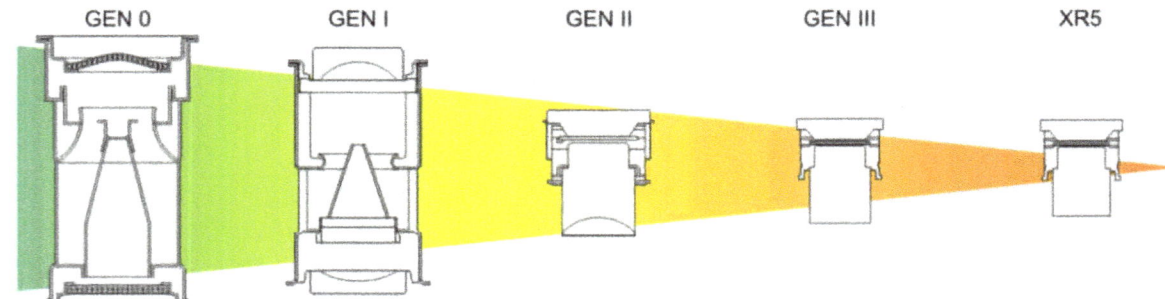

GENERATION 0

S1 photocathode with peak photoresponse in the blue-green region

Photosensitivity of 60uA/lm

Electrostatic inversion and electron acceleration to achieve gain (photomultiplier)

Suffer from geometric distortion and require IR illumination

GENERATION I

S20 photocathode with the photosensitivity expanding into the green-yellow region

Photosensitivity of 180-200uA/lm

Electrostatic inversion and electron acceleration to achieve gain (photomultiplier)

Suffers from geometric distortion and suffers from blooming but does not require IR illumination

GENERATION II

S25 photocathode with the photosensitivity expanding into the red region

Photosensitivity of 240+uA/lm

Microchannel plate to achieve gain

Very little distortion and operates at low light levels

GENERATION III

Gallium Arsenide photocathode expanding further into the red and infrared region

Photosensitivity of 800uA/lm

Microchannel plate to achieve gain but ion barrier film to extend tube life

Very little to no distortion and very good performance at low light levels

GENERATION IV/XR5

Multi alkalide photocathode equal in performance to the Generation III gallium arsenide

Photosensitivity of 800uA/lm

Curved microchannel plate to achieve gain with NO ion barrier film

Very little to no distortion with good performance in both high and low light

Autogated technology

Aeromedical Factors When Using NVGS

Although NVGs are obviously used at night unless you revert to night unaided flight, you are not using all your night vision. Instead, you are effectively viewing a television screen essentially while flying at night. The only time you need your night vision is if you de-goggle and fly unaided.

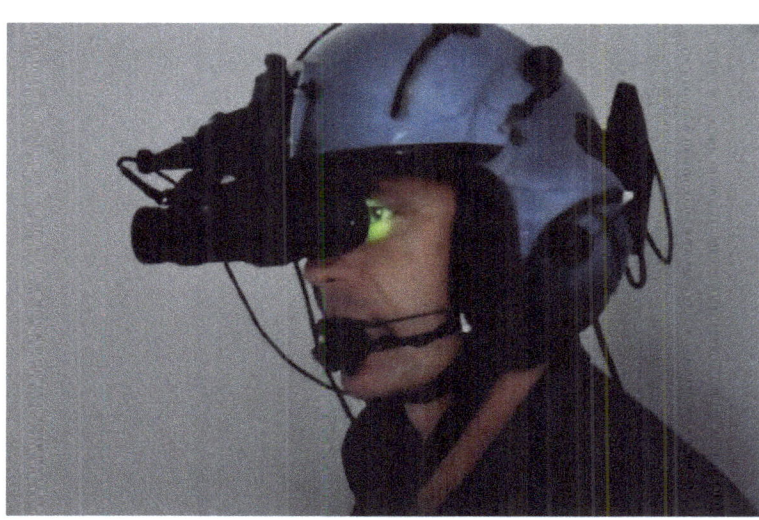

The most significant difference, therefore, is getting used to flying with:

- **a limited field of view** (only 40 degrees circular),
- a monochromatic (one colour) image, and
- **a limited sense of depth perception** as you are now only seeing the outside world in 2 dimensions.

For these reasons, it is more important than ever that crew resource management (CRM) techniques are utilised.

Eyes When Using NVGs

As we know, cones are located around the centre of the retina, are sensitive to light and responsible for the definition of colour and fine detail.

Rods are located at the outer edges of the retina and are used in our peripheral vision, and are responsible for recognising movement. Rods do not respond to light in the 600 nm wavelength or longer (orange to red spectrum), so red light is commonly used at night because it will not affect our night vision adaptation.

> **Example**
>
> In the classrooms at Becker Helicopters, we have red lights for use at night. This allows aircrew to conduct flight planning while not losing their night vision adaptation.
>
>

Rods will detect light of a shorter wavelength, such as a blue-green in the 400-580 nm region, even at very low light levels, and as a result, some of your night vision may be lost.

When using NVGs, we are essentially viewing a green television screen, so we are viewing the image with our cones and not our rods. This is an important fact to remember. We are viewing a colour (green) image at night through the NVGs using the cones in the retina.

Because it is a low light image and because our peripheral image is essentially dark, our cones are partially night-adapted so that when we de-goggle, it only takes seconds or, at the most several minutes to be fully night-adapted. So, when using NVGs both our rods and our cones are being used.

Field of View (FOV)

The field of view (FOV) is the angular extent (horizontal and vertical) of the observable world at any given moment. The human eye typically has *approximately (some people have more, some less)*:

- a 130-degree forward-facing horizontal view, and
- a 120-degree forward-facing vertical view.

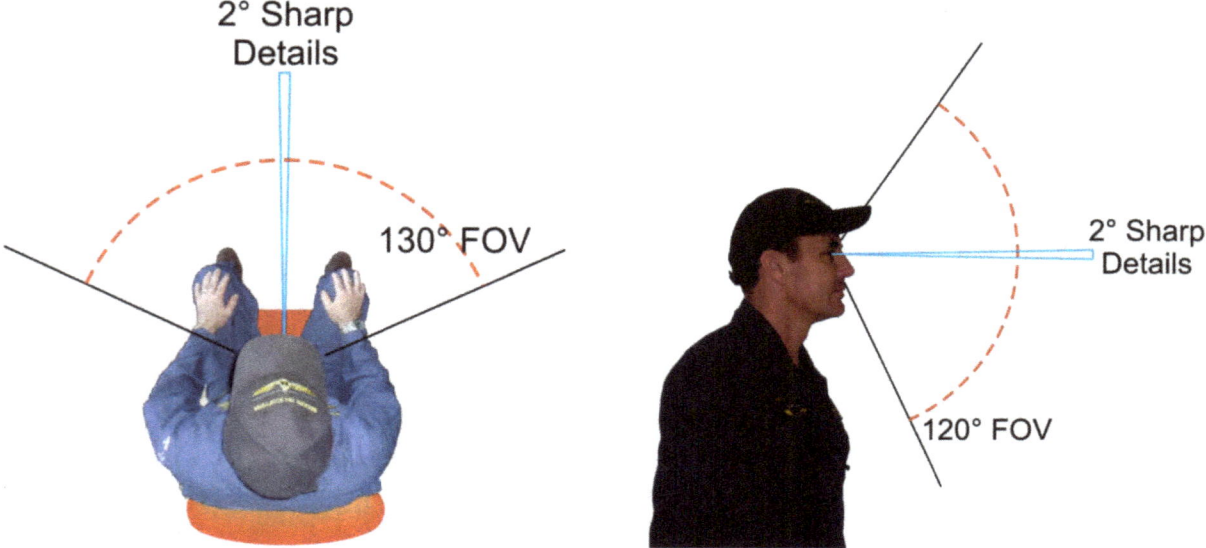

Figure 80 Horizontal field of view   Figure 81 Vertical field of view

This allows us to have a view similar to the image below:

While flying IFR or at night, our field of view unaided remains the same; however, what we can see can be limited due to reduced visibility caused by clouds or darkness.

However, when using NVGs, the goggle itself only has a limited FOV. Therefore, the image of our perceivable world reduces. When the information we receive reduces, our ability to operate within our environment also reduces. Therefore, using NVGs requires different scanning techniques and procedures.

Night Vision Goggles *for Helicopter Pilots*

To demonstrate what a limited FOV is, bring your hands up to your face and look through them as though you were holding an imaginary pair of binoculars.

You have now effectively limited your FOV. What you see through the holes you have made with your hands is all you can see. To look to the side now, instead of using your eyes, you have to move your head.

Below are two images. The one on the left shows a FOV as we would typically experience, the one on the right shows a limited FOV of the same landscape.

Figure 82 Normal field of view

Figure 83 Limited field of view

If we now use the same FOV image discussed previously, it becomes obvious that what we can see is much reduced.

Figure 84 Limited horizontal field of view

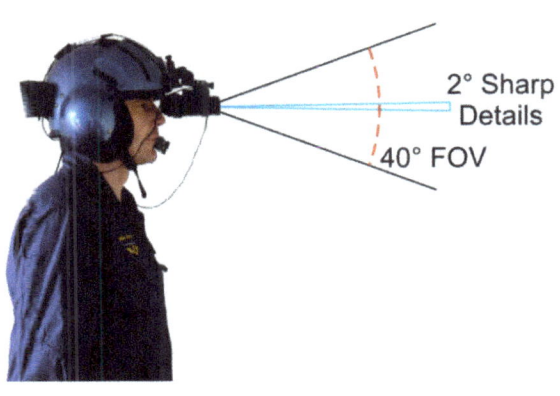
Figure 85 Limited vertical field of view

Field of Regard (FOR)

Although the use of NVGs limits our field of view, because it is mounted on the pilot's helmet, the FOV can be altered when viewing the outside scene by moving your head. The total area that the FOV can cover is called the Field of Regard (FOR). The FOR will vary depending on several factors, including:

- The physiological limit of the individual's head movement
    - A healthy, flexible neck with flexible, healthy shoulders and back should give an average FOR of 180 degrees horizontally and 180 degrees vertically
    - An unhealthy or stiff neck, stiff shoulders and back can reduce this FOR significantly
- Design of the NVG such as
    - Protrusion of the binocular housing from the mount
    - Size of the FOV
    - Number of tubes
    - Placement of the tubes
- Cockpit design and placement, such as
    - Seat adjustment
    - Distance of the window, canopy, pillars, instrument panel
    - Door and number of windows

Scanning Techniques

When flying utilising NVGs, it is common practice to do this with a two-pilot or one pilot and one crewman crew. This requires the sharing of responsibilities in the cockpit, including the scan.

Regulations may also specify limits. For example, in Australia at the time of publishing, single pilot NVG operations are only allowed above 1000 ft AGL or LSALT, whereas multi-crew NVG operations are allowed to operate below 1000 ft AGL and LSALT.

In general, the techniques that are used during the day and at night are used with NVGs, but with a few key differences.

Slow methodical head movements

The eyes are not able to change the FOV. Instead, they can only view various parts of the NVG image as projected onto the eyepiece. For the user to change the FOV, **the head must be moved** to look in another area to cover the FOR. This must be done in a **slow, methodical manner** using either the side to side or front to side scan.

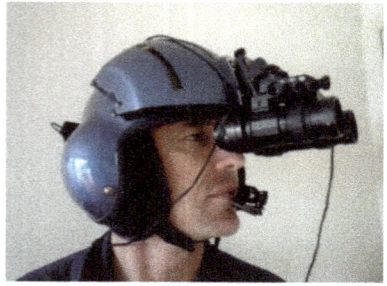 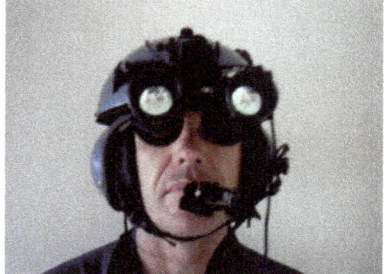 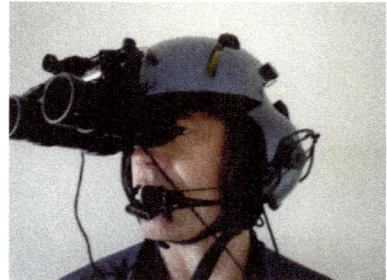

Additionally, if one pilot must look at the instruments and cannot look outside, then he has to notify the other pilot, who will take up the additional scan on the opposite side of the helicopter in addition to the side they are responsible for until the other pilot can again take up their scan.

Night Vision Goggles for Helicopter Pilots

Multi-crew overlapping scanning

There are two sets of eyes in the cockpit when there is two crew; therefore, each pilot will have an area of responsibility on which they are able to focus their scan rather than have to scan the entire sky. The pilot on the left will complete a scan covering the left side of the helicopter from approximately 8 o'clock to 1 o'clock. The pilot on the right will complete a scan covering the right side of the helicopter from approximately 11 o'clock to 4 o'clock. This overlap allows both pilots to cover any blind spot that may be occurring straight ahead.

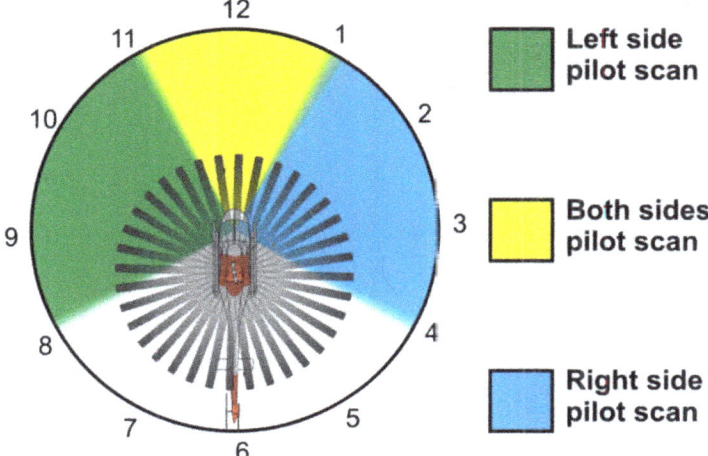

Other crew member scanning

If there are other crewmembers in the back, they will be given scanning responsibilities for their area that will overlap with each of the pilots in the front.

Crew coordination and communication

Crew coordination and communication are critical to a successful NVG operation. It is important to note here that when looking at the instruments, the pilot does so by looking under the NVGs. You do not look at the instruments using NVGs as they are focused to infinity; instead, you use normal vision to view the instruments under the NVGs. Viewing the instruments will be done with the cockpit lighting; therefore, the cones can detect colour and bright light.

Scanning Patterns

Environmental factors will influence the scan by limiting what may be seen in specific directions or by degrading the overall image. If the image is degraded, aircrew may scan more aggressively in a subconscious attempt to obtain more information or to avoid the chance of missing information that suddenly appears and/or disappears.

The operation itself may influence the scan pattern.

Example
Consider looking for another aircraft, landing zone, or airport, which may require focusing the scan in a particular direction.
The restrictions to scan and the variables affecting the scan pattern are not specific to night operations or the use of NVGs, but due to the limited FOV, the degree of impact is magnified.

Unaided Scan

Under certain circumstances, it may be beneficial for one or more crew members to de-goggle and conduct the scan unaided (not with NVG). Under the right conditions, this can improve depth perception, distance estimation and closure rates. If close to the ground and particularly over low contrast surfaces, then the unaided scan should be done using white light from the searchlight. When in cruise flight, the unaided scan does not necessarily require the white light to be effective.

> **Example**
>
> Consider flying in close proximity to another aircraft, and the external lights are causing a halo effect on the NVG, causing the external lights to mask the other aircraft while on NVGs. If one of the pilots was to de-goggle and look at the other aircraft unaided, he would be more readily able to detect distance and closure rate.
>
> Another good example is when operating within a tight basic helicopter landing site approved for NVG use. With the use of white light, one pilot that is de-goggled will be able to have a better scan and a better scan rate and be able to judge distance and depth better than the pilot that is goggled up.

Ambient or Artificial Light

As we know, NVGs require some form of ambient or artificial light to function suitably. Low light levels, non-compatible aircraft lighting and poor windshield light transmissibility, can all reduce the performance capability of the NVGs. It is the responsibility of the crew to determine when a transition from aided (NVG) to unaided is required due to unacceptable NVG performance.

NVG Eye Factors

Monochromatic Image

NVG images are currently projected from either a green or a white phosphor screen. Almost all of the NVGs available in the civil market are the green type. Because there is only one colour, the image is said to be monochromatic. Green was the initial colour selected because the human eye can see more detail at lower brightness levels when viewing shades of green.

Colour differences between components in a scene help the viewer to discriminate between objects and aids in object recognition, depth perception and distance estimation. The lack of colour variation in the NVG image will decrease these capabilities to varying degrees.

White phosphor NVGs are relatively new. They are not yet common because the manufacturing process is not as reliable, making them more expensive. When they do become readily available, because you will effectively be looking at a black and white screen, you will have a greater range of shades and possibly better definition.

Eye Stress and Fatigue

For those of us who watch a lot of TV or sit in front of a computer for a long period of time, it will be noticed that our eyes suffer from fatigue.

We blink less, we are constantly looking at a brightly lit screen, and we tend to focus on a closer image. The eyes may begin to water, they start to feel hot, it becomes harder to focus, and we could end up with a headache. These symptoms are all possible when using NVGs because we are watching the image through two small TV screens.

Figure 86 Computer screen

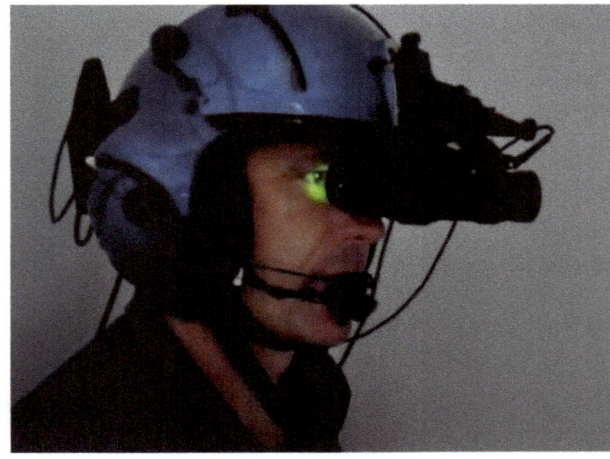

Figure 87 TV screen in NVGs

Night Vision Goggles *for Helicopter Pilots*

To minimise these effects, an aircrew member using NVGs should:

- Ensure they blink regularly
- Develop a scan that includes looking under the NVGs and away from the eyepiece occasionally
- Limit the number of NVG hours in a continuous sortie
- On long sorties, if possible, occasionally de-goggle to give the eyes a short rest
- Remain hydrated

Night Adaptation

When using NVGs, the pilot may need to de-goggle and revert to night unaided flight, at which point they will be required to rely on their natural night vision. This will require a period for the eyes to become night-adapted. Because NVGs are used at night, the cockpit is dimmed down, and there are not likely to be any bright light sources. Therefore, the eyes will already have partially night-adapted. However, when de-goggling, it can still take between **30 seconds to 5 minutes to achieve sufficient night adaptation** to see sufficiently unaided.

The most common scenario for this is when on approach into a Helicopter Landing Site (HLS) using NVGs. In some operational sorties, particularly when the HLS is very tight and the pilots can use white light, it may be appropriate for one pilot to de-goggle to have better depth perception and a greater FOV while in the tight HLS; this also allows the scan rate to be increased as the natural eye can take in fine detail faster than a moving NVG.

On de-goggling, the pilot or crew member must make allowance for the time it will take for the eyes to gain night adaptation before being able to offer useful information to the flying pilot or before taking over the flying duties.

Figure 88 HLS using NVGs

Figure 89 Same HLS at night unaided (NUA)

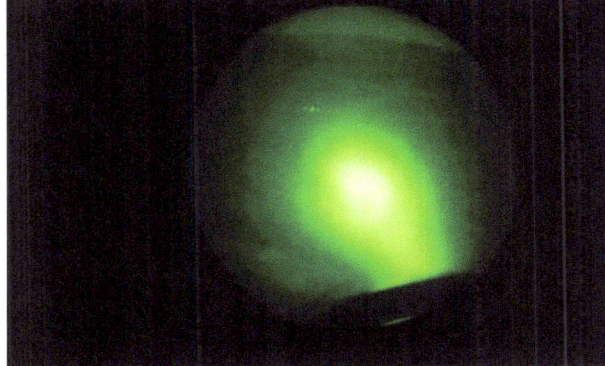

Figure 90 Same HLS NVG with light

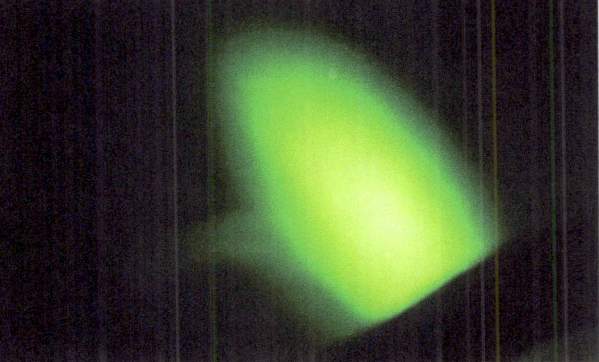

Figure 91 Same HLS NUA with light

If transitioning the other way from unaided flight to NVGs, there is no time required to adapt to see the image through the NVG correctly. The only change is a mental one as the pilot goes from a 3-dimensional image with a wider FOV to a 2-dimensional image and a 40-degree FOV.

Eyes That Need Corrective Lenses

The NVG has two areas that can be focused. The outer objective ring allows the lens to be focused to infinity or some lesser distance, and the eyepiece or dioptre is focused to make allowances for each pilot's eye requirements.

Figure 92 Objective lens

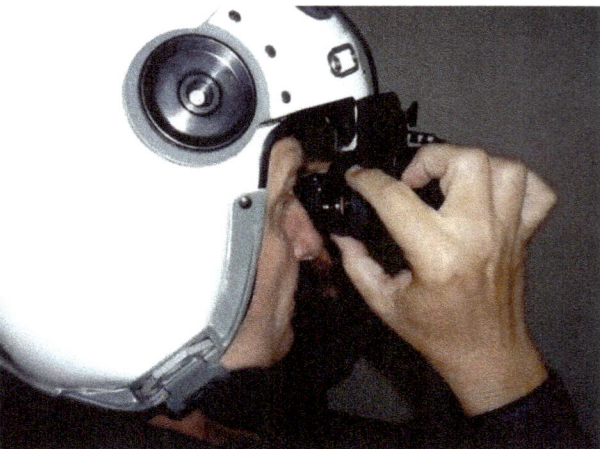

Figure 93 Dioptic lens

If a pilot is long-sighted, they can see long distances but struggle to focus on close objects; they can wear their glasses or contact lenses while using NVGs. Doing this will allow the pilot to focus the NVGs to infinity but still allow the pilot to look under the NVG and read the instruments and view a map.

If a pilot is short-sighted, that is, they can see objects that are close but cannot see images that are a long distance away, then they do not need to wear any corrective lens as the NVG can be focused to suit their particular needs and when looking under the goggles at the instruments, their normal vision is sufficient.

As each person is different, it may take some experimentation to discover which combination works best for you.

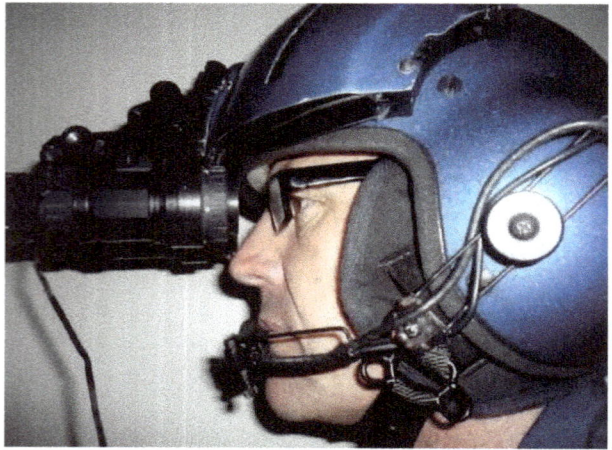

Figure 94 Long-sighted (needs reading glasses)

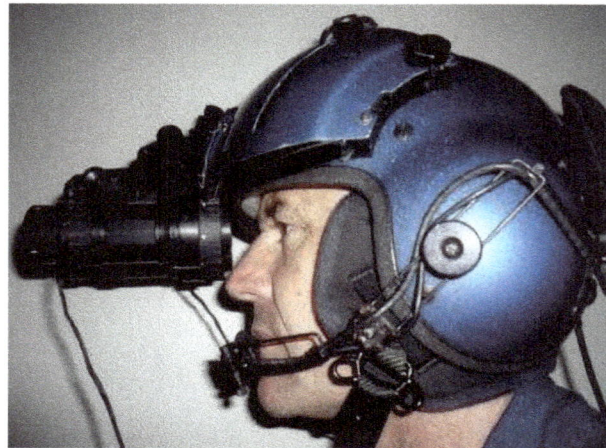

Figure 95 Short-sighted (no reading glasses)

Visual Illusions

All the visual illusions relating to the eye during the day and NUA operations are relevant to the eye when on NVG operations, with subtle differences. At this time, we will introduce a common acronym used by the military to help remember the visual illusions, that is:

FFF CRASH SAR CL

There are a few ways to remember this acronym, but we will use the following mnemonic (sentence) to help us remember it.

Fly Fly Fly Crash SAR Checklist

Each letter in the acronym represents an illusion; in this section, we will review these visual illusions and discuss any differences because we are now using NVGs.

False Horizons

A false horizon can occur when the natural horizon is obscured or not readily apparent. It can be generated by confusing bright stars and city lights because of a line of clouds or a shoreline. It is most common when the pilot has been looking down inside the cockpit for a prolonged period and then looks up and references the helicopter's attitude with the horizon and incorrectly identifies a false horizon.

Hovering over sloping terrain, especially when using NVGs because of the lack of depth perception, could lead to the pilot trying to level the skids with the ground and therefore start a sideways movement.

Crew coordination and instrument cross-referencing and scanning are critical in overcoming this illusion.

Flicker Vertigo

A light flickering at a rate of 4 to 20 cycles per second can cause the pilot to suffer from nausea, vomiting, vertigo and, on rare occasions, convulsions and unconsciousness. When using NVGs, the anti-collision lights and strobe lights, especially if they are not NVG compatible, should be turned off as they will be the main source of flicker vertigo.

Another common source of light contributing to flicker vertigo is rotating beacons on the ground from police or emergency vehicles, reversing trucks and utility equipment, which often have a rotating warning light and sometimes infrared alarm systems. If you can have these turned off before landing, then that will help; otherwise, you should look or turn away from the flickering source.

Fascination (Fixation)

Because NVGs have a limited field of view, this is one illusion that the crew has to be particularly aware of. It occurs when orientation cues are ignored, and instead, the crews' attention is solely fixated on their goal or the object, to the detriment of everything else.

> **Example**
>
> Consider an attack helicopter aiming at a target on a run in. They could delay the break-off point because they were so focused on hitting the target that they forgot where they were. This is sometimes referred to as target hypnosis and, in the military environment, is the most common form of fascination illusion.
>
> Another example is the use of the searchlight on an approach to an HLS on a very dark night. If all you can see is within the searchlight area, the crew could become so fixated on what is within the searchlight beam that they forget to move it around and scan for other obstacles causing them to drift sideways or come into contact with the ground or other obstacles on approach. Good crew coordination, movement of the searchlight, and movement of the head and eyes will help avoid this illusion.

Confusion of Ground Lights

Confusion of ground lights, sometimes referred to as Ground Light Misinterpretation, is when light from stars is confused with lights on the ground and vice versa, and the helicopter is put in an unusual attitude as the pilot has identified a false horizon. This is more common when flying over very low contrast terrain, such as the ocean or a lake, particularly when the stars are reflected off the surface.

A good instrument scan, use of the AH and the RAD ALT to confirm altitude AGL, and crew coordination and communication are important in avoiding this illusion.

Relative Motion Illusion

Relative Motion Illusion consists of several illusions that may be experienced, including the Lack of Motion illusion, Wave Drift illusion and Waterfall illusion.

The most common example of relative motion illusion using NVGs is a helicopter hovering while another helicopter hovers into position alongside the first one. When the second helicopter appears in the peripheral vision (both from the unaided and the aided vision), the movement of the second helicopter can be misinterpreted as movement of your helicopter, and the pilot can put in an incorrect control input to stop the perceived movement.

Lack of Motion Illusion

When flying over low contrast terrain at low level, the crew can get the incorrect perception that they are not moving. This may result in the pilot trying to increase speed with forward cyclic, which can lead to an inadvertent descent and ultimately contact with the ground (CFIT – controlled flight into terrain).

This can also be apparent at the hover over a surface with low contrast terrain where the helicopter may drift, and the crew may not realise it.

To overcome this, a good instrument scan and crew communication is important. At the hover, good use of white light and moving to an area with good contrast will help.

This illusion is most noticeable and dangerous when on approach to land.

> **Example**
>
> Consider a helicopter on approach to a landing site. Our peripheral vision will pick up the movement, as we get closer to the ground, things appear to go faster, so we slow down, it is a good cue to help us realise our closure rate.

A lack of motion parallax denies us the ability to determine depth and motion. This means we find it more difficult to gauge our closure rate. This can occur especially over low contrast terrains such as water, desert sand, or snow and particularly occurs at night when we cannot see motion in our peripheral vision because it is dark.

To avoid this, the NVG pilot needs to be moving the searchlight and moving his/her head to cover a large FOR so that movement can be realised. Additionally, a good cross-reference with the instruments to confirm the expected movement, rate of descent, and height AGL is vital.

Wave Drift Illusion

If hovering over water at night, particularly if there are no discernable reference points close to the helicopter, then the motion of the waves blowing away from the helicopter can create the illusion that the helicopter is actually moving in the opposite direction. To correct for this, the pilot may start to follow the waves and, therefore, inadvertently cause the helicopter to move. This illusion is also possible during the day, but because there are often reference points in the distance, it is easily countered. At night, and particularly using NVGs, this illusion is more pronounced, so hovering over water at night should be avoided if possible. The illusion may also be caused by long grass, a loose surface such as sand or snow, or by an unanchored chemical light placed in the water as a marker being affected by the downwash.

Crew communication, a good instrument scan and preferably a solid reference point will help avoid this illusion.

Waterfall Illusion

Waterfall Illusion is where particles of water, dust, salt, snow, etc. are seen at night, often reflected in the search or landing light. They will present to the crew as a downward movement that is caused by the downwash of the rotor blades; however, they present as an illusion to the crew that the helicopter is rising vertically. To prevent this, the pilot may incorrectly lower the collective to stop the upward movement but in doing so, will inadvertently land or come into contact with the terrain or water.

Crew communication, cross-checking of the RAD ALT and the other instruments such as the VSI, and movement of the searchlight to new areas of the scan will help avoid this illusion.

Autokinesis

When a static light source is stared at in the dark, the light may appear to move, called Autokinesis. This is very common when flying unaided but less common when flying on NVG operations because when viewing through the NVG, the surrounding light is intensified, and the eyes tend to move within the FOV, so they do not get to fixate on only one small static light source for a long period.

Correct scanning techniques avoid this illusion.

Structural Illusion

Heat waves, rain, snow, sleet, dust, windscreen curvature or other similar factors that can obscure or affect vision can promote this illusion. At night and when using NVGs, one of the greatest causes can be a dirty windscreen. Straight lines can appear curved; position lights may appear double. Crew awareness of structural illusion, clean windows, crew communication and correct scanning techniques help avoid this illusion.

Height Perception Illusion

When flying over areas of low contrast such as desert, snow, water, pine forests, fields, etc., the crew may get the illusion that they are higher than they actually are.

When using NVGs, this is particularly important to know because of the reduced FOV and the lack of depth perception due to viewing a 2-dimensional image through the NVG.

Good use of the landing and searchlight, correct instrument scan and use of the RAD ALT, crew communication and outside scanning is very important. If hovering, then the use of shadows or even throwing some light source out the door may help the crew in gaining a better perception of the height AGL.

Size Distance Illusion

At night it is very difficult to judge distance and in particular, the distance of lights. In general, the brighter the light, the closer it is perceived to be and the dimmer the light, the further away it is perceived to be.

For NVG operations, this illusion is amplified because any light source is intensified through use of the NVG. Additionally, if viewing a stationary source of light that is increasing or decreasing in brightness, this could be interpreted as coming closer or moving further away; in other words, varying brightness can incorrectly be perceived as movement.

Occasionally looking under the NVGs to use unaided vision can help in gaining a perception and good use of the map and local knowledge to correlate what you are seeing to a scale of what is real, referenced to other known features, all help avoid this illusion.

Altered Planes of Reference

When approaching a line of hills or clouds or other obstacles, the crew often will perceive that they have a requirement to climb to ensure adequate clearance over the obstacle. This feeling may be apparent even if you know the helicopter is higher than the obstacle.

This is much more of a problem unaided than using NVGs because when using NVGs, you usually get to see more of the surrounding area. Good scanning, cross-checking the instruments, and crew communication will avoid this illusion.

Reversible Perspective Illusion

At night an aircraft can appear to be moving away when in fact, it is moving closer. This illusion can often occur when the other aircraft is flying parallel to the first aircraft. Usually, at night to determine the actual course of the other aircraft, the crew would look at the position lights for colour and configuration and assess their position to the horizon.

Additionally, if the brightness intensity of the lights begins to increase, then it is assumed that the aircraft is getting closer; if the brightness intensity decreases, then it is assumed that the aircraft is moving away.

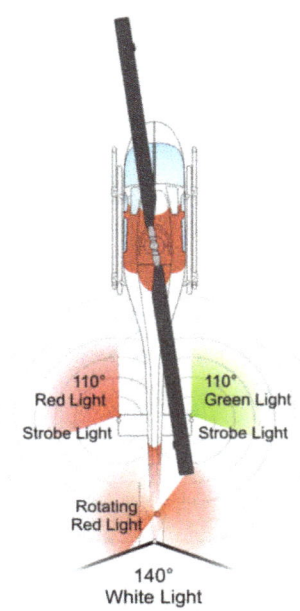

To determine the aircraft's direction of travel, remember the three **R**s

Red lights are on the **R**ight side, indicating the aircraft is **R**eturning

When using NVGs, we cannot see colour; therefore, the red and green position lights will not display. In fact, the green position light may not even be visible through the NVGs.

To see position lights, look under or around the goggles; however, this requires the use of our peripheral vision. Because our eyes have adapted to seeing only a monochromatic image, when we look around the goggles, the position lights may be distorted, whereby white lights appear pinkish and the red and green can appear fuzzy.

Also remember that other aircraft using NVG may have dimmed position lights or may not be displaying any position lights at all or be using infrared lights or any combination.

Keeping all this in mind, to avoid this illusion, the crew communicate internally and identify any other aircraft. The pilots should broadcast their intentions and communicate with other aircraft on the radio. If an aircraft appears to be remaining static in the windscreen, then the two aircraft are on a converging course, and it will be very hard to tell if the second aircraft is getting closer or moving away, so you should alter your course and height if possible so that the second aircraft starts to move across your vision. If possible, have one of the crew de-goggle to get an un-aided sense of the other aircraft. If your position lights are off, turn them on.

Crater Illusion

When approaching a confined area, particularly when using NVGs, the crew can feel that they are descending or dropping into a crater or hole in the ground. This is more common when using an Infrared (IR) searchlight than a white searchlight and is more common on a very dark night than a night with a good moon.

Good crew communication, good use of white light and moving the searchlight along with a good instrument cross-check and calling of the RAD ALT will help avoid this illusion.

Light

Infrared Light

Infrared (IR) light can only be seen through the NVGs. When using an IR searchlight, you can see an image clearly through the NVGs, but when looking under the goggles it is completely black. It can be disconcerting when used to using white light, especially on short finals or when in a confined area.

Good crew communication, faith in the NVGs, and an instrument cross-check help avoid the disorientation that can occur when only using infrared light.

Monochromatic Adaptation

Because most NVGs use a green phosphor screen, we get to see only in shades of green to which our eyes adapt. When we look away from the NVGs, all objects we view unaided will be affected by this, and it will take time for our eyes to re-adjust to the real world.

Ears When using NVGs

No additional aeromedical factors apply to the ear when using NVGs. All the information regarding the vestibular system relevant to IFR and NUA applies to NVG use.

Proprioceptive System When Using NVGs

The proprioceptive system can be fooled more readily when using NVGs. This is because what we see with our eyes is not as useful because of the restricted FOV and the 2-dimensional image, which may not be as accurate to help resolve any unwanted ambiguity in the normal manner.

The postural righting reflex and the vestibular ocular reflex are two that can lead to inappropriate movement.

Postural Right Reflex

You may recall that you automatically move your hands and feet to try to counter the fall if you trip over. As a pilot wearing NVGs, if the image you are seeing moves or appears to move for some reason, you may make a control correction that is not required. This is more applicable to using NVGs alongside a large independent structure such as a ship that can move. If it moves, you may try to maintain your position relative to the ship, this could cause you to be in an excessive nose up, or roll left or right situations leading to unwanted movement. Crew coordination and communication and an instrument scan mainly using the AI, and RAD ALT will help guard against this.

Vestibular Ocular Reflex

When we move our head, our eyes initially stay still, then they start to move in the same direction as the turning head in anticipation of looking in the new area.

When wearing NVGs and we move our head to look in a new area, our eyes naturally want to move in the same direction, which means we may inadvertently look past the goggles and temporarily see nothing but blackness. This could lead to the leans, vertigo or wrongly perceived motion.

Experience using NVGs, slow head movements, and a well-lit cockpit help guard against this.

Fatigue When Using NVGs

NVG operations require a reverse cycle, the same as night unaided flight and therefore, consideration needs to be given to acute, chronic and cumulative fatigue in the usual manner.

NVG Fitting

The most significant source of physical fatigue is the presence of extra weight on your head in the form of the NVG, mount, power pack and any ballast weight.

Before commencing an NVG flight, take care to:

- properly fit your helmet to your head, and
- balance the NVGs and battery pack.

Fitting Your Helmet

A tight fit is best, making sure the helmet does not wobble or shift on the head. Ensure there are no hotspots that will cause irritation leading to distraction and fatigue. A hot spot is where one part of

the helmet puts pressure on your head, and that position gets hot, sore and uncomfortable. It can often take a bit of experimentation and trial and error to eliminate all the hot spots.

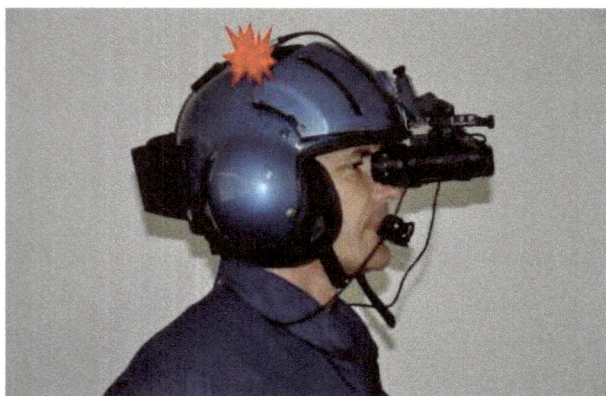

Some helmets sit quite low on a person's head, others sit quite high, so additional packing may be required so that the NVGs themselves are placed in a position where they do not come in contact with the helmet and can be adjusted suitably to the pilot's eyes.

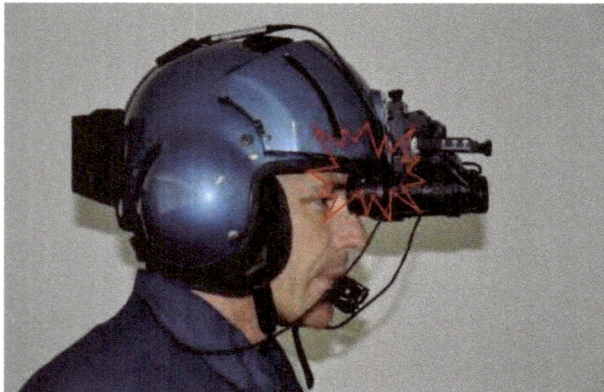

Make sure the power pack, cabling and ballast do not interfere with seating, helmet drop leads, seatbelts, pillars, power levers and anything else in the cockpit.

Ensure lip lights, volume controls, chin straps, and ear cups are all suitably attached, fitted and secured.

Night Vision Goggles *for Helicopter Pilots*

Balance Your Helmet

Balance the NVGs and battery pack so that the helmet does not want to flop forward or backward. This may take some experimentation with varying ballast weights. The NVG system Centre of Gravity (C of G) should feel neutral when placed on your helmet. If it is not neutral, pressure and strain points can develop on your head and neck. This will lead to fatigue and ultimately injury if not corrected.

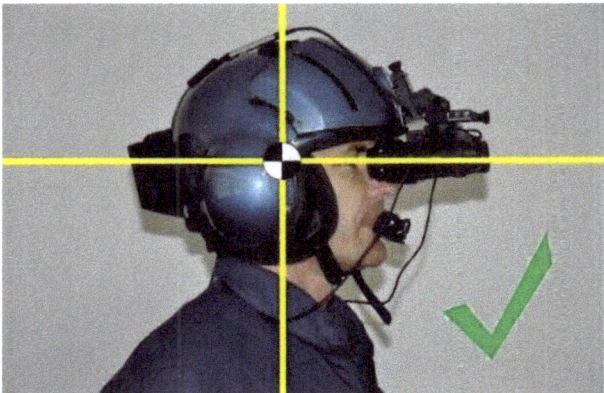

Figure 96 Neutral Centre of Gravity

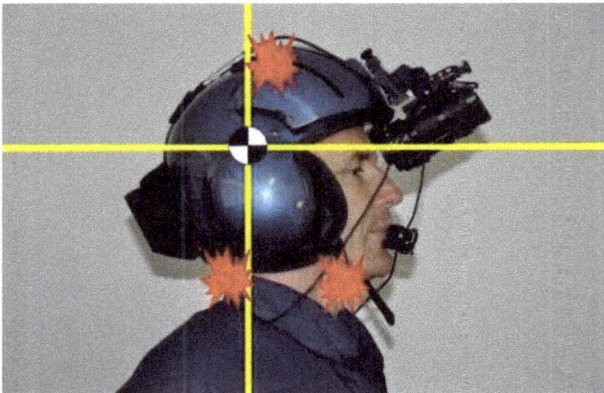

Figure 97 Aft Centre of Gravity

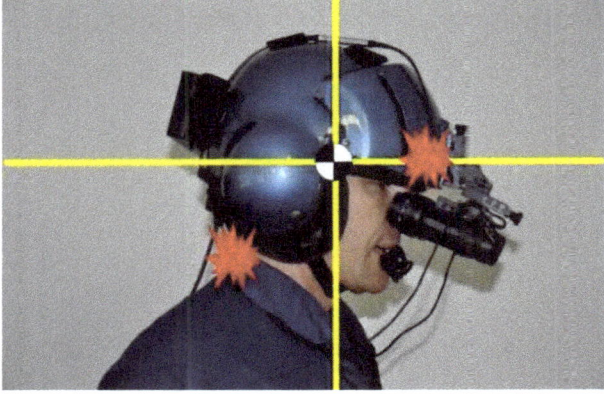

Figure 98 Forward Centre of Gravity

Building Your Fitness

Be healthy and if necessary, do some neck stretching and strengthening exercises to build up for the additional weight you will have to manage on your head.

Side Effects

After the first few flights, it is not unusual to get a headache from the additional neck and eye strain. This will typically pass as you become used to your new operating environment and your body learns to cope with the extra stress.

If headaches persist, seek medical advice.

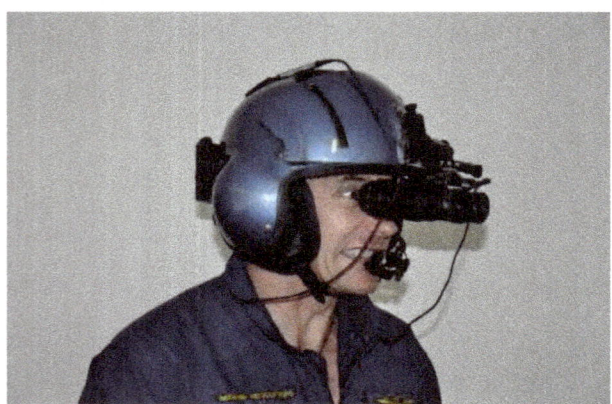

Terrain and Environmental Factors

A range of factors in our operating environment can affect NVG performance.

- Illumination at night can either come from natural sources such as the sun, moon and stars or artificial sources such as cities, ground-based lighting or aircraft.
- The type of terrain being flown over will affect NVG performance as each surface can have a differing reflectivity (known as albedo), affecting its luminance qualities, contrast, and shadowing effect based on the illumination.
- Factors in the atmosphere such as cloud, fog, humidity, rain, snow, dust, salt and any other form of interference that can affect light will reduce the amount of light available to the NVG for intensifying, will affect overall NVG performance.
- Factors within the aircraft or outside the aircraft, such as the windshield, aircraft lighting (both internal and external), and cockpit design, can reduce visibility.

These are all considered to be "Environmental Factors" because they are items that make up our operating environment.

Illumination

As we know, illumination (sometimes referred to as illuminance) is the amount of light coming from a source that arrives at a surface. It is commonly measured in Lumens but is still often referred to as LUX or Footcandles as well. All these measurements are measuring the same thing, just using a different scale depending on the needs of the manufacturer or user.

- A Footcandle (ftcd) is an imperial measurement based on the number of Lumens (the amount or intensity of light) within a 1 x 1 foot square area 1 foot away from the light source.
- A LUX is the metric equivalent based on the number of Lumens (the amount or intensity of light) within a 1 x 1 meter square area 1 meter away from the light source.

The terms Footcandle and LUX are interchangeable when describing illumination; the result will just be a different number because of the differing scales.

The term Lumen is also an indication of illumination because the Lumen is the basis of both the Footcandle and LUX calculation.

For comparison sake:

1 LUX = 0.0929 Footcandles (ftcd)

1 ftcd = 1 LUX divided by 10.752

1 Lumen per square foot = 1 Footcandle

Example
Consider the sun, our greatest source of illumination. On a clear day it generates 10,000 Footcandles or 107,527 LUX.
Source: 42

---

42 Williams. B. 1999, ' Footcandles and Lux for Architectural Lighting' Ed. 2.1, online article, viewed 11 November 2011, www.mts.net/~william5/library/illum.htm#7

Below is a table showing typical illumination levels 43:

Condition	Illumination	
	Footcandle	LUX
Direct sunlight	10,000	107,527
Full daylight	1,000	10,752
Overcast day	100	1,075
Very dark day	10	107
Twilight	1	10.8
Deep twilight	.1	1.08
Full moon	.01	.108
Quarter moon	.001	.0108
Starlight	.0001	.0011
Overcast night	.00001	.0001

Lumination

As we know, lumination (sometimes referred to as luminance) is the amount of light that leaves a surface after it has been illuminated. It is also measured in Footcandles or LUX and can provide illumination depending on the luminance properties of the surface.

Example
For example: Consider the moon, our greatest source of illumination at night. It is illuminated by the sun and, because of its light grey colour, has good luminance properties so that its redirected (reflected) light, in turn, provides illumination.
A full moon on a clear night can generate 0.01 Footcandles or 0.108 LUX.

Natural Sources

The natural sources of light available to a pilot at night originate from:

- the moon
- the night sky
- influence from the sun.

When using NVGs, knowing what light is available, when, and for how long can be important in pre-flight planning.

---

43 Source: The Engineering Toolbox, online table, viewed 30 July 2013, www.engineeringtoolbox.com/light-level-rooms-d_708.html

Moon

The NVG pilot needs to know the current phase of the moon. This will give an indication of its illumination. When it is rising, setting and where it will be in the sky during the NVG operation is important. This information can be easily obtained from weather or meteorology bureaus on the internet, from tables or Almanacs which may be made available to you by the operator, or, more commonly these days, through smart phones and applications, for example:

- https://geodesyapps.ga.gov.au/moonrise
- https://apps.apple.com/au/app/moonrise/id390606204

The position and amount of illumination provided by the moon can influence flight planning, pilot preparation for the best techniques that may be used to conduct the NVG operation, and potential NVG performance.

Example

For example: Consider flying into a full moon low on the horizon. This can be distracting and can provide too much light to the NVGs; in some instances, the NVGs could bloom out, or the intensity of the light may obscure terrain and obstacles, similar to flying into a setting sun. Flying away from the moon may be a better option depending on your operational requirements.

Important

It is important to note that a very bright full moon high in the sky (directly overhead), although providing maximum illumination, may not provide shadows, and therefore the contrast of the terrain may be reduced, making depth perception more difficult.

A low moon will cast long shadows and give good terrain contrast, giving better depth perception.

Night Sky Illumination

There will be some nights during which the moon will not be available, and, as we know, NVGs require some light to function. The night sky, which consists of airglow, stars, moons, and other light coming from space, provides enough infrared light within the same sensitivity range of the NVGs to allow them to work.

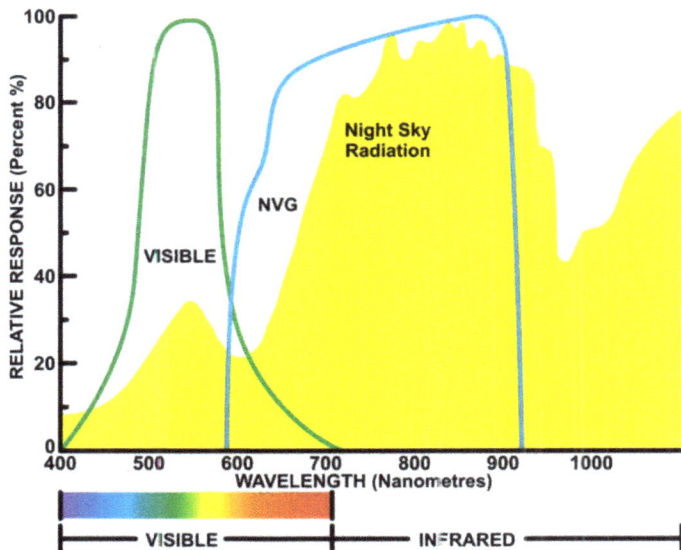

The graph above shows the IR radiation within the night sky and the wavelengths that are detectable by the NVG and the eye. As can be seen, the night sky radiation is well within the NVG detection range. The overlap between the visual and the NVG between around 600 and 700 nm represents the spectrum within the cockpit (red and orange warning lights) that needs to be filtered so that the eye can still see them, but they do not overly influence the NVGs.

Starlight

Starlight provides the equivalent of approximately 1/10 the illumination level of a quarter moon and about 40% of the night sky illumination. The remaining 60% of the night sky illumination comes from particles in the atmosphere and space that produce light, particularly infrared light These particles can be made up of gegenscheins, auroras, zodiac light and noctilucent clouds. Gegenscheins refer to sunlight reflecting off interplanetary dust within the earth's upper atmosphere (Figure 99).

Figure 99 Illustration of Gegenscheins [44]

Aurora

An aurora is a natural display of light, usually seen in the Polar Regions, caused by the collision of charged particles interacting with the earth's magnetic field.

[45]

---

44 ESO/Stéphane Guisard (www.eso.org/~sguisard), Paranal-Gegenschein, European Southern Observatory/Stéphane Guisard, 2013, online image, viewed 26 June 2013,: www.eso.org/public/images/paranal_gegenschein/

45 Parviainen, P, 2006, digital image collection, viewed 21 November 2011, www.polarimage.fi/

Night Vision Goggles *for Helicopter Pilots*

Zodiac

Zodiac light is a faint whitish/yellow glow seen in the atmosphere in the vicinity of the setting sun. It is caused by sunlight scattered by space dust in the zodiac cloud which is space particles following the path of the sun. On very dark nights, the zodiac cloud is responsible for most of the 60% of the night sky illumination generated by reflected particles.

Noctilucent Cloud

A noctilucent cloud is a polar type of cloud found in the upper atmosphere and made of crystals of ice water. They are the highest clouds in the earth's atmosphere and are visible only when illuminated by sunlight.

---

46 European Southern Observatory/Y Beletsky, online image, viewed news.nationalgeographic.com/news/2010/01/photogalleries/100112-week-in-space-pictures-77/

47 Parviainen, P, 2006 digital image collection, viewed 21 November 2011, www.polarimage.fi/

Solar Influence

The sun can supply adequate light for NVG operations; however, the sun can also provide too much light and be detrimental to NVG operations. For the NVG pilot, knowing when the sun is setting and rising is essential in the planning phase. Like the moon, this information is available on the internet through smartphone applications, but it is also available on TSO GPS units such as he Garmen 430, if installed within the aircraft.

With the sunup or just setting, there is usually too much light to warrant NVG use, and it can also damage the intensifier tubes. As the sun moves to 0 to 6 degrees below the horizon into the area called *Civil Twilight*, again, the influence of the sun on NVGs is significant to the point that flying into a setting sun is providing far too much light. Flying away from a setting sun at civil twilight would be acceptable.

When the sun is 7 to 12 degrees below the horizon, this is an area called *Nautical Twilight*. This is the best position of the sun for NVG operations, and it will provide ample light to increase NVG performance. When the sun is 13 to 18 degrees below the horizon, it has moved into an area called *Astronomical Twilight*, and the influence of the sun on NVG operations is minimal.

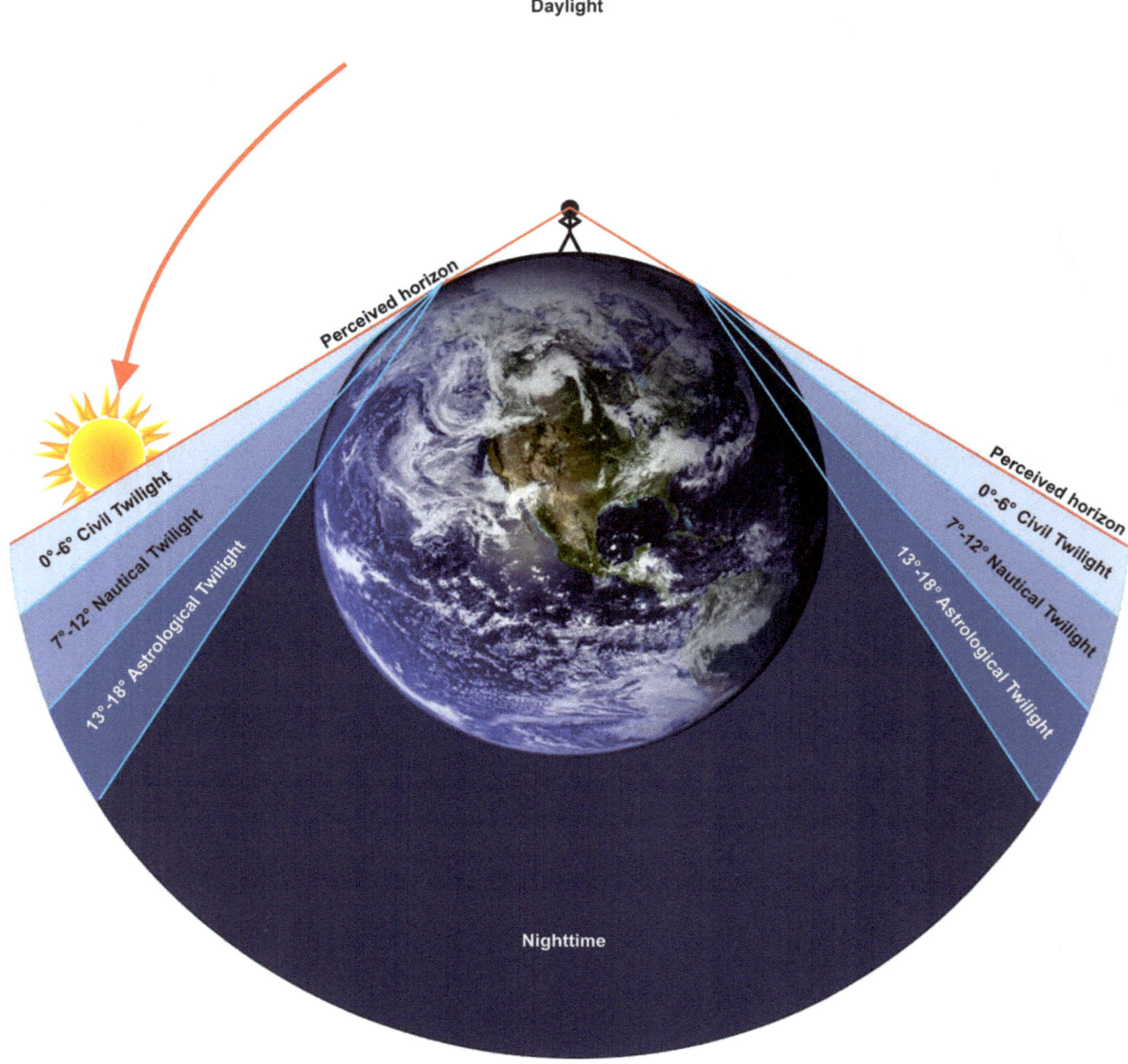

Night Vision Goggles *for Helicopter Pilots*

Artificial Sources of Light

Light can be generated artificially. Sources of artificial light include lights from:

- cities, towns and villages and factories, which in turn can be reflected by low cloud cover
- vehicles
- flares
- weapons
- ground-based lights
- other aircraft
- internal aircraft sources.

In addition to these, fires or light generated from volcanoes or similar natural occurrences can all be deemed to be artificial sources of light for NVG purposes. Artificial lights that the crew can control can be of great benefit. Artificial lights that the crew cannot control can be either good or bad, depending on the situation.

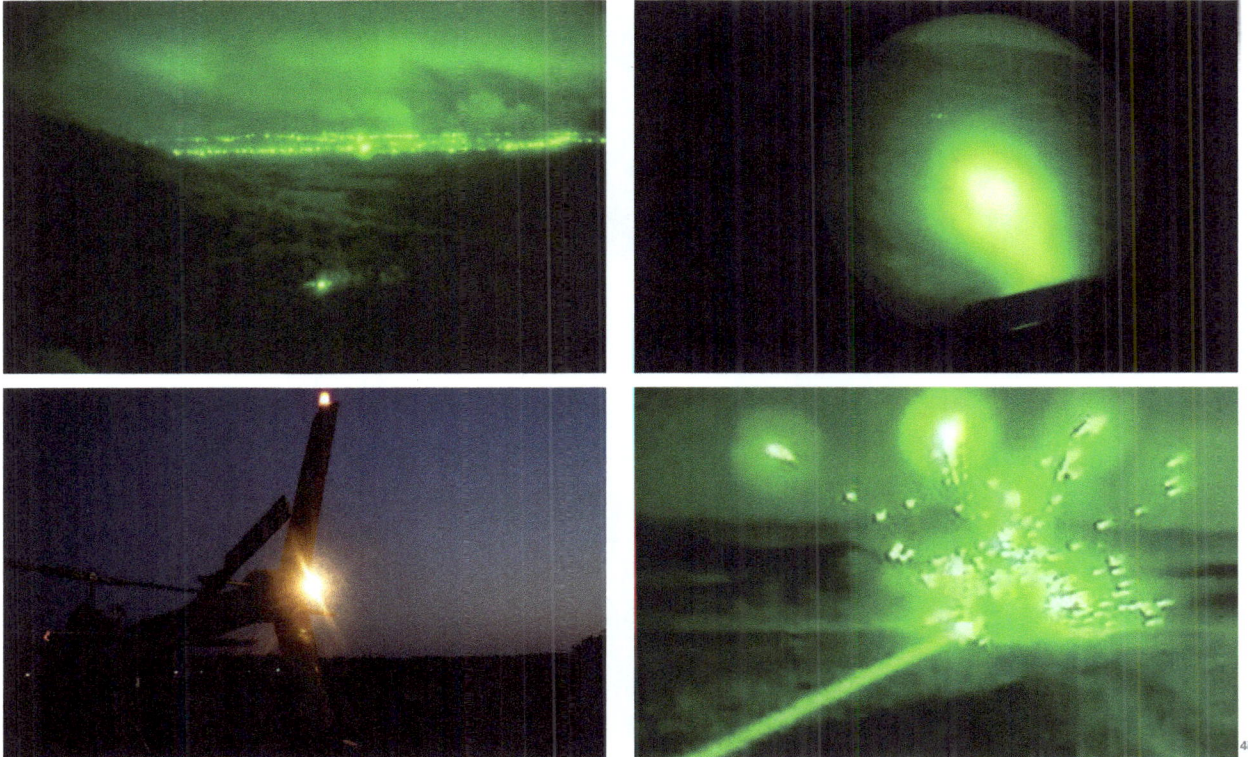

Terrain

The type of terrain being flown over while using NVGs will have varying abilities to reflect any light, whether coming from natural sources such as the moon and stars or artificial sources such as the aircraft's landing lights, ground lights or others. When considering the terrain and its effect on NVG performance on any given night, we need to consider:

- Terrain reflectivity (referred to as the surface's albedo)
- Terrain contrast
- Terrain shadowing.

---

48 Military.com, online image, viewed 24 June 2013, www.military.com/video/guns/artillery/usmc-artillery-in-action/1409864868001/

Terrain Reflectivity (Albedo)

As discussed previously, the surface of an object will have varying degrees of reflectivity. This ability to reflect light will influence the luminance of the surface. White or very smooth surfaces will reflect more light when compared to dark, rough surfaces.

Example

For example: Compare flying over snow on a moonlit night to flying over a dark ploughed field of soil. The snow will reflect more light when compared to the dark field, and the NVGs will therefore perform better because they have more reflected light with which to work.

Figure 100 Snow [49]

Figure 101 Field [50]

Another example is flying over a still water source such as a lake. The water will reflect more light from a light source compared to flying over, say, a jungle and, again, the NVGs will perform better because they have more light to work with.

Figure 102 Lake [51]

Figure 103 Jungle [52]

The scientific term for the amount of light that any particular object can reflect is termed its **"*albedo*"** which is expressed as a decimal of one or a percentage.

---

49 Corvatsch, 2011, online image, viewed 11 November 2011, www.corvatsch.ch/en/winter/snow-night.html

50 UnderThreeHundred 2009, online image viewed 11 November 2011, underthreehundred.blogspot.com/2009/12/good-morning-judge.html

51 Wallpapers-for-free.com, online image, viewed 11 November 2011, : www.wallpapers-for-free.com/sky/lake-by-night-4.htm

52 Flickr.com, online image, viewed 11 November 2011, www.flickr.com/photos/33823163@N03/3499308165/

> **Example**
>
> *For example*: Consider a light source being directed onto an object and the object absorbed all of the light (no light at all was reflected back), then it would be considered to have an albedo of zero (0) or zero percent (0%). If light was shone onto an object and it reflected back all of the light, then it would have an albedo of one (1) or one hundred percent (100%).
>
> Most objects are somewhere in between, and therefore the albedo would be somewhere in the middle. The earth, for example, has an albedo of 0.35, which is equivalent to 35%; in other words, the earth will reflect 35% of the light it receives from the sun, the remaining 65% is absorbed.

Below is a table comparing the reflective values of various terrain surfaces and giving their albedo calculation. The higher the number, the greater the albedo, and the greater the amount of light that is able to be redirected for use by the NVGs and, therefore, the greater the NVGs' performance.

Surface type	Condition	Albedo
Soil	Dark and wet	0.05
	Light and Dry	0.40
Sand	Dark and wet	0.15
	Light and Dry	0.45
Grass	Long	0.16
	Short	0.26
Agricultural crops		0.18 - 0.25
Tundra (wild grasses)		0.18 - 0.25
Forests	Coniferous (evergreen)	0.05 - 0.15
	Deciduous (lose their leaves)	0.15 – 0.20
Water	Light source is low on the horizon	0.03 - 0.10
	Light source is high above the horizon	0.10 – 1.0
Snow	Old (dirty)	0.40
	Fresh (clean)	0.95
Ice	Sea	0.30 – 0.45
	Glacier	0.20 – 0.40
Clouds	Thick	0.60 – 0.90
	Thin	0.30 – 0.50

Terrain Contrast

Terrain contrast is a measure of the difference between the albedo of two or more adjacent surfaces. In general, the greater the difference, the better the contrast. Therefore, the better the perception of depth and the easier it is to see the terrain and objects.

The contrast will be good when using NVGs in high light conditions (such as a full moon about 45 degrees above the horizon). Contrast can be dramatically reduced in low light conditions (such as an overcast night and no moon).

The perception of contrast can also be affected by the texture of the surface. If you are viewing only one type of surface that is even and the same, it will have much less texture than an undulating surface with various different shaped objects at varying heights.

> **Example**
>
> Consider flying over water, snow or a desert, the texture of the surface is similar, and there is very little contrast compared to flying over mountain ranges or cattle country.
>
> Imagine flying over the water compared to flying over the hills in the background in the image below. Which one will give you better visual cues?
>
>

Flight over low contrast terrain should be avoided if possible. If it is unavoidable, then the pilot will have to be extra vigilant in cross-checking the instruments, particularly the Radar Altimeter, to ensure that the helicopter is not inadvertently descending towards the surface. If a manoeuvre is required over low contrast terrain, then only one manoeuvre at a time should be completed.

> **Example**
>
> *For* example: If wishing to do a 180 degree turn away from the area of low contrast and at the same time you wish to climb or descend, then either conduct the turn or the change in altitude first. Do not try to do both at the same time.

In summary, if flying over low contrast terrain you can climb or descend or turn, but not together.

Following are several NVG images. Can you identify the areas of low contrast within each image?

Most of this image is low contrast. Good reference points around the landing lights and where the airframe runs across the image give some contrast and a sense of altitude and distance. In this case, there is good contrast between the land and the sky, giving a good horizon line for visual flying.

This image shows low contrast in the foreground due to short grass and low contrast in the background due to low light levels. The centre of the image around the trees has good contrast and, therefore, good depth perception allowing a good sense of your situation.

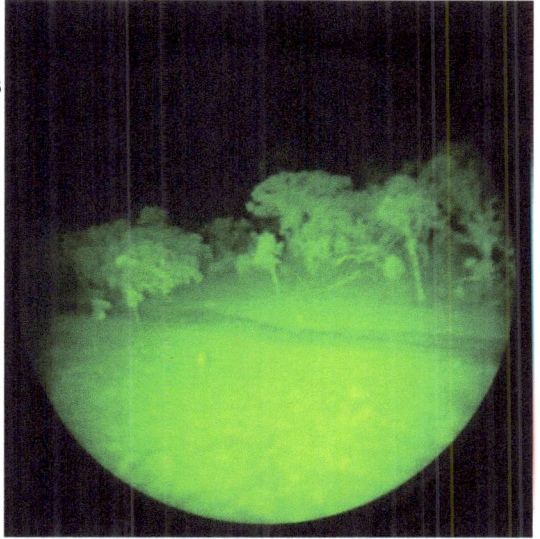

This image has reasonable contrast, especially in the foreground, where you can see the texture of the trees. The background starts to display low contrast due to lower light levels.

The lake in the image above represents an area of low contrast. Good contrast can be seen along the lake's edge.

The table below shows the percentage of contrast between some common terrain surfaces. Obviously, the higher the percentage value, the greater the contrast.

Surfaces	Contrast in %
Asphalt against grass	18%
Asphalt against snow	73%
Dirt against grass	41%
Grass against leaf	11%
Sand against leaf	39%

Terrain Shadowing

Terrain shadowing can happen at night in exactly the same way it does during the day, except that the shadows we see at night will always be away from whatever light source is available, whereas, during the day, the sun is our primary light source shadowing usually relates to that.

Anything blocking light will create a shadow; if there is a moon then shadows will fall away from the moon; if the aircraft landing light is on, shadows will fall away from the object in the same direction as the direction of the landing light. If there are conflicting light sources coming from various directions, then there can be multiple shadows on the same object at the same time.

53

Shadowing will assist in the perception of texture and, therefore, the contrast of a surface. In general, if a surface has multiple irregular shadows, the surface will appear to be high contrast. If there are few or no shadows, the surface is likely to be of lower contrast.

---

53 J.-M. Hasenfratz, J.M., Lapierre, M, Holzschuch, N, and Sillion, F., 2003, A Survey of Real-time So ft Shadows Algorithms, online article, viewed 21 November 2011, artis.imag.fr/Publications/2003/HLHS03/

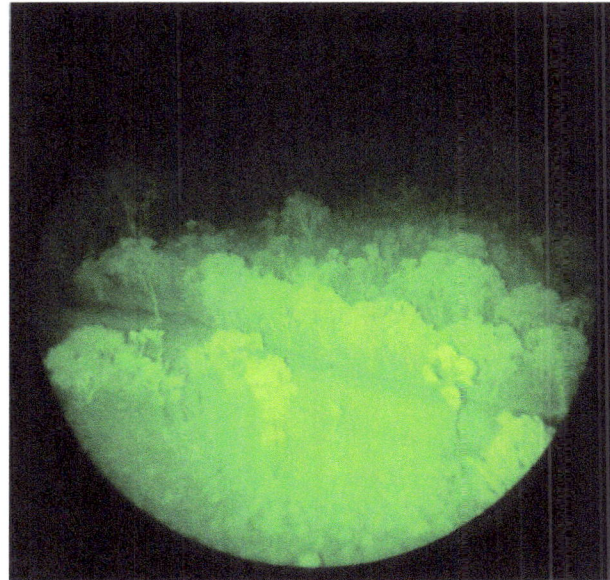
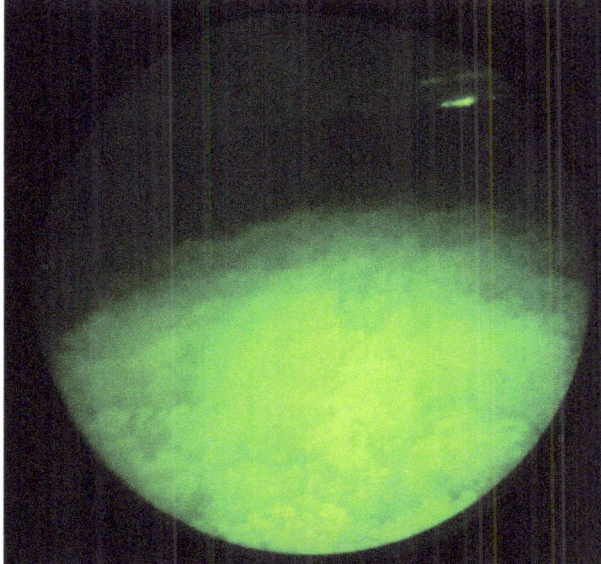

Figure 104 Shadows/High contrast

Figure 105 No shadows/Low contrast

Terrain shadowing from a fixed light source (e.g., the moon) can be a great advantage. Conversely, shadowing from a moving light source (another aircraft) can be a great disadvantage as it can give the observer the illusion that the object viewed is moving.

For NVG operations, areas that are in shadow can hide obstacles. For this reason, areas of shadow should be treated as an obstacle and should either be avoided or inspected with a searchlight before operating into the area. The image below shows an area on the left in shadow. Use of the searchlight to look into the area will expose any obstacles before operations.

Weather and Atmospheric Obscurants

The state of the atmosphere can be one of the most important factors contributing to NVG performance, as anything within the atmosphere has the ability to absorb, scatter, reflect and/or refract (bend) light.

Atmospheric Absorption

Usually, atmospheric absorption is discussed globally, where light from the sun is absorbed, scattered, reflected or refracted by the earth's atmosphere before it reaches the surface. Only a small portion of the sun's rays make it to the surface.

When discussing NVGs, we are more concerned with the light sources that we need at night, namely the moon, the aircraft's lighting and the effect from any ground-based lights. In the following discussion about absorption, scattering, reflection and refraction, we will be relating it to particles in the earth's lower atmosphere and how they can affect the light sources, we need and use at night and not on the total atmospheric absorption of the sun.

Absorption

Absorption is where any radiant energy in the form of light, either from a natural or an artificial source, is retained or "absorbed" by the substance it is striking. For the NVG pilot, a light directed at a surface with low luminescence will have the effect of absorbing light and projecting back a dark image. Absorption will be a regular occurrence within the NVG environment and is considered to be the main reason NVG performance can reduce.

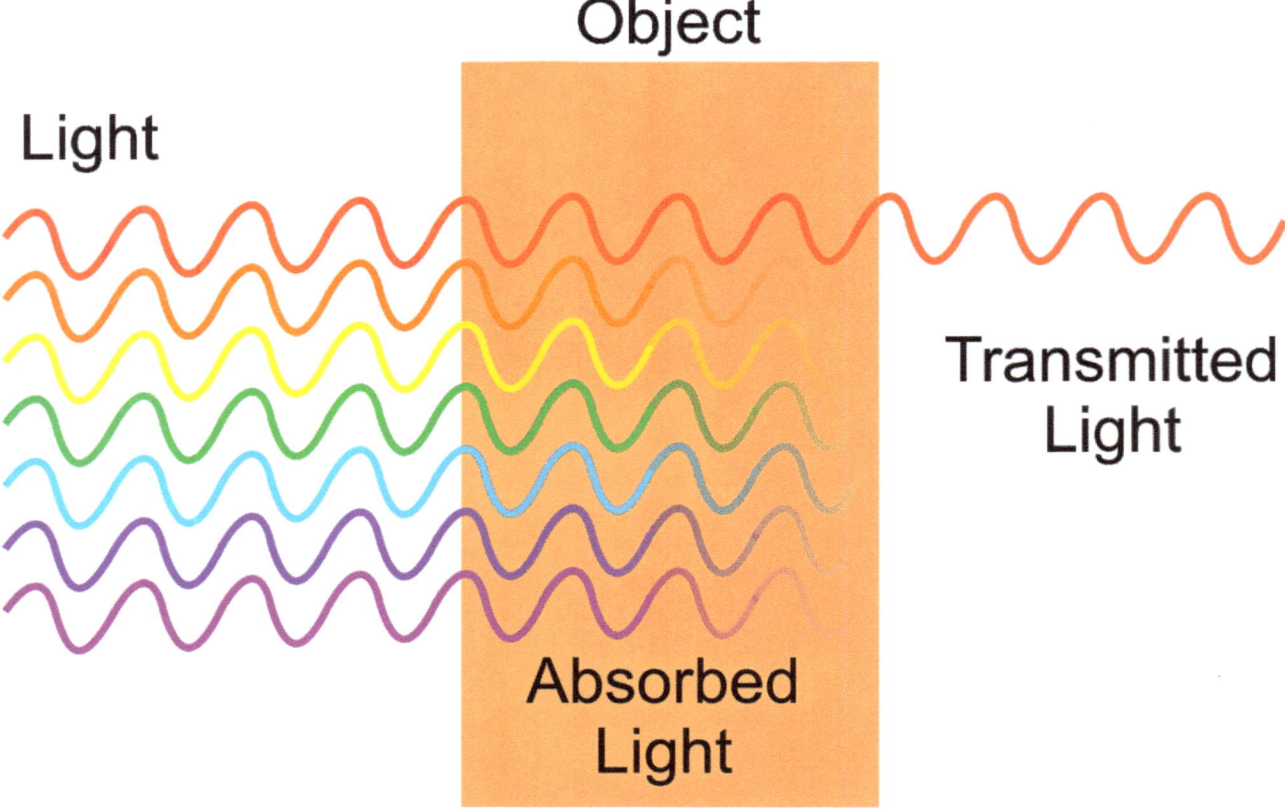

Scattering

Any radiant energy in the form of light travelling through the atmosphere can strike a particle. In doing so, the particle can change the light energy's path, scattering it.

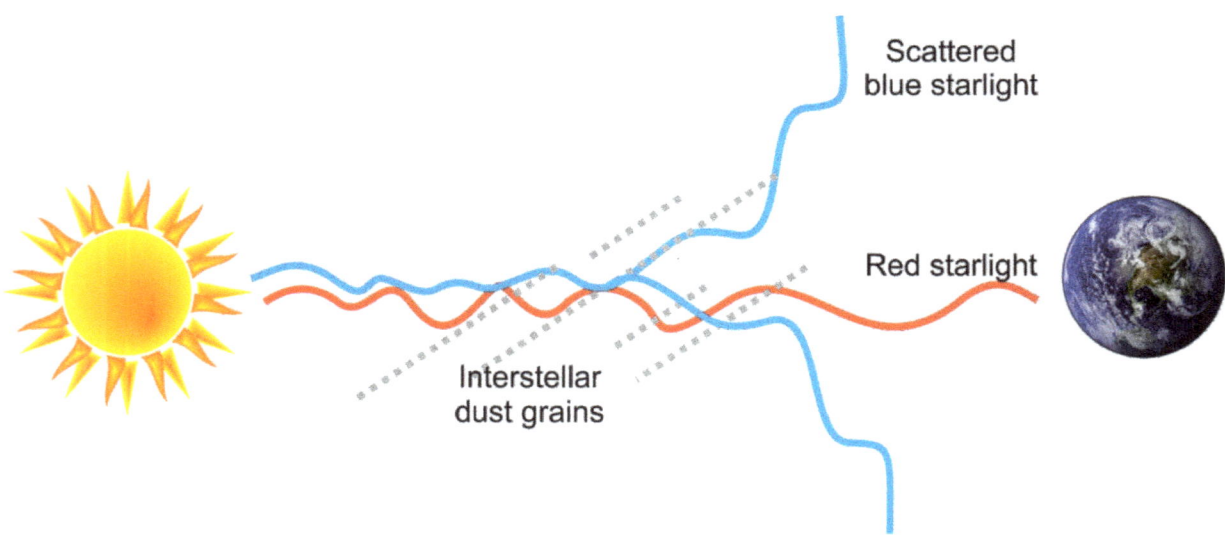

Night Vision Goggles *for Helicopter Pilots*

Because there will be multiple photons of light and because there will be multiple particles, they will not all act uniformly.

This means that the image that you might otherwise see on a clear night in good lighting conditions can start to appear fuzzy as the light is scattered in various random directions.

Refraction

Refraction refers to the bending of light. This is most common when light passes through water, and for the NVG user, that means clouds, fog, mist, haze, snow and especially rain on a wet windscreen.

Refraction can distort the image and make you think part of it is somewhere it is not.

Reflection

Related to the particle's albedo, the greater the luminance properties of the particle, the more likely light is reflected directly back to the source. The greatest natural source of reflection is dark, still water. The greatest manufactured source of reflection is a mirror.

Weather

During NVG operations, the crew can usually see areas of moisture that are dense such as thick clouds, fog, heavy rain showers etc., but they may not be able to see areas that are less dense such as thin fog, wispy clouds, light rain etc.

---

54 American Physical Society, 2011, online image, viewed 21 November 2011, physicsbuzz.physicscentral.com/2009_12_01_archive.html

55 Moultworld.com, online image, viewed 21 November 2011,: www.moultworld.com/?p=156

Understanding how the differing types of moisture in the atmosphere can affect NVG performance is important. Additionally, the crew should be vigilant in maintaining an awareness of changes in the weather while in flight. This can be aided by being attentive to changes in the NVG image, that is looking for:

- **Halos**: The halos around a light source may start to get bigger and more diffused. This is due to increased moisture content such as rain or fog etc.
- **Scintillation**: This background electrical noise may start to become obvious in the image due to the decreasing amount of light available as it is being absorbed, scattered, reflected or refracted by clouds.
- **Loss of scene**: What you can actually see in the image detail may start to reduce as the level of light reduces and the moisture becomes thicker.

Obtain a thorough pre-flight weather briefing and apply the NVG weather minima prior to the flight. Discuss the flight and the weather with the crew to consider all opinions and thoughts. Local knowledge of the local weather patterns can be a real advantage as the crew can apply the weather forecast to actual conditions to known weather patterns.

It is a good idea when using NVGs to occasionally look under the goggles to view the outside scene unaided. The unaided eye may just pick up bad weather that the NVGs are not seeing.

Despite planning for inadvertent weather, the crew should have an IIMC (Inadvertent Instrument Meteorological Conditions) recovery plan and be certain that the weather minima for this recovery are applied to the instrument approaches available at the destination.

Airborne Obscurants

Moisture (weather) is not the only consideration, as there may be other particles that can absorb, scatter, reflect or refract light within the atmosphere before it reaches the NVG. Haze, dust, smoke, ash, pollen, sand, leaves, salt, pollutants, and anything else circulated within the atmosphere are examples of obscurants that can affect light.

Airborne obscurants are similar to moisture in that the size, concentration, colour and shape of the particles will determine the degree of impact on NVG performance.

- high winds can stir up dust
- forest fires can produce smoke
- pollution around major cities or industrial areas
- even the helicopter's downwash, acting on surface material can produce airborne particles.

Atmospheric Influence

Below are some of the more common items found in the atmosphere and a general discussion on how they may affect NVG performance.

Low Temperatures

As a pilot, it is important that you obtain a weather forecast, and for NVG operations, we know this is mandatory. Obtaining the weather will give the crew valuable information on the state of the atmosphere, and this information can be used in pre-flight planning so that conditions can be planned for and expected. One of the key elements to look for in the forecast is the temperature and the freezing level because one of our main concerns is moisture in the air (clouds, rain, snow, fog, etc.). If this water gets to freeze, that can be very dangerous to helicopter flight. So relating all the weather to the freezing level is critical to the pilot.

Airframe Icing

Airframe icing is difficult to detect while on NVG operations. Firstly, flight in icing conditions is not permitted. However, if conditions are marginal, the crew will need to develop a good cross-check to ensure the airframe icing does not exceed the operating limits of the aircraft.

Low Ambient Cockpit Temperatures

Depending on the cockpit heating or defogging system, fogging on the NVGs can be a problem, and this will significantly reduce NVG performance, as will fogging of the windscreen.

In the tropics, the opposite problem can occur when the NVGs are stored in an air-conditioned room and are cool, then taken outside for use. The NVGs will instantly fog up due to the warm and moist air condensing on the colder goggles. To avoid these issues, it is best to allow some time for the NVGs to acclimatise to the outside ambient conditions before use.

Clouds

Clouds can come in all different sorts, shapes and sizes, and each will have a different effect. Therefore, it is impossible to accurately predict how any particular cloud will affect NVG performance. Water content, temperature, and ice within a cloud will all have an effect. The NVG pilot needs to develop experience in becoming attuned to a degrading image so that appropriate actions may be taken.

Summer clouds, particularly in the tropics where it is warmer, will tend to have a higher water content when compared to winter clouds. Generally, the water droplets are of a size that, when affected by a light source, will appear opaque to visible in the near IR wavelength; therefore, these wavelengths will be reflected. For this reason, thick clouds can easily be seen with NVG, particularly when they are silhouetted against the night sky.

A cover of clouds can reduce illumination from the moon and the night sky; however, if low enough and close to an artificial source like a city can increase illumination by reflecting and then scattering the ground lights.

If a cloud is thin and wispy, then the water particles are further apart; this may allow the NVG pilot to see through the clouds. This can be an advantage when operating in poor weather conditions but can also be dangerous as the image may slowly degrade and not be noticed as the pilot flies into the cloud. Therefore, particular attention should be given to a degrading image and crew communication about this will lead to an early decision to continue or change height, heading, airspeed etc. to allow for the reducing visibility.

Sometimes thin clouds can be seen unaided but not seen with NVGs. Low-level clouds may be masked by terrain or themselves be masking the terrain. This can be more prevalent in very high or very low light conditions. This can be an issue if flying low level and you inadvertently fly into a low cloud that you did not see that was masking terrain, and you now have reduced visibility.

Clouds can also produce shadows. As we know, a shadow is to be considered an obstacle. Another illusion of a cloud shadow is that it can be perceived as rising terrain or a structure in the distance. A line of clouds can also give a false horizon illusion.

Thunderstorms and Lightning

Thunderstorms are particularly nasty to flying, day or night and should be avoided. The associated lightning, turbulence, microbursts and hail are not conducive to helicopter flight. Because thunderstorms are avoided, the only real effect they may have is lightning which can be seen through the NVGs many miles away. If you happen to be looking directly at the lightning strike, then goggles may bloom out temporarily as they receive very intense light that overstimulates the intensifier tube. You may have to turn away from the storm to prevent it from happening again and revert to instrument flying for a short time.

If the lightning happens behind you or off to the side, then often there is a short-term benefit as the lightning provides a large burst of light energy and therefore gives the NVGs more light to work with.

The bottom line is if operating around thunderstorms, be sensible and keep your distance. A good rule of thumb is to avoid thunderstorms by approximately 25 NM.

Rain

Rain comes from clouds, so if you are flying through rain it will usually be a dark night with not a lot of illumination from the night sky or moon. Rain droplets are quite large and are not seen by NVGs unless the white landing light is turned on.

With the landing light off, NVG operations often seem normal with reasonable visibility particularly if there is a good source of cultural lighting. If the landing light is turned on, the pilot can often get a bit of a shock as the rain suddenly appears as fast, hard-driving water droplets racing towards the helicopter at high speed.

The best suggestion is to turn the landing light off and go back to not seeing the rain.

Light rain is not going to be a problem; however, very heavy driving rain can become a problem, as it can be associated with increasing cloud cover. Good crew communication, monitoring the visibility still available and early decision making are required when flying in rain.

Snow

Snow usually falls in large gentle white flakes. This makes them very susceptible to reflecting back large amounts of light. Similar to rain, snow may go unnoticed until a landing light is turned on.

During the lift-off and landing, snow can be affected by the downwash, causing a whiteout condition. This may require either an aborted lift-off or a Reduced Instrument Flight Take Off (RIFTO) procedure.

Haze, Mist, Fog

Haze, mist and fog are usually associated with low-level flight. For the NVG pilot, they should be avoided as they can not only reduce visibility but hide obstacles and terrain.

When flying low level in the mountains, a bank of fog can hide a ridgeline or the pilot could falsely think that a fog bank is a ridgeline.

If the fog, haze or mist is very light, the NVG pilot can often see through it to the ground, particularly if there is good lighting on the ground. The main problem comes on finals, when the landing light is turned on, and all the light is scattered, reflected and absorbed so that suddenly the pilot can no longer see the ground. This can lead to disorientation.

Salt, Dust, Smoke, Ash, Pollen, Leaves, Grass and Bugs

Salt, dust, smoke, ash, pollen, leaves, grass and bugs can differently absorb, scatter, reflect and/or refract light. Using the landing light can make the situation worse. Bugs also tend to splatter on the windshield, which can be distracting and reduce visibility.

When getting close to the ground, the downwash from the rotor system can further induce these types of particles leading to a "brown out"; therefore, the subsequent RIFTO drills need to be utilised.

Wind

Wind has the effect of stirring up the atmosphere and circulating more particles. Picking up ground or sea-based particles as described above and reducing visibility.

Aircraft Configuration

Most aircraft were not initially designed by the OEM (Original Equipment Manufacturer) with NVG operations in mind. In the domain of the military, the aircraft have been modified at great research and cost and the information to do this, until recently, has been kept closely guarded or restricted.

In the Civil world, SAR/EMS and Police operators were typically the only ones able to use NVG and usually with ex-Military crews. Typically, when a helicopter was to be modified for NVG, it was for a specific operation and done by organisations that had very little knowledge or access to NVG lighting equipment. Therefore, the cockpit NVG configurations were often of a lower standard than desired.

Finding the correct lighting configuration, the suitable filters and finding all those little areas that can cause reflecting issues often takes a lot of trial and error. Thankfully, this is becoming easier as the flow of information and the levels of experience in the Civil sector increase. Below are the most common areas to address when looking at the aircraft's environmental effects on NVG performance.

Windshield

Several issues regarding the windshield can affect NVG performance; they include the windshield shape, the wavelengths of light it will transmit, its distance from the user, and its condition.

Before an NVG flight, the windshield of a helicopter shall:

- be cleaned and polished
- not have excessive scratching or damage, and
- be shielded from reflected light from the inside (cockpit) and the outside (nav lights, strobes and beacons).

Shape

The shape of the windshield can affect light as it passes through it. If the windshield is flat, then light can usually pass straight through it. If the windscreen is curved, then the light may be refracted, giving a false image to the NVG.

Wavelengths

Most windscreens are manufactured to allow the visible spectrum (400-700 nm) to pass through for normal unaided flight, day or night. Unfortunately, some windscreens, particularly those with a "tint" built into them, may absorb some light in the infrared spectrum (700-900 nm) and thus can significantly reduce NVG performance.

Distance from User

Distance from the user is more of a problem in small cockpits where the NVGs attached to the helmet protrude a distance from the face. If trying to scan to the side, the pilot may accidentally contact the windscreen. This can cause several things:

- Annoyance and distraction to the pilot, to the point where he may not scan that area anymore just because the NVGs keep hitting the windscreen
- The goggles could be knocked from their mount, and the pilot could inadvertently lose the NVG image
- The goggles can scratch the windscreen causing permanent damage and reducing the quality of the image viewed through the window.

Condition

If the windscreen is dirty, foggy, scratched, cracked or otherwise not in a good clear condition, this can reduce NVG performance by absorbing, scattering, reflecting or refracting the light. It is good airmanship to make sure your windscreen is clean before departure.

Lighting

Cockpit Lighting

When NVGs are first integrated into a helicopter, one of the first issues that have to be addressed is the modification of the internal cockpit lighting.

Normal cockpit lighting utilises incandescent bulbs filtered to produce red, orange, white, green or blue-white lighting for use during unaided night and IFR flights.

Even though these incandescent bulbs are filtered, they still emit large amounts of infrared energy. Even if the lights are dimmed down to the unaided eye, when using NVGs, they will produce massive amounts of cockpit light pollution. This, in turn, will reflect off the windscreen and bloom out the goggles so that the user is unable to look out the window.

Following is an image with the white non-NVG modified instrument lights turned on and the subsequent reflection on the window rendering the NVGs ineffective.

Over time, engineers have developed compatible lighting systems to easily see cockpit lighting with the unaided eye but do not degrade NVG performance.

Below are two images. The one on the left is an unmodified cockpit; the one on the right is the same aircraft after its lighting has been modified. It's interesting to note that both cockpits appeared to have the same brightness level to the unaided eye, but when viewed through the NVGs we have the results as shown below.

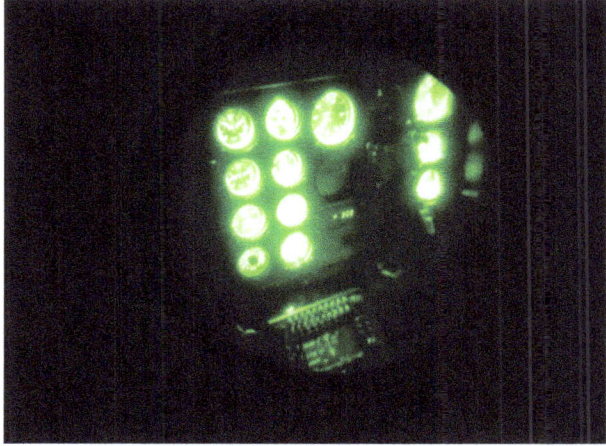
Figure 106 Unmodified cockpit lighting

Figure 107 Modified cockpit lighting

External Lighting

External lighting presents similar issues. The navigation lights, particularly the red nav light and the anti-collision lights and strobes, produce too much infrared energy that will cause reflections within the cabin.

There are several ways around this:

- Modify the navigation lights so that they are NVG compatible
- Turn the anti-collision and strobe lights off
- Paint or tape up the side windows that allow the entry of reflected infrared energy into the cabin
- Paint or tape up the windows that are reflecting infrared energy off the windscreens

Cockpit Design

While wearing NVGs, the cockpit ergonomics (seating design) could restrict the movement of the head and the viewing of the applicable instruments, gauges and switches.

Viewing an overhead panel, reaching forward to adjust the flight controls, accessing map pockets, and conducting normal checks may all have to be modified and coordinated with the crew to achieve the same result in a different environment.

Risk Management for NVG Operations

Before commencing any NVG operations, it would be expected that the pilot would have at least a reasonable understanding of what Risk Management and Threat Error Management (TEM) are and how to apply them. This chapter will only review some basics and relate Risk Management and Threat Error Management specifically to NVG operations.

Quick Review of Risk Management

To understand risk management, we need to understand what a *hazard* is and then relate this to the *risk* and then to the *management* of the risk.

Hazard

A hazard is an event or a situation that could result in damage or injury.

Risk

A risk is the chance of something happening that could impact a desired outcome. It could be either a positive or negative risk.

Risk is measured in terms of the consequence versus the likelihood of the event.

Risk = Likelihood x Consequence

In aviation, we tend to only consider the negative aspects of risk as they relate to the safety of the flight.

Management

Management is the act of collating all the relevant information and resources (including people) and then putting this together to accomplish a desired goal or objective. Management encompasses planning, organising, resourcing, staffing, leading, directing and controlling an organisation or group or effort to accomplish a goal.

Example

Consider the image below. What are the hazard and the risk, and how could this be managed?

The *hazard* is the snake.

The *risk* is getting bitten by the snake.

The *management* process is to identify the hazard and develop a method to manage the risk. Which, in this case, is to put and keep the snake in a sealed cage.

Night Vision Goggles *for Helicopter Pilots*

Risk Management for NVG

Therefore, risk management with regards to NVG is the coordinated effort to direct and control an organisation in relation to events that could have a positive or negative impact on that organisation and, in particular, on an NVG sortie.

Risk Management Plans

Flight using NVGs has unique hazards and risks. These can include goggle failure, blooming, battery failure, crew fatigue, new crew, transition to NVGs and potential loss of situational awareness, breakdown of the scan, breakdown in crew coordination, deterioration of weather, low-level flight, unknown obstacles, etc.

Because flights using NVGs are typically very controlled and pre-planned, operators can go about the usual process of identifying standard risks and produce a **Risk Management Plan (RMP).** This plan can then be published so that all stakeholders can assess these risks against the particular flight.

Additionally, crews can identify additional risks that may not have been covered in the RMP and put in place strategies that will guard against the risk of those events happening.

Risk Management Plan (RMP) Process

To create a RMP, the following steps should be considered.

1. Communicate the need for risk management to the organisation.
2. Establish the context for risk management within the organisation.
3. Identify and list the risks.
4. Analyse the risks.
5. Evaluate the risks.
6. Treat the risks.
7. Monitor and review the risks.

Risk Management Plan (RMP) Content

A RMP is usually made up of the following content:

1. Risk context: This will state where the risk may be encountered. On the ground, in-flight, during planning, organisational, etc.
2. The risk: This will state what the risk is.
3. The context: This describes where in the organisation the risk is appropriate.
    (a) Is it a safety issue?
    (b) Is it money, people or resource issue?
    (c) Is it an issue due to outside influences, etc.?
4. Analyse the risk: This is broken down into several categories, including what mitigating strategies are in place to control the risk, rating the risk in the event that it is going to happen, rating its likelihood and the level of the risk. The evaluation is usually the result of a team of people putting in their thoughts regarding the risk.
5. Evaluate the risk: After the risk has been identified and analysed, the team will decide whether it is acceptable or not.
6. Treat or mitigate the risk: This is the plan to avoid or manage the risk. It may include a statement, an action, a process or procedure, the purchase of equipment, the modification of equipment or similar. It is simply the method desired to avoid and manage the risk.

RMP Headings

For example, the RMPs may contain the following headings:

- Task Analysis
    - Sortie Element / Sub-Element - a description of the task(s).
- Identify Risk
    - Before a flight, all crews, and in particular NVG crews, are to sit down, discuss, identify and evaluate any potential risks. This can be aided by the use of any of the following:
        - Checklists
        - Scenario analysis
        - Decision trees
        - Brainstorming between pilots, crews, instructors
        - Interview/focus group discussion
        - Examination of local or overseas experience
        - Expert judgment, peer review
        - SWOT analysis (Strengths, Weaknesses, Opportunities, Threats)
        - History/failure analysis
        - Audits or physical inspections
        - Operational modelling
        - Risk - a description of the risk.
        - Dimension / Context - Identify the context of the risk, for example, safety, fatigue, etc.
- Analyse Risks
    - Existing Controls - Review the current procedures and standards in place to prevent or limit this risk
    - Consequences - Review the potential consequences of this risk
    - Likelihood - Evaluate the likelihood of this risk occurring
    - Risk Level – Determine what the resulting risk level is based on the risk matrix
- Evaluate Risks
    - Meet Criteria? - Is this risk level within the criteria for acceptable risk?
    - ALARP - Is this risk **A**s **L**ow **A**s **R**easonably **P**racticable?
    - Decision - Is this risk accepted?
    - Priority - What is the priority of this risk?
- Treat Risks
    - Treatments - What additional actions will be taken to reduce this risk?
    - Consequences - Based on the suggested treatments, what is the adjusted consequence score?
    - Likelihood - Based on the suggested treatments, what is the adjusted likelihood score?
    - Risk Level - Based on the suggested treatments, what is the adjusted risk score?
    - Meet Criteria - Is this adjusted risk level within are criteria for acceptable risk?
    - ALARP - Is this risk **A**s **L**ow **A**s **R**easonably **P**racticable?
    - Final Decision - Is this risk acceptable with this additional treatment(s)?

Night Vision Goggles *for Helicopter Pilots*

Risk Matrix

The matrix below is a method used to categorise risk. Once the risk is identified, it can be placed within this matrix depending on its likelihood of happening and the consequence if it did happen. Based on the score, the organisation or individual can decide to continue or abort the proposed activity. Additionally, companies can then set rules to help pilots and employees make go or no go decisions.

	Catastrophic	Critical	Major	Moderate	Minor
Likely	Ext	V.Hi	Hi	Med	Med
Probable	Ext	V.Hi	Hi	Med	Med
Possible	Hi	Hi	Med	Med	Low
Improbable	Med	Med	Med	Low	Low
Rare	Low	Low	Low	Low	Low

Consequence Rating

Rating	Consequence	Consequence Definition
5	Catastrophic	Capability: Indefinite loss of business capability provided by an aviation system.
		Safety: Many fatalities or numerous aircraft lost.
		Task: Failure to achieve a task that is essential to a business objective and/or goal.
		Public Relations/Image/Morale: Widespread public condemnation of the business. Long term Media condemnation or an Aviation Industry inquiry.
4	Critical	Capability: Long-term degradation to business capability provided by an aviation system.
		Safety: Few fatalities or single aircraft loss.
		Task: Failure to achieve an essential business operational objective with significant business strategic implications.
		Public Relations/Image/Morale: Widespread public discontent of the business. Prolonged national media condemnation or a coronial inquest.
3	Major	Capability: Temporary loss or severe degradation to business capability provided by an aviation system.
		Safety: Serious injuries that could result in permanent disability or long term aircraft unserviceability requiring more than 6 months and/or 3/4 of the original purchase price to repair.
		Task: Failure to achieve an important business operational objective with serious business implications.

Rating	Consequence	Consequence Definition
		Public Relations/Image/Morale: Negative public reaction by public aviation interest groups and short term national media attention. Company morale seriously affected but recoverable.
2	Moderate	Capability: Substantial temporary degradation to the business capability provided by an aviation system.
		Safety: Injuries that could result in temporary disability and/or short term aircraft unserviceability requiring more than 3 months and/or 1/2 of the original purchase price to repair.
		Task: Failure to achieve an important business operational objective with significant business implications.
		Public Relations/Image/Morale: Local prolonged media attention and negative public reaction. Company morale slightly affected.
1	Minor	Capability: Temporary degradation to business capability provided by an aircraft system.
		Safety: Minor injuries requiring medical attention and/or short term aircraft unserviceability requiring more than <=3 months and/or <=1/4 of the original purchase price to repair.
		Task: Partial achievement of a business task with significant company implications but does not affect a business operational objective.
		Public Relations/Image/Morale: Local short-term media attention and negative public reaction. Company individual's morale slightly affected.

Likelihood Rating

Rating	Likelihood	Likelihood Definition
5	Likely	Expected to occur during the activity under consideration.
4	Probable	Could occur during the activity under consideration.
3	Possible	Occurrence is conceivable but only expected infrequently during the aviation system life. (nominally 20 years)
2	Improbable	Occurrence is conceivable but only expected on a few occasions during the aviation system life. (nominally 20 years)
1	Rare	Occurrence is conceivable but only expected no more than once during the aviation system life. (nominally 20 years)

RMP Example

An example extract of an RMP is shown below.

			Risk 1	Risk 2	Risk 3
Identify Risks	Task Analysis — Sortie Element / Sub-Element		All airborne sequences	All airborne sequences	Operations into HLS- NVG Basic
	Risk		**Changing NVG operations.** NVG crews could be expected to undertake NVG operations in a variety of tasks. Due to seasonal variations there could be some tasks that the NVG crewmember has not undertaken for some time and therefore could lack proficiency that could lead to a breakdown in NVG procedures. This could lead to a breakdown in scan due to time taken with a cockpit task. Traffic/ terrain confliction, IIMC, CFIT. Loss of aircraft, crew injury or fatality.	**Crew fatigue leading into a breakdown in ability to operate the aircraft safely.** All NVG crew members under high work load cockpit environment. Breakdown in external scan and operating in marginal weather. Disorientation, IIMC. Loss of aircraft, crew injury or fatality.	**Crews are operating into unlit and often unprepared landing sites.** It is possible for crews to become overwhelmed by visual illusions possibly not see potential obstacles during the conduct of operations info or out of an HLS. Damage to aircraft both on ground and in air leading to possible aircraft damage and or injury to personnel which could be fatal.
Analyse Risks	Existing Controls		All NVG crew must conform to the currency and experience requirements as detailed in the Ops Man. Before any BHS NVG personnel undertake the NVG operation they will have to be checked for suitable training and qualifications together with currency and finally proficiency. All BHS NVG crew members will undertake ongoing NVG training to maintain levels of experience and proficiency. Those members who lack suitable currency or proficiency will receive training to elevate their levels to ensure they are capable of completing the assigned task.	Detailed understanding and application of the requirements contained within the BHS Ops Man concerning endurance calculations and fatigue management. All staff will use the BHS FTD Ver 8 program and apply the PSWR process prior to any NVG operation.	Where possible crews will operate into known NVG HLSs as detailed in the BHS Ops Manual. When Operating to areas unknown by crews they will be required to use their white light sources as soon as they are below LSALT and at a speed as detailed within the Stds Manual. Where possible, crews will make maximum use of onboard crewmembers as observers as well as using any air ground communications that may assist.
Evaluate Risks		Cons	Critical	Critical	Moderate
		Like	Improbable	Improbable	Improbable
		Risk Level	Med	Med	Low
		Meet Criteria?	Yes	Yes	Yes
		ALARP?	Yes	Yes	Yes
		Decision	Accept	Accept	Accept
Treat Risks		Treatment	Not Required	Not required	Not required
		Cons	Critical	Critical	Moderate
		Like	Improbable	Improbable	Rare
		Like #	5	5	6
		Risk Level	Low	Low	Low
		Risk #	5	5	5
		Meet Criteria	Yes	Yes	Yes
		ALARP?	Yes	Yes	Yes
		Final Decision	Accept	Accept	Accept

Threat Error Management (TEM) for NVG Operations

Most aircraft accidents are linked to deficiencies in human performance. These deficiencies may involve a variety of factors which can include but are not be limited to

- poor lookout
- loss of situation awareness (SA)
- poor decision-making
- lack of task organisation
- breakdown of communication, both in the cockpit and externally
- failure to recognise threats to safety
- creeping in of small errors that compound.

TEM is an operational concept applied to the conduct of a flight that is more than the traditional role of airmanship, as it provides for a structured and proactive approach for pilots to use in identifying and managing threats and errors that may affect the safety of the flight. To achieve this, TEM uses many tools, including training, standard operating procedures, checklists, briefings and single-pilot human factor principles.

There is some overlap between Risk Management, TEM and Human Factors (HF), particularly at the stage of developing and implementing plans to mitigate risks and in reviewing the conduct of a flight.

Threat

A *threat* is a situation or event that has the potential to negatively impact the safety of a flight or any influence that promotes the opportunity for pilot errors.

External Threats

Some typical external threats to NVG operations might include:

- adverse weather
- deteriorating weather
- weight and balance
- density altitude
- runway length
- other traffic
- artificial light
- high terrain or obstacles
- the condition of the aircraft
- low-level operations.

Internal Threats

Some typical internal threats to NVG operations might include:

- fatigue
- complacency
- visual disorientation
- over or under confidence
- lack of flight discipline, including poor use of white light, phones and a non-sterile cockpit (talking about the weekend while on short finals into a basic HLS)
- lack of NVG phraseology
- hazardous behaviour
- lack of recency and proficiency.

Organisational Threats

Some typical organisational threats to NVG operations might include:

- operational pressure, such as tight scheduling of flights
- aircraft – poor serviceability or incorrect lighting for NVGs
- NVGs – poor storage and servicing
- maintenance – maintenance error or event
- documentation error – incorrect or expired charts, incomplete or erroneous maintenance release.

Error

An *error* is an action or inaction that leads to deviations from the organisation or the person's intention or expectation. In other words, someone makes a mistake because they did not follow the correct procedure, and you did not get what you were expecting.

While errors may be inevitable, the safety of flight requires that errors that occur are identified and managed before flight safety margins are compromised.

Typical errors in-flight might include:

- incorrect performance calculations
- inaccurate flight planning
- non-standard communications
- aircraft mishandling
- incorrect systems operation or management
- failure to meet flight standards, e.g. poor power and airspeed control.

Management

Management is the ability to plan, direct and control an operation or situation and specifically, in this case, an NVG operation.

Because we are able to identify various threats and anticipate some of the errors that could potentially be made, the crew is able to better manage them. Just being aware of the threats and errors possible can go a long way to reducing the possibility of them occurring.

Therefore, management can stand back and plan for these adverse events before the flight.

Pre-flight Brief

In a flight training organisation, the management of threats and errors can be discussed during the pre-flight brief for each training sortie. This is a time when all the crew members are getting together to discuss the actual specifics of the flight, and you can take the time to allow everyone to have input in discussing possible threats and errors that may be applicable and how to mitigate (manage) against them.

For non-training operations, it is still a good idea to conduct a pre-flight brief with all the crew. This would include the non-NVG equipped crew as well as doctors, fire crew, photographers, etc., as they need to be made aware of the possible threats and errors that could potentially affect the flight. These threats or errors may potentially come from them, and they may potentially be part of the solution. Additionally, if they are aware of the potential threats and errors that may affect the flight crew or the aircraft, again, they may be able to be part of the solution. Good communication and a thorough understanding of the NVG flight are paramount to a safe flight.

Mike Becker

Crew Resource Management and Phraseology

It is assumed that basic Crew Resource Management (CRM) principles and procedures ae already well understood by the trainee NVG crew. This chapter focuses on CRM and Phraseology techniques specific to NVG operations.

It is important that each crew member learns specific words, phrases and crew coordination techniques so that everyone involved in the NVG flight is working from the same "mental model". The term "mental model" is used to describe the picture you have in your mind of what is going on around you and what you are expecting to see in the future.

Having the entire crew with the same "mental model" ensures that everyone knows exactly what is going on in, around and outside the helicopter at all times.

Standard Phraseology

Using industry-standard phraseology means that any crew member should be able to fly with crews from another base, company or military organisation and still have the same, or at least very similar, procedures.

Good verbal communication skills within the crew are crucial in NVG operations; because you cannot see each other due to the limited light and the reduced field of view of the NVGs. Correct verbal communication and feedback between crew members are imperative for the conduct of a safe NVG flight.

The following pages outline recommended procedures that could be applied to a variety of situations that can occur during various NVG operational and/or helicopter malfunctions and emergency situations. You may already be doing something similar, you may wish to adopt some of them, or you may create something new that is more specific and relevant to your situation. Either way, you need to set the guidelines for your crews prior to commencing any NVG operation.

Note:

All aircrew are reminded of the need to complete all relevant Rotorcraft Flight Manual or checklist requirements. It is the helicopter captain's decision as to whether the malfunction or emergency procedure is to be conducted with the NVGs goggled-up or de-goggled, depending on the situation. These stated procedures are either:

- a new procedure for a situation specific to NVGs where a checklist action does not exist, or
- an extension of an existing procedure where a checklist action does exist but may vary due to the use of NVG.

The procedures assume the transition is during the conduct of an NVG, IFR or NFVR flight, as appropriate, and not whilst on the ground or stationary.

Crew Resource Management (CRM)

Any helicopter pilot would know that there is a lot to do in managing a helicopter. This is compounded at night when using NVGs. In general, an NVG operation is a minimum two (2) pilot crew. Although legally, you can go single pilot on NVG, there are more restrictions, and it is very seldom exercised, so it will not be discussed here. Instead, we will assume a minimum of a two (2) pilot crew and will designate the pilot on the controls as the **Flying Pilot (FP)** and the pilot not on the controls as the **Non-Flying Pilot (NFP)**.

In general, the NFP shall make all the radio calls and be responsible for managing the radio and navigation equipment. The NFP is responsible for the bulk of the administration and for directing or telling the FP what to do; this allows the FP to concentrate on only controlling the helicopter. Remember, because of the reduced field of vision, it is important that each crew member verbally tells the other(s) what is going on and what they are doing because there is no other way to know.

Because you cannot see each other, each crew member is *assuming* that the other is either conducting a systematic scan outside of their allotted area while they are attending to their allotted duties (flying, administration, etc) or they have their eyes inside the cockpit after notifying the other crew that this is what they are doing to complete some administration task. Without good verbal communication, the crew will not have the same "mental model" of their current situation.

It is also important to note here that the designation of FP and NFP has nothing to do with who is the designated Captain or co-pilot (First pilot or PIC and second pilot or co-pilot). The crew will, prior to the flight, designate who fulfils these roles separate from who may actually assume the FP or NFP duties at any given time.

Eyes Inside/Outside Drill

For various reasons, a crew member may have to look inside the cockpit for a prolonged period of time. This can be for changing radio frequencies, setting up navigation aids, reading through an instrument approach, reading a map or similar. It is important to tell the other crew members this so they can then take up this crew member's scan during this time.

If a crew member looks inside for a prolonged period (greater than approximately 1 minute), then the following drill applies:

Step	Action
1	NFP or crew member prior to looking inside announces: *"eyes inside front/back left/right"*
2	FP or other appropriate crew member announces: *"taking up the scan"*
3	Once completed and ready to look outside again, then the NFP or crew member will announce: *"eyes outside front/rear left/right"*
4	FP or other appropriate crew member announces: *"Roger"*

NVG Scanning Procedures

Scanning

The movement of the NVGs to accommodate the whole viewing area is known as the NVG scan. The total area able to be scanned using the NVG is called the Field of Regard (FOR).

The scan should be constant and methodical with smooth head movements to minimise disruption to the vestibular system and potential spatial disorientation. Periods of high workload may lead to a scan breakdown that detracts from accurate helicopter control. This includes hovering, where it is difficult to detect drift due to the reduced peripheral vision.

All crew members should begin scanning at the greatest distance an object can be perceived (top) and move inward toward the position of the helicopter (bottom). For each stop, an area approximately 40 degrees wide should be scanned. The duration of each stop is based on the degree of detail that is required; that is, the stop should be long enough to interpret the image.

Different phases of flight require different applications of the NVG scan to isolate areas of interest. In transit below LSALT, the scan should be concentrated in the direction of flight to detect and avoid obstacles. When manoeuvring at lower altitudes, crews should include consistent scanning to the side of the helicopter. When hovering in an NVG HLS Basic area, the scan should encompass the immediate area around the entire helicopter equally to avoid drift and subsequent collision with obstacles.

In addition to the NVG scan, aircrew should continue to conduct a normal instrument crosscheck scan. This is achieved by looking under the NVGs to see the instrument panel. Specific items may be illuminated by lip or finger lights to seek information. NVGs should be adjusted so there is minimal head movement required to scan under the NVGs inside the cockpit.

An unaided scan can also be incorporated to identify objects with the naked eye. Red obstacle lights can stand out better unaided, especially when the obstacle is surrounded by cultural lighting. Distances and rates of closure with other helicopters may also be easier under certain conditions using an unaided scan.

In the Military environment, there is great reluctance to have an unaided scan when using NVGs and rightly so. Operationally they are not using any white light, but infrared light, and usually, they do not want to be seen themselves, so using an unaided scan would not be effective. But a civilian operator has the ability to use white light and is often operating in areas that have more light that can be distracting, such as flashing emergency services lights or household or HLS lights, so an unaided scan can actually be of great benefit. Whichever one is used at the time will be at the discretion of the helicopter captain and in accordance with whatever guidelines and procedures the operator may determine is appropriate.

NVG Scanning Arcs Of Responsibility

To ensure that the area of flight is scanned efficiently, each member is allocated an 'arc of responsibility'. The area for each member of the aircrew will vary according to the helicopter type and number of crew on board and should be briefed prior to flight.

The standard arcs for NVG flights are as follows; the left front member of the aircrew will have an arc of responsibility from the 8 o'clock position through to the 1 o'clock position, and the right front member of the aircrew will have an arc of responsibility from the 11 o'clock position through to the 4 o'clock position. These arcs overlap between the 11 o'clock and 1 o'clock position.

Scanning Arcs for NVG Flight

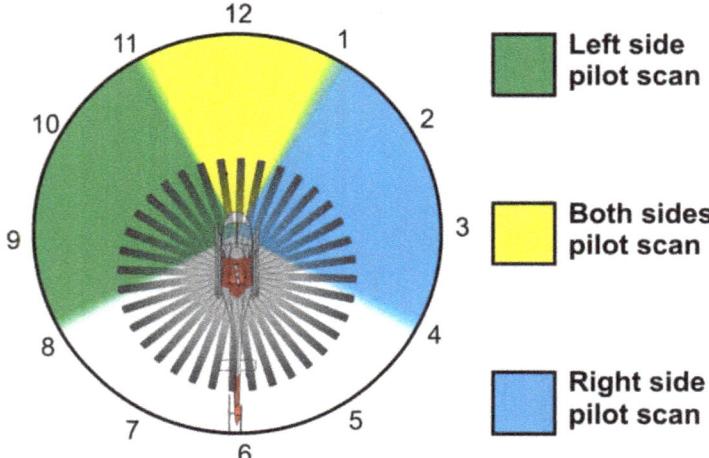

Bear in mind that if you can move your head and actually see to the 7 or 4 o'clock position, you may do so. The arcs of responsibility are a guide only, and helicopter design may play a role in determining what you can physically do.

Standard Words and Phrases

Aided flight	A flight in which NVGs are used in an operational position by trained personnel to enhance night vision. Note: Aided flight is associated with the procedure of goggle-up, where the crewmember places NVGs in the operational position.
De-goggle	The action of transferring from NVG flight (aided) to non-NVG (unaided) flight by removing the NVGs from a usable position. Note: The expression is also used as a command and is opposite to goggle-up.
Look under (under view)	Is the ability of operators to look under or around the NVGs to view inside and outside the helicopter.
Abort	Terminate a pre-planned manoeuvre.
Altitude	Announcement by any crewmember for FP to immediately check altitude/height AMSL or AGL.
Braking	Announcement by FP or NFP who intends to apply brake pressure.
Break left/right/up/down	Immediate action command to perform an emergency manoeuvre to deviate from the present track.
Call Out	Command from either AC or FP for a specified procedure to be read from the checklist by another member of the crew.
Caution	Used in conjunction with a Warning. It allows other crewmembers to develop a mental picture of what is happening during an approach/departure, when manoeuvring around a pad or persons/vehicles within the vicinity of the landing area.
Clear to Ground	A clearance to facilitate a more efficient approach. It is given when the helicopter is two to three lengths from the landing point. It indicates that both the touchdown point and the landing area beyond are clear of obstacles and that a run-on landing can be made, if required.
Clear to Roll	A clearance to commence forward movement. It is given after checking the rear, above and forward for obstacles and other aircraft.
Come up/down	Command to change the altitude up or down.
Controls	Helicopter flight controls.
Distance to Run	Information referring to distance from the helicopter to the desired set down point or to obstacles on the approach path.
Drifting	An alert of the unintentional or undirected movement of the helicopter - will be followed by the direction of the move.
Egress	Emergency command to leave the helicopter.
Execute	Initiate an action.
Expect	Anticipate further instructions or guidance.

Eyes Inside	Primary focus of the announcing crewmember is inside the helicopter for an extended period and obstacle clearance duties for that crew position need to be reallocated.
Eyes Outside	Primary focus of the announcing crewmember is back outside the helicopter and obstacle clearance duties for that crew position are accepted.
Fly Heading	Command to fly an assigned compass heading.
Height Below the Helicopter/Load	An estimation of the height below the helicopter or external load to the closest obstacles on the approach angle, or to the ground.
Hold	Command given by crew member to ensure any helicopter movement is stopped immediately.
Jettison	Command for the emergency release of an external load or stores.
Losing Sight	The point at which the FP has lost sight of the termination point and requires the crew member to commence providing advice intended to position the helicopter.
Maintain	Command to continue or keep the same.
Maintain Your Height	Clearance given when it appears that the helicopter, if it continues on the same line, will encroach safety limits to obstacles.
Monitor	Command to maintain constant watch or observation.
Move	Command to hover "forward, Aft, left or right" followed by a distance.
Move Left/Right on Line	Command given during an approach to a pad if the helicopter is left or right of the line required to remain clear of obstacles on the approach path. Once the desired line is acquired, the call "Line's good" is given.
Negative	Incorrect or permission not granted.
Nil / Negative Contact	Unable to establish communications.
Not Sighted	Target, traffic, or obstacle not positively seen or identified.
Now	An immediate action is required.
Passengers (crew) clear in/out	Command to have personnel enter or exit the helicopter or disc.
Release	Command for the planned or expected release of an external load or store.
Roger	Message received and understood.
Say Again	Repeat your transmission.
Set in the Back	Call given when the crew member has completed cabin safety checks of passengers, cargo security, loose articles, door security and personal harnesses.
Slow Down	Command to decrease ground speed.

Speed Up	Command to increase ground speed.
Stand By	Wait – duties of higher priority are being performed and the request cannot be complied with at this time.
Stop	Command to go no further – cease the present action.
Taking Over	Command by the pilot assuming control of his/her helicopter. The term is also used as an acknowledgment of duties being assumed for a particular crew member's activity after he/she has used the term "Handing Over".
Traffic	Refers to friendly helicopter that presents a potential hazard to the current route of flight; will be followed by an approximate clock position and the distance from the helicopter with a reference to altitude.
Turn	Command to deviate from the present ground track; will be followed by words left or right and clock ray indication for low-level flight (to ensure FP does not bring attention inside the helicopter) or compass heading.
Unable	Indicates the inability to comply with a specific instruction or request.
Up On	Indicates primary radio selected; will be followed by radio selector position.
Wilco	Message received and understood and I will comply.

Standard Crew Interactions

Manoeuvring requirements

NFP   *'Start left turn'*

FP   Initiates left turn, remaining eyes outside.

NFP   Referencing compass/RMI, anticipates turn by 10 degrees.

'Stop the turn'

FP   Stops the turn, remaining eyes outside throughout the manoeuvre.

Hover and taxi calls include

'Drifting left / right' – 'Hold'
'Move left / right' – 'Hold'
'Move nose left / right' – 'Stop'
'Move tail left / right' – 'Stop'
'Go up/down' – 'Hold'
'Move about the tail left / right' – 'Stop'
'Move about the nose left / right' – 'Stop'.

Identifying and avoiding obstacles

Aircrew or crew member identifying the obstacle.

'Obstacle'	Alerts crew.
'Left'	Immediate left/right obstacle direction indicator
'10 o'clock'	Clock code to pinpoint obstacle direction
'1km'	Distance indicator to adjust viewing range
'Radio tower'	Description to cue other members of the crew
'Terrain - Left'	Description to cue other members of the crew
'Stop the left turn'	Steering cues to the FP to avoid, if necessary

NVG Standard Phraseology

The tables below outline the standard words and phrases used for NVG operations.

Remember that:

- the Flying Pilot (FP) is responsible for flying the helicopter, whereas
- the Non-Flying Pilot (NFP) is responsible for directing the FP and managing everything else.

In the table below, the NFP will state what he wants the FP to do, and the column on the right describes what the FP will do in response to the instructions.

The NFP will monitor the instruments and gauges and keep the FP informed on the progress. The FP can maintain his visual reference and not look inside at the instruments. The NFP will help the FP manage the power demands by limiting the amount of collective the FP can use. This can be done by simply putting pressure on the collective to stop the FP from pulling over a limit.

Hover And Taxi Management Phraseology

Non-Flying Pilot Giving the direction	Flying Pilot Taking the action
Drifting left	Stop drifting left
Drifting right	Stop drifting right
Hold	Hold position
Slide left	Slide sideways to the left
Slide right	Slide sideways to the right
Nose left	Pedal turn to the left
Nose right	Pedal turn to the right
Go up	Increase hover height
Go down	Decrease hover height
Move about the tail left	Do a left turn about the tail
Stop	Stop
Move about the tail right	Do a right-hand turn about the tail

In-Flight Phraseology

Non-Flying Pilot Giving the direction	Flying Pilot Taking the action
Start right turn	Roll right and commence rate one turn
Start left turn	Roll left and commence a rate one turn
Stop turn NFP will monitor instruments and will anticipate the "*Stop turn*" command by 10 degrees.	Roll out of turn and maintain straight and level
Start steep left turn	Roll left and commence a 30-degree angle of bank turn
Start steep right turn	Roll right and commence a 30-degree angle of bank turn
Start Climb	Commence a standard climb
Start Descent	Commence a standard descent
Stop Climb	Level out and return to straight and level
Stop Descent	Level out and return to straight and level

Identifying and Avoiding Obstacles Phraseology

Challenge (any crew member)	Response (usually by the FP)
"Caution" then: Description of the obstacle or traffic The position of the obstacle or hazard using the clock code Distance of the obstacle or hazard Movement (if applicable) of the obstacle or hazard Conflict of the obstacle or the hazard to the helicopter Recommendation by the crew member giving the caution if applicable.	*"Sighted"* Response (if applicable)

Example

For example: Consider a helicopter on NVG operations flying at 1000 ft AGL and the NFP sights another helicopter at the 10 o'clock position, 5 NM away moving from left to right. The correct way to announce this would be as follows:

Challenge	Response
Crewmember sighting the helicopter would announce: *Caution* *Aircraft 10 o'clock high approximately 5 NM away moving from left to right possible conflict* *Suggest left turn and maintain altitude.*	The FP should respond with: *Sighted. Turning left, maintaining altitude.*

Another example: Consider a helicopter on short finals in a HLS that has a sandy surface and looks to have some slope. The correct way to announce this would be as follows

Challenge	Response
Crewmember sighting the hazard would announce *Caution* *Sand and slope.*	The FP should respond with: *Sighted.*

Take-Off And Landing Phase Below 500 ft AGL Phraseology

Once below 500 ft AGL on NVGs, the psychology within the cockpit needs to change as you are now operating in a very challenging environment where an unexpected change in circumstances could lead to an emergency. The following rules should always apply when flying on NVGs below 500 ft AGL:

- A sterile cockpit environment is essential. This means no unnecessary or irrelevant chatter in the cockpit. You are to remain 100% focused on the job at hand.
- The NFP needs to put away any maps and clutter they may have on their lap and be ready to immediately take over from the FP in the event that the FP has an NVG failure, needs to hand over or is otherwise incapacitated.
- All crew must be ready to conduct a RIFTO or IIMC drill and have the same mental model of what is going to happen in that event. These plans must be in place BEFORE descending below 500 ft AGL.

NFP shall monitor and articulate	FP shall listen only
Radio altimeter height at 100' increments until 100', then at 20' increments (discretionary use here dependant on the requirement of the FP and the situation as you do not want too much verbal communication close to the ground.)	The FP can ask for other relevant information from the NFP at their discretion if needed.
Rates of descent in excess of 500' per minute as a caution.	
Airspeed passing 40 & 60 KIAS.	
Any other parameters, as directed by the AC.	

Checks

Pre-lift-off and Pre-landing checks

Pre-lift-off and Pre-landing checks remain unchanged from standard day operations by using the acronym **HEFFR**. The only addition is the crew must confirm the lighting requirements for NVG operations and the helipad from which they are lifting is suitable for NVG operations and/or decide whether they have to taxi somewhere for the goggle up procedure.

Hover Checks

Because the FP and the NFP are goggled up and each have a reduced field of view, the hover and instrument checks are now shared, allowing each to concentrate on a specific task at hand rather than having to multi-task. The FP will fly the helicopter, and the NFP will call and confirm the checks as follows:

1. The FP lifts the helicopter off the surface to a stabilised hover and will announce
   (a) Controls feel normal
   (b) C of G feels normal
2. The NFP will check then announce
   (a) Warning lights out
   (b) Ts and Ps in the green
   (c) RPM top of the green
   (d) Power required to hover (stating the margin and category) and
   (e) Pedal position noted

At this point, the NFP shall direct the FP where to taxi and also direct the FP through the instrument performance checks.

Instrument Performance Checks

The NFP is to run through a series of instrument checks. This is done by asking the FP to turn, climb and adjust the attitude, whereby the NFP is to confirm that the attitude instruments are responding in the correct manner. After ensuring the tail is clear, the NFP shall call the instrument checks and direct the FP to:

1. Turn left and right, noting HSI numbers and compass numbers are either increasing/decreasing, as appropriate, and the ADF is tracking to the station if applicable. The turn indicator (bat) moves left or right in the turn, and the balance ball is free in the race. Climb vertically in the hover to 50 feet noting the VSI showing a ROC, RAD ALT increasing and altimeter increasing.
2. Change the helicopters attitude by moving the nose up/down and rolling left/right, noting the AI's response.
3. Descend vertically back to the IGE hover, noting VSI showing a ROD, RAD ALT decreasing and altimeter decreasing.
4. The airspeed indicator will then be checked on take-off by the NFP as speed increases through the transition.

Power Wind Plan (PWP) Statement

The Power Wind Plan (PWP) statement which, as we know, is a method of assessing the HLS take-off or landing parameters (referred to as the HLS assessment plan) remains the same with the addition of two items that are specific to NVG operations. Prior to an NVG take-off, the crew need to also consider wires and obstacles. Although this is done on every flight (including day) it is not necessarily articulated.

Because NVGs have a much-reduced field of view, the crew must confirm with each other that each has looked in their area of responsibility and report back to the others that there are no wires or obstacles that need to be considered or guarded against for the take-off or landing. Additionally, the crew need to know where the last safe point of hover is so that if the take-off has to be aborted, a predetermined landing area has been chosen.

For this reason, the PWP becomes PWPWOH and is specifically articulated for a NVG flight:

- **P**ower – state the margin or category
- **W**ind – state where it is coming from and estimation of strength
- **P**lan – based on the above two items, state the type and direction of take-off
- **W**ires – state where the wires are
- **O**bstacles – state where the obstacles are
- **H**over – state where the last safe point of hover is going to be on the take-off run

Use of Lights For NVG

External Lights in General

When the helicopter is on the ground, visible external lights must be activated for the safety of ground personnel and other helicopters that are unaided or are unfamiliar with NVG operations or helicopter operations generally. As a minimum for ground operations, the position lights and the anti-collision lights are to be on whenever the rotor is in motion.

If the helicopter's exterior lighting adversely affects NVG performance in flight and satisfied there is no risk of collision with another aircraft, the pilot may:

- Turn off the exterior lighting; or
- Cease NVG operations until the risk has abated.

Position Lights

Position Lights are turned on before engine(s) start and remain on until the rotor blades stop turning unless they adversely affect NVG performance, and the pilot makes the decision to turn them off.

Anti-Collision Light

Anti-Collision Lights turned on before engine(s) start and remain on until the rotor blades stop turning unless they adversely affect NVG performance, and the pilot makes the decision to turn them off.

When airborne, the anti-collision light may be turned off in the following circumstances:

- When operating as the only helicopter within an area; or
- When distracting the crew or otherwise adversely affecting NVG performance.

Strobe Lights

Strobe lights fitted to a helicopter tend to cause a significant distraction to crews operating NVGs. Because of this, the pilot is to determine when and if the strobe lights are to be used.

Landing Light / Searchlight / Night Scanner

Crews should make maximum use of landing lights, searchlight, or night scanner below LSALT, which may improve the detection of wires and other obstacles and the maintenance of terrain separation. This includes scanning horizontally and vertically for obstacles with a steerable searchlight when on final approach and immediately before departure. A steerable light may also be used in the direction of turns at low level, as for night unaided operations.

In some conditions, the use of searchlights and landing lights may degrade the NVG image. In these circumstances, the pilot may elect to turn these lights off.

The use of non-NVG-compatible lights does not preclude the use of NVGs by other crew members. A mix of white lights, NVGs and unaided techniques should be used, where it improves the ability to see and avoid obstacles. For example, consider a white light searchlight with a broad beam, this may be used to increase the available illumination for an NVG approach to an HLS NVG area at night.

A visible landing light should be on for all air taxi, ground taxi or air transit at an HLS, airfield or tarmac area as applicable to the helicopter type.

On very bright nights (full moon), the landing light may not be necessary, so it is still at the discretion of the FP on when and how to use these lights.

Torch

Use a clear lens (white light) torch for tarmac, pre-flight, crew change, refuel, entry or exit under the rotor disk. Use only NVG compatible torches (blue-green filtered or super white) in the helicopter for NVG operations. Each crew member should have their own torch.

Lip Light / Finger Light

The small blue/green and super white LEDs used in lip and finger lights are NVG 'friendly' but may not be fully NVG compatible. NVG crew members are encouraged to use these lights to aid switch selection and map reading in the helicopter but are cautioned against their indiscriminate use in the cockpit.

Goggle Up/De-Goggle Procedure

The goggle up/de-goggle procedures can be conducted on the ground or when airborne and are usually initiated by the helicopter captain.

On the Ground

If applicable, the goggle up procedure may be used prior to taxi and, therefore, the hover checks and the instrument checks will have to be completed while goggled up. If the helicopter needs to be taxied to a more appropriate position prior to goggle up, then the helicopter captain will make this decision. Circumstances that may determine this include a helicopter on a trolley or platform and excessive cultural lighting on the HLS.

The same is true when returning from a flight and conducting the de-goggle procedure. It may or may not be more appropriate to land at a specific point, de-goggle, and then taxi to the dispersal area unaided.

Goggle Up Procedure : On the Ground

Step	Action
1	Taxi to the goggle up point unaided
2	Carry out the Instrument and Hover Checks
3	Land at the goggle up point
4	Pre-Take-off Checks
5	**P**ALE Check **P**osition Lights — ON **A**nti-collision Lights — ON **L**anding Light — As required **E**nabler Switch — White or for IR light if installed as required
6	Pilot announces "Crew goggle up"
7	NFP announces "Goggling up front/back left/right", then lowers his/her NVGs and confirms the fit, eye relief and focus of the NVGs on an appropriate object near the helicopter
8	When complete, the NFP announces "Goggled up front/back left/right – Taking over"
9	After conducting a hand over/take over drill the remaining pilot announces "Goggling up front/back left/right", then lowers his/her NVGs and confirms the fit, eye relief and focus of the NVGs on an appropriate object near the helicopter
10	When satisfied with the condition of his/her NVGs, the remaining pilot announces "Goggled up front/back left/right"

The crew is now goggled up established in the aided condition and ready for departure.

De-Goggle Procedure : On the Ground

The de-goggle procedure is the reverse of the goggle up procedure as follows:

Step	Action
1	Taxi to and land at the de-goggle point during aided flight
2	The pilot announces "Crew De-Goggle"
3	NFP announces "De-Goggling front/back left/right", then raises his/her NVGs
4	When complete the NFP announces "De-Goggled front/back left/right – Taking over"
5	After conducting a hand-over/take-over drill, the remaining pilot announces "De-Goggling front/back left/right", then raises his/her NVGs
6	After raising his/her NVGs, the remaining pilot announces "De-Goggled front/back left/right"
7	Conduct the PALE Check **P**osition Lights — ON **A**nti-collision Lights — ON **L**anding Light — As required **E**nabler Switch — White or for IR light if installed as required

The crew is now de-goggled and established in the night un-aided condition and ready for taxi to the dispersal area. Prior to taxi, the crew should conduct the PALE checks to put the appropriate lighting in the correct configuration for NUA flight. In military operations this may be relevant because of the use of IR light. In civil operations, it may be relevant because the position lights etc., had been turned off for the NVG flight.

Goggle Up Procedure : In The Air

The helicopter is to be **at or above LSALT** before conducting the goggle up procedure in the air.

Step	Action
1	The pilot will announce the helicopter's parameters of Altitude, heading and airspeed, and these parameters are to be maintained until all crew members are goggled up.
2	Pilot announces "Crew goggle up."
3	NFP announces "Goggling up front/back left/right", then lowers his/her NVGs and confirms the fit, eye relief and focus of the NVGs on an appropriate object near the helicopter.
4	When complete, the NFP announces "Goggled up front/back left/right – Taking over."
5	After conducting a hand over/take over drill, the remaining pilot announces "Goggling up front/back left/right", then lowers his/her NVGs and confirms the fit, eye relief and focus of the NVGs on an appropriate object near the helicopter.
6	When satisfied with the condition of his/her NVGs, the remaining pilot announces "Goggled up front/back left/right".

The crew is now goggled up and able to descend below LSALT for NVG operations.

De-Goggle Procedure : In The Air

The De-Goggle Procedure is the reverse of the goggle up procedure as follows:

Step	Action
1	The helicopter is to be at or above LSALT prior to conducting the procedure
2	The pilot will announce the helicopter's parameters of Altitude, heading and airspeed and these parameters are to be maintained until all crew members are goggled up
3	The pilot announces "Crew De-Goggle"
4	NFP announces "De-Goggling front/back left/right", then raises his/her NVGs
5	When complete the NFP announces "De-Goggled front/back left/right – Taking over"
6	After conducting a hand-over/take-over drill, the remaining pilot announces "De-Goggling front/back left/right", then raises his/her NVGs
7	After raising his/her NVGs, the remaining pilot announces "De-Goggled front/back left/right"
8	Conduct the PALE Check. **P**osition Lights — ON **A**nti-collision Lights — ON **L**anding Light — As required **E**nabler Switch — White or for IR light if installed as required

The crew is now de-goggled and established in the night un-aided or IFR condition.

NVG Departure Profile

Part of the plan is determining what sort of a departure profile the FP is going to use based on the power and the conditions. Because with NVGs, we are better able to see at night, we can use any type of departure profile as we would during the day as appropriate. In general, the three departure profiles used for NVG operations include:

1. Restricted Instrument Flight Take-off (RIFTO), also referred to as the instrument take-off
2. Constant Angle Take-off
3. Standard Airfield Departure

Standard NVG take-off profiles

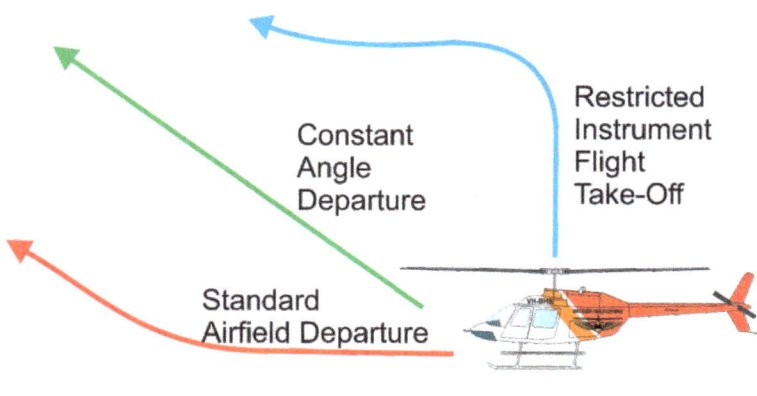

Restricted Instrument Flight Take-off (RIFTO)

A Restricted Instrument Flight Take-Off (RIFTO) departure should be flown when

- ambient light levels are low
- the departure area has obstacles in the general vicinity
- the surface may produce reduced visibility (sand, snow, dust, bulldust, etc.).

The profile for the departure is the same as for the preferred night unaided departure. The aim of the departure is to clear the obstacles, hazards or ground prior to the transition into forward flight. As with the night unaided departure and general NVG flight, the searchlight should be used to identify and avoid obstacles. The RIFTO profile is also to be used to counter brownout/whiteout conditions in a landing or manoeuvring area.

Constant Angle and Standard Airfield Departure

When illumination levels are high, and the departure area is free of obstacles, either a standard airfield departure or a constant profile departure may be flown. The techniques for these departures are the same as for day.

Encountering Low Contrast Situations

There will be certain terrain and lighting conditions that can cause low contrast situations. This may not be uniform across the helicopter, so effective communication is important.

For example, consider a helicopter flying low level on NVG operations along the edge of a lake on a still night. The crew on one side of the helicopter may have good contrast if viewing the lake's edge, whereas the crew facing the lake may have very poor contrast.

For this reason, crew members should announce a warning regarding low contrast situations as follows:

1. NVG crewmember identifying or experiencing a low contrast situation shall announce 'Caution: low contrast front/back left/right'.
2. The remaining crew will respond with "Roger" and are to assist with determining height AGL, airspeed, rates of closure, obstacle clearance, or orientation as appropriate, both visually and with cross-reference to the instruments.
3. The pilot is responsible for determining when and how to use available external white or IR light to help control the flight during low contrast situations.
4. Depending on the operational requirement, the FP is to either:
   (a) maintain straight and level
   (b) turn the helicopter around
   (c) descend to a lower altitude that offers clearer air
   (d) enter a climb to a safer height
   (e) decelerate to a slower speed, or
   (f) any one of these options whilst continuing to cross-reference the flight instruments.
5. The FP and crew are to remain vigilant to their height, speeds, rates of closure, obstacle clearance and orientation until a higher level of contrast can be restored.
6. The FP must not conduct a descent and turn at the same time whilst they are operating in a low contrast situation.

NVG Approach Profiles

When making an approach to an NVG HLS Standard or NVG HLS Basic, conduct the PSWATP drill as done for a confined area by day, but do not descend below 500 ft AGL till within 3 NM of the HLS and it is positively identified.

Additionally, the PSWATP drill is slightly amended because there is obviously no sun. The drill therefore, uses the word "shadows" (of the moon or light source) instead of "sun". A Quick Recap of the PSWATP:

P	Power, Pilot, Payload
S	Size, Shape, Slope, Surface, **SHADOWS *(moon or other lighting)***, Surrounds, Stock
W	Wind, Wires, Wires, Wires, Way in, Way out
A	Approval, approach type and abort point
T	Turning and Termination points (this is where you select the line-up feature, base feature, to far feature, etc.)
P	Plan

NVG approach profiles used for operations to unsurveyed HLS (NVG-basic) should be the same as the constant angle approach technique used for night unaided approaches. As for unaided approaches, NVG crews should use a height/distance comparison to cross-check the approach profile to ensure they are controlling the descent prior to having proper visual reference to the ground for landing.

Although in light wind conditions, this height and speed comparison can be done using airspeed and the airspeed indicator, in strong wind conditions it would be more relevant to use ground speed off the GPS.

Example
For example: Consider making an approach into an HLS with a 20 kt headwind.
If using airspeed referenced of the ASI all the way to the ground, you would be very slow and not making headway into the pad. At 500 ft you may have 60 kt airspeed, but you would only be going 30 kt over the ground; at 100 ft you may actually stop with 20 kt airspeed, but no ground speed.

Standard NVG Approach Profile

The desired descent profile is reviewed below.

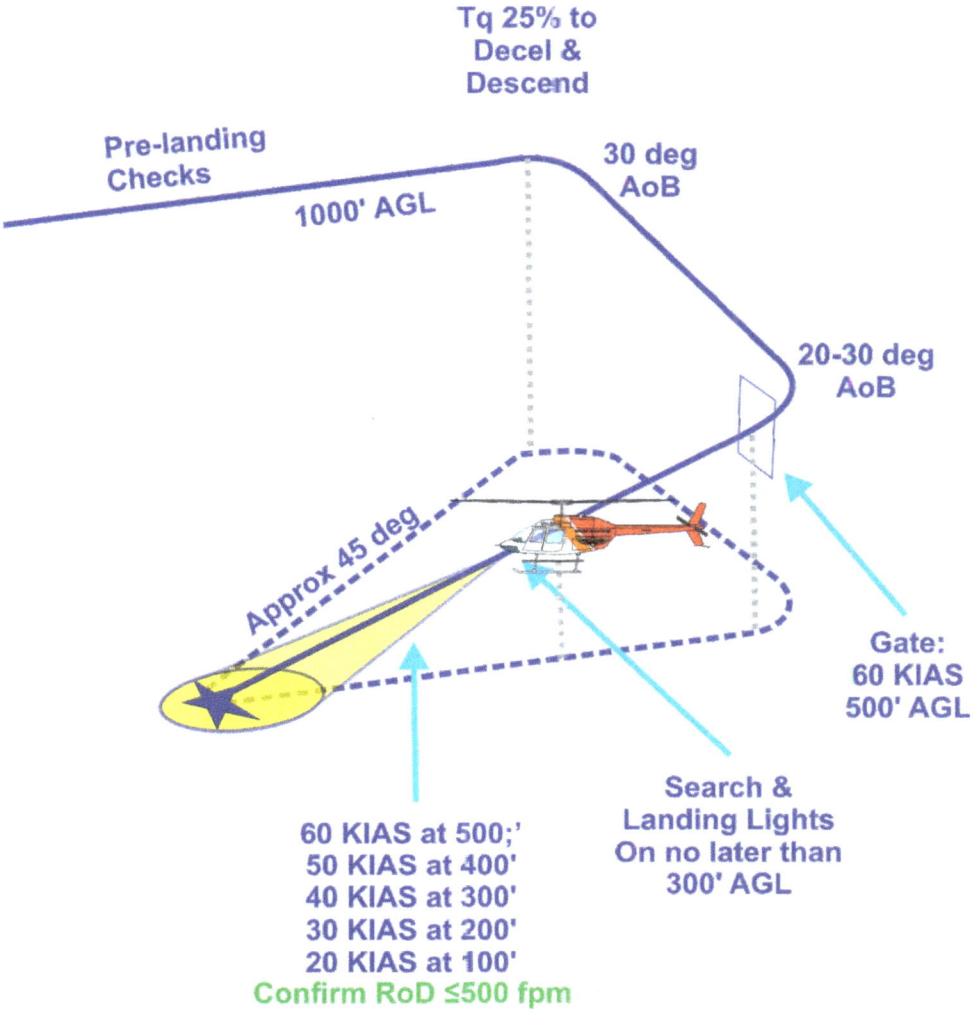

With a ROD less than 500 feet per minute then at:

- 500 ft AGL the helicopter should be 60 kt ground speed
- 400 ft AGL the helicopter should be 50 kt ground speed
- 300 ft AGL the helicopter should be 40 kt ground speed
- 200 ft AGL the helicopter should be 30 kt ground speed
- 100 ft AGL the helicopter should be 20 kt ground speed

From approximately 200 ft AGL, the crew should be visual with the ground with the searchlight on so the closure rate can be estimated physically with ground references rather than having to rely accurately on the set of numbers above.

Remember the numbers above are a guide only to assist your approach. Once properly visual with the HLS, a landing is a visual manoeuvre.

NVG crews may arrive at a landing site below LSALT and are to conduct a reconnaissance of the landing area prior to committing to an approach. Throughout the reconnaissance and approach, the searchlight(s) should be used to scan the helicopter flight path for wires and other obstacles. The decision as to when the searchlight(s) and landing light(s) are to be used rests with the pilot. In civil operations, external white lights must be used during any approach or departure unless, due to the lighting conditions, they reduce the NVGs' performance (such as in a full moon or bright landing site where the FP can decide not to use landing lights.

NVG HLS

The use of NVG HLS Standard and NVG HLS Basic locations may require the use of both day and night unaided confined area techniques previously taught. The restricted FOV increases the difficulty of HLS operations. In low visibility conditions, the landing area may not actually be visible until established on the final approach. As with day operations, NVG aircrews should attempt to identify the following lead-in features (also referred to as circuit markers) while conducting the PSWATP to ensure obstacle clearance and correct positioning for the approach and subsequent landing:

1. A too-far feature - this alerts the crew if they have inadvertently overflown the HLS and to commence a crosswind turn;
2. A base turn feature - this cues the FP to commence the base turn and achieve the correct spacing and profile for the approach;
3. An approach line-up feature - when intercepting the final approach leg having a line-up feature allows the FP to be approaching the HLS from the correct direction even if unable to actually see the HLS;
4. An abort point - this is a predetermined point on the approach where the crew can make a decision to either go around or continue in for the landing based on either meeting or not meeting the landing criteria on finals; and
5. A termination point or area within the HLS - this is the area identified during the PSWAT as the most suitable area to come to a hover and most probably land within the HLS.

Like day operations when conducting the reconnaissance, it is often better to do a square circuit at 60 kt IAS to conduct the PSWATP to keep the HLS insight initially, then once the PSWATP is completed, join the racetrack pattern to make the approach using the selected markers.

Night Vision Goggles *for Helicopter Pilots*

As we know, every landing site will be different with different obstacles and hills and shapes etc. For this reason, the actual shape of the circuit may have to vary depending on the situation. Although a racetrack pattern is depicted in the image below, the crew may elect to conduct a different shape to suit the situation. This is where the correct and clever use of the course bar on the HSI, use of the OBS function on the GPS and the correct selection of the lead in features will be of great benefit.

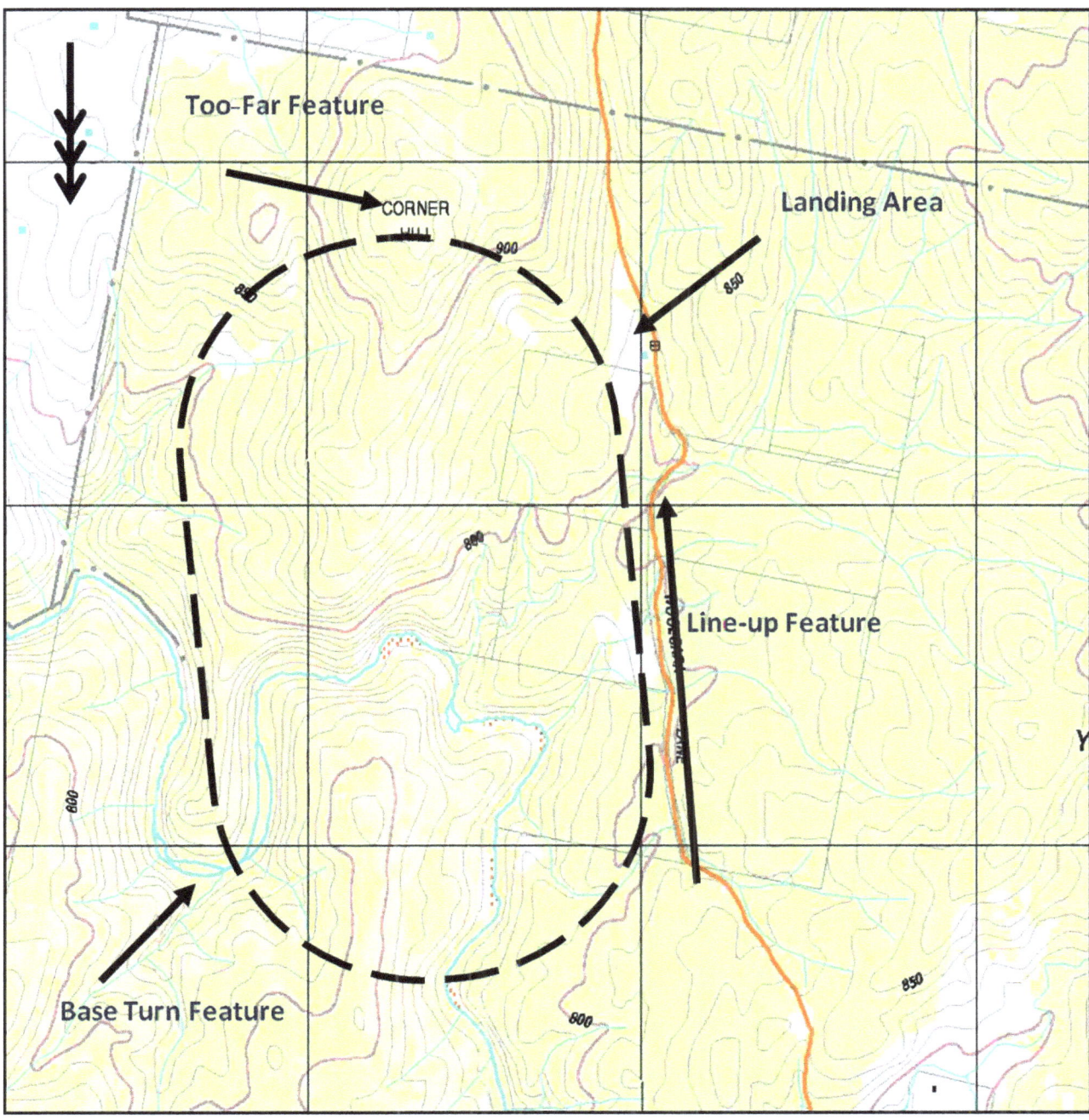

Figure 108 Circuit for a Helicopter Landing Site (HLS)

HLS NVG Pinnacle Approaches

When making an approach to a pinnacle at night using NVGs, there may not be any visual cues because of the height of the pinnacle relative to the surrounding terrain, and therefore depth perception is greatly reduced. The preferred method to arrive at a pinnacle is to follow the contours of any ridgeline that leads up to the pinnacle. This will give the crew the best visual cues to determine the closure rate. If this is not possible and the crew now need to make an approach directly to a pinnacle, then close referencing of the instruments to attain the proper descent profile is required to achieve this.

Approaching 200 ft above the pinnacle, the FP will then focus 100% outside and use the visual cue of the pinnacle to determine the closure rate, with the NFP spending approximately 75% of his time looking outside but 25% of his time looking inside and cross-referencing the instruments to ensure the descent and speed are correctly under control. He needs to confirm that what they are seeing outside is reflected inside on the instruments and vice versa.

Depending on the wind, a shallow approach is preferred as the helicopter can move forward with a low ROD towards the pinnacle. If the winds are strong, this may not be possible, and a steeper approach may be required above the wind demarcation line.

A PWASTP will be conducted in the normal manner. A race track pattern circuit can then be established, but because ground features may be too far below, the good use of the GPS to select the pinnacle as a way point and the use of the Course bar and OBS function will help maintain the circuit shape.

Departing an HLS

Step	Action
1	Based on the crew's decision, external helicopter lights may be turned on or off depending on the circumstances and operational requirements.
2	The crew are to conduct an HLS assessment before lift-off using existing techniques, processes and procedures (PWPWOH).
3	If this is going to be the first take-off for the night, then the crew need to conduct the instrument performance check during the taxi and prior to take-off, ensuring all attitude instruments are working properly. If it is a subsequent flight, then the instrument performance check does not have to be repeated.
4	The FP is then to conduct the departure in accordance with the HLS assessment plan as discussed with the crew (PWPWOH) with the NFP monitoring and to read out the performance parameters as well as acting as a limiter on the collective to prevent the FP from pulling inadvertently overt a limit while focusing 100% outside.
5	All other crew members are to perform their assigned tasks and duties as discussed during the crew's pre-flight briefing.
6	If visual reference is lost during the take-off, the FP is required to either abort the take-off and return to the hover or continue with the take-off by performing the RIFTO drill of AHTA.
7	If visual reference is lost during the take-off, there are very few reasons to try to come back to the hover, and this can in fact, be very dangerous as you literally cannot see the ground at this point. It would only be applicable to return to the ground if either of the pilots had visual reference with the ground or if an emergency required the aborted take-off. An aborted take-off when you have lost sight of the ground is dangerous and should be avoided.

Step	Action
8	The best and automatic course of action if losing visual reference on take-off is to conduct the RIFTO drill of AHTA: <table><tr><td>A</td><td>Attitude</td><td>Select an attitude that allows the helicopter to continue with the take-off transitioning into a forward climb. In most cases, while on take-off, simply maintain your current attitude, but this will now be with reference to the AIs inside the cockpit instead of visually outside.</td></tr><tr><td>H</td><td>Heading</td><td>Maintain the current heading or turn onto a safe heading to avoid known obstacles. This will be with reference to the HSI.</td></tr><tr><td>T</td><td>Torque</td><td>Select climb power or 100% depending on the requirement for performance. You need to establish and maintain a positive ROC on the VSI then.</td></tr><tr><td>A</td><td>Airspeed</td><td>Adjust the attitude to obtain the best climb speed for the configuration.</td></tr></table> *OR* the FP can decide to abort the take-off as appropriate to the circumstances, conditions and crew experience.
9	During the performance of the RIFTO, the NFP is to assist the FP by monitoring and advising of the AHTA performance parameters.
10	All other crew members are to assist the flight crew where, when and how appropriate to the circumstances.
11	The helicopter is to be flown to achieve a climb to a designated height whilst remaining within 3 NM of the HLS.

Arriving at an HLS

Step	Action
1	The crew are to commence a NVG visual letdown ensuring they arrive at the HLS no lower than 500 ft AGL and within 3 NM of the location.
2	Prior to descending below 500 ft AGL and based on the crew's decision, external helicopter lights may be turned on or off depending on the circumstances and operational requirements. The helicopter should be decelerated to 80 KIAS.
3	At the pilot's discretion, the helicopter may be descended no lower than 300 ft AGL within 3 NM of the intended HLS whilst carefully scanning for obstacles and wires.
4	The crew are to positively identify the intended HLS.
5	The crew are to identify all potential obstacles, including terrain, before letting down to not below 200 ft AGL. The helicopter should be flown between 60 kt to 80 kt at the FP's discretion when not below 200 ft.

Step	Action
6	The determination as to which height AGL is best to conduct the PSWATP and other checks is going to be dependent on several factors, including but not limited to - The quality of the white or IR lighting used to look into the HLS and scan the area for obstacles and hazards. A powerful light may allow you to be higher as opposed to a weak landing light which may not be of much use. - The atmospheric conditions on the night. If there are obscurants in the air (smoke, dust haze, cloud, rain etc) then you may need to be lower to actually see - The geographical conditions that may need to be negotiated, such as hills, valleys, ridgelines etc - The current phase and position of the moon. In general, the darker the night, the lower you need to be able to see. - The local knowledge that the crew may have of the area. If it is a new area that you have never been to before, it would be wise to stay higher until you have cleared the area. If the area is well known, then the crew may be more comfortable close to the ground.
7	The crew are to commence an HLS assessment using the PSWATP before commencing the approach. If below 200 ft AGL the helicopter should be flown no faster than 60 KIAS.
8	On approach, the NFP calls: - Airspeed passing 60 kt and 40 kt - Rates of decent if greater than 500 feet per minute - Radar Altimeter heights when below 500 feet AGL in increments of 100 ft and then in increments of 50 or 20 ft below 100 ft AGL as appropriate or required by the FP - Power demand on short finals and passing through translational lift and terminating at the hover - Any "Cautions" noticed and that need to be articulated - Any other parameters as directed or requested by the FP.
9	If a RIFTO event occurs during the landing the FP is required to either commence an abort of the landing by performing the RIFTO drill of AHTA: | A	Attitude	Select an attitude that allows the helicopter to abort the approach and commence transition into a forward climb. In most cases while on approach or take-off simply maintain your current attitude but this will now be with reference to the AIs inside the cockpit instead of visually outside.
H	Heading	Maintain the current heading or turn onto a safe heading to avoid known obstacles. This will now be with reference to the HSI.
T	Torque	Select climb power or 100% depending on the requirement for performance. You need to establish a positive ROC on the VSI then.
A	Airspeed	Adjust the attitude to obtain the best climb speed for the configuration.	 **OR** the FP can decide to continue with the landing as appropriate to the circumstances, conditions and crew experience.
10	During the performance of the AHTA drill, the NFP is to assist the FP by monitoring and advising of the AHTA performance parameters and limits.

Step	Action
11	All other crew members are to assist the flight crew where, when and how appropriate to the circumstances.
12	The helicopter is to be flown to achieve a climb to a designated height whilst remaining within 3 NM of the HLS. The pilot will decide the best course of action to be taken following the RIFTO event.

NVG Navigation

NVG navigation is no different to Day, Night Unaided and FR navigation. Because the NVG pilot has usually already done all three, they are able to plan and make the best use of any of the techniques to support the NVG operation at their discretion and preference.

Typically, Night Unaided planning is conducted with the backup of IFR planning in the event that the helicopter inadvertently flies into IMC conditions with the benefit of being able to visually identify navigation waypoints visually with the NVG as would be done during the day.

During NVG navigation sorties, it is usually the responsibility of the NFP to manage the navigation, and it is the NFP who will call out the heights and headings to fly as well as calculate the EETs and the ETAs. The NFP will tell the FP what features to look for and when to turn. The FP is responsible for flying the helicopter. Either pilot may make the radio calls at the crew's discretion, but it is usually the NFP who will make the frequency and transponder changes.

All the usual checks used during Day, Night Unaided and IFR are still relevant and used for the NVG flight. (*The next chapter, "Planning an NVG Flight", will look at the flight planning and map reading techniques applicable to NVG in more detail*).

On dark nights it may not be possible to see all the way to the horizon or to identify tracking features that are further away as would normally be seen on brighter nights. The NFP should, therefore, nominate tracking features that are close to the helicopter for the FP and continue with time, distance and heading when there are no useful tracking features. Maintenance of tracks by good heading holding and accurate timings should aid in avoiding disorientation.

If disorientation does occur and the location of the helicopter becomes temporarily unknown, the NFP should inform the crew, who can give their input and assist. The crew should then also take particular care to scan outside to help avoid inadvertent flight into obstacles or airspace. Climbing to height may not be an option on a dark night as visual cues reduce, or the cloud base may be low. If lost, the FP should return to the last known point and use whatever aids are available to determine the current location; this includes using obvious ground features such as towns, factories, roads, etc., as well as navigation aids, GPS and radar vectoring if available. Although getting lost in the modern helicopter world is difficult due to the use of GPS, crews can still become disorientated.

The NFP will often be looking inside to refer to the map. This reduces the capacity to scan outside. During navigation, the FP should be informed that the NFP's scan will be in and out continuously. The FP acknowledges and increases the scan to cover the arc of responsibility of the NFP. This negates the requirement for the NFP to continuously call "eyes inside/outside" when referring to the map.

NVG Low-level Flight

For the experienced pilot operating at low level (usually below 300 ft AGL) while on NVGs, there is very little difference compared to doing it during the day except that there is a much-reduced field of view (FOV), depth perception is reduced, and the ability to see obstacles in a reasonable time frame is also reduced. For the inexperienced pilot, it can be a very daunting thing to do, to be flying around at 60 kt in the pitch black.

I say that it is like day operations because the lower you are, the more you have to fly to the conditions and the environment and low-level NVG operations are no different.

Local knowledge of the area you are operating in will be the single greatest benefit an NVG pilot could have and will allow operations and tasks that you would otherwise not think of doing in an unknown area.

Plan the low-level component of the flight. If possible, have a look at the area during the daytime. Fly at speeds that allow you to see and avoid obstacles and hazards. Increase your scan rate and ensure all crew members are focused on scanning outside and are communicating effectively. In general, it is best to fly from an obvious feature to another obvious feature staying above the tallest obstacle within your sphere of influence (this is an imaginary bubble surrounding you that you can do something about).

Treat shadow areas with caution as they may be hiding an unknown obstacle or hazard. Good use of the searchlight into the shadow areas is imperative.

When the moon is bright but low on the horizon (usually up to about 30 degrees above the horizon), this will create longer shadows and provide better contrast between the shadows and the surrounding terrain. This is good for the NVG pilot as it helps with depth perception and realising just how far away obstacles and hazards actually are. Conversely, a full moon high in the sky (as in overhead) will provide no shadows and possibly too much light, effectively "washing" the scene out with too much light and therefore providing no contrast at all.

The limited FOV and the low flying may prevent NVG pilots from maintaining a horizon or attitude reference while manoeuvring. Remember, at low level, the crew are focused more on looking outside than they are inside, and this can significantly inhibit the instrument crosscheck scan by the NFP. To maintain awareness of the helicopter's attitude while manoeuvring at low level, the FP can be helped by positioning their scan to include some part of the helicopter structure, such as a windscreen pillar or instrument console. This helps the mental picture of what attitude the helicopter is currently in without the need to look inside.

Frames of Reference

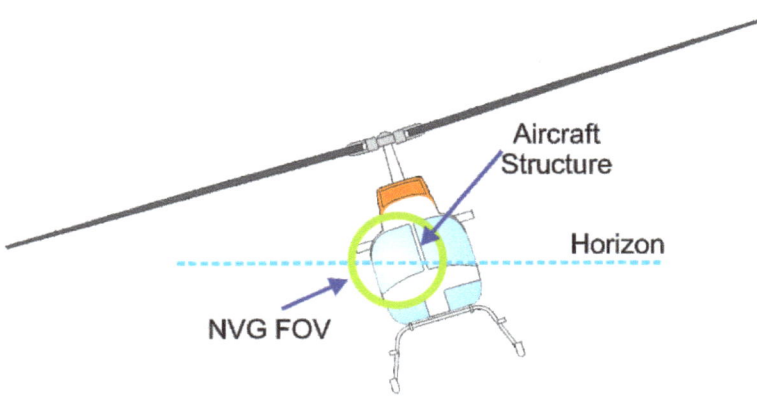

With helicopter reference **Without helicopter reference**

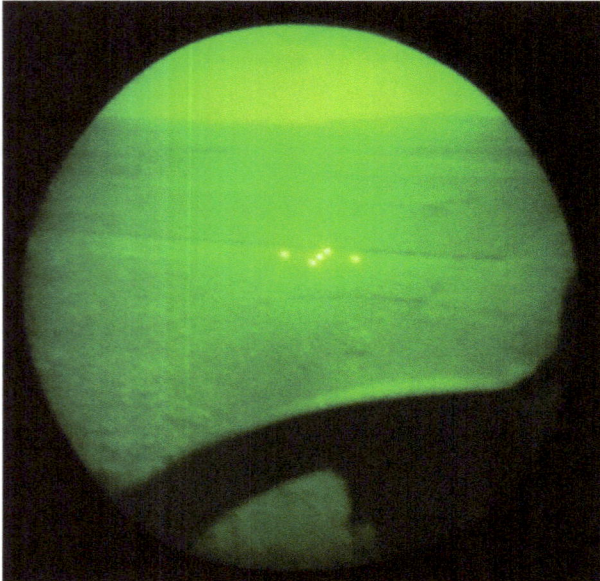 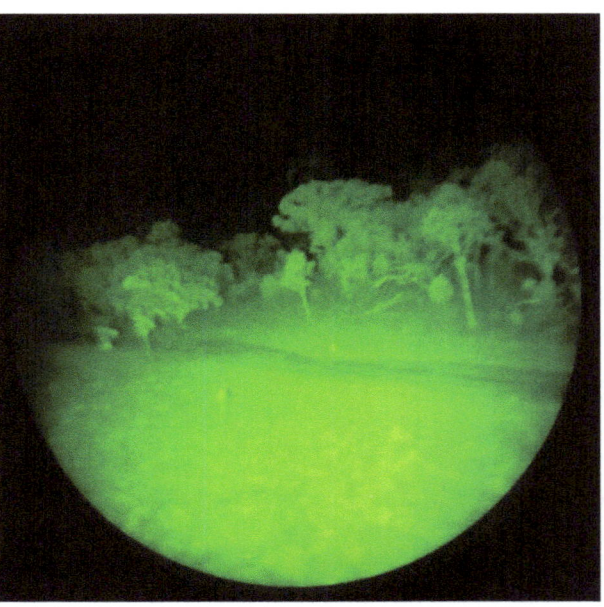

Looking at this picture, you can see that the helicopter is level and probably on approach   Looking at this picture, you are not able to determine the attitude of the helicopter

Transition Between Flight Categories

The use of NVGs is conducted under either the Night Visual Flight Rules (NVFR) or Instrument Flight Rules (IFR) rules. This means that there may be differences in the equipment you need to have installed in the aircraft, the training and qualifications you may need to have completed and the subsequent differences in the flight planning requirements.

Typically an NVG operation is conducted under the NVFR. However, provision has to be made in the event that the crew inadvertently fly into IMC conditions and have to notify Air Traffic Control and change category. In some operations, changing categories may be planned so that the helicopter may depart on NVG using the NVFR but then transition into IFR to transit to a location then change their category to an NVFR (NVG) flight again on descent if they become visual above LSALT.

Although this sounds complicated, once you have done it a few times, it can become routine. To make the transitions as smooth as possible, it is a requirement at Becker Helicopters that all NVFR and NVFR NVG flights submit a flight plan to Air Traffic Control. This means that when contacting Air Traffic Control to change category, they will already have all your details, and this will speed up the process time. If a flight plan is not lodged, then you will have to transmit all these details over the radio. This can be time-consuming and will absorb much of your effort that should be directed to flying and managing the helicopter.

The following pages outline the procedures which can be used to achieve this.

Transition from NVG Flight to IFR Flight

Step	Action
1	Assuming this is a planned transition (not inadvertent or accidental flight into IMC) and all weather minima and fuel requirements have been met and planned for then, before making the decision, the Aircraft Captain (AC) should initiate a discussion among the entire crew as to the reason why and all should agree before the command to transition to IFR flight is given.
2	Before transitioning from NVFR NVG to IFR flight, the crew shall: - Contact Air Traffic Control on the Area Frequency and notify them of the requirement to change category and ask for a Transponder Code and, if applicable, an Airways Clearance prior to going IFR if controlled airspace is going to be entered or is close. This should be made easier if the NVFR NVG flight had a flight plan lodged before departure; all the controller has to do in this case is change the category. - Configure the helicopter for IFR, tuning, identifying and testing the applicable navigation aids and readying the autopilot for use under the IFR. - Ready the appropriate IFR maps and charts as applicable. - Consider when to initiate a climb to LSALT or above and then when to commence the transition procedure. - Once the decision is made, the Airways Clearance is received and the category has been changed, the Aircraft Captain will issue the command "Transition to IFR flight".
3	All members of the crew are to acknowledge the command with the response "Roger".
4	The FP then commences the Attitude, Heading, Torque, Airspeed (AHTA) drill to commence the climb using Instrument flight (IF) techniques with the NVGs still in the goggled or down position.
5	The NFP may then announce "de-goggling front left/right" and de-goggles at which point the NFP will announce "de-goggled front left/right".
6	The NFP commences using Instrument flight (IF) techniques by scanning inside. When ready, commence taking control of the helicopter, including activating the autopilot if that is the preferred method by the crew, and then running through the usual "Hand Over / Take Over" (HOTO) drill.

Step	Action
7	At this point, the helicopter is considered to be now operating under the IFR.
8	When control of the helicopter is transferred to the new FP, then the new NFP is to announce "de-goggling front left/right" and de-goggles. The new NFP will then resume an instrument scan and NFP duties under the IFR whilst assisting the FP.
9	The remaining NVG crew members should continue to use the NVGs and visual scanning techniques until such time that the helicopters enters IMC and is at a height that the NVG are no longer of any practical use. At that time the crew may individually de-goggle and notify the remaining crew by announcing "de-goggling back left/right" etc.
10	It is the Aircraft Captain's (AC) decision as to whether other crew members in the back are to remain goggled up or not if there are operational reasons to do so.
11	It is the Aircraft Captain's (AC) decision as to who should continue to act as the FP and NFP in the normal manner.
12	The flight will now continue as an IFR flight.

Transition from IFR Flight to NVG Flight

Step	Action
1	Assuming this is a planned transition and all weather minimas and fuel requirements have been met and planned for then, before making the decision, the Aircraft Captain (AC) should initiate a discussion among the entire crew as to the reason why and all should agree before the command to transition to NVG flight is given.
2	Before the transition from IFR to NVG flight, the crew shall: ■ Contact Air Traffic Control and notify them of the requirement to change. This should be relatively easy as being an IFR flight, you will already be on an active flight plan and currently being controlled, so two-way communication will be easy. ■ Configure the helicopter for NVG, adjust the lighting as applicable and any other operational requirements for NVG operations. ■ Ready the appropriate NVG maps and charts as applicable. ■ Consider when to initiate a descent below LSALT and then when to commence the transition procedure. ■ Once the decision is made, the Air Traffic Control has been notified, and if applicable, a clearance for the descent is received, the Aircraft Captain will issue the command "Transition to NVG flight".
3	All members of the crew are to acknowledge the command with the response "Roger".
4	The NFP will then announce "goggling up front left/right" and goggles up at which point the NFP will announce "goggled up front left/right".
5	The remaining crew members will also announce "goggling up front/back left/right" and go through the goggle up procedure. Once goggled up, they will all in turn announce "goggled up front/back left/right" as applicable.
6	The FP then announces and commences a descent to the LSALT. It is important to note that the FP is not yet goggled up but is still flying the helicopter under the IFR. The NFP is also cross-checking the instruments under the goggles on descent but is also bringing his scan outside looking to come visual as are the other crew members.

Step	Action
7	The FP will then either level off at the LSALT and wait for the NFP to call visual (possibly with the assistance and confirmation of other crew members), or if the crew do not become visual, they may have to remain under the IFR and initiate a climb and return to base (after communicating this with Air Traffic Control).
8	Once reaching the LSALT and becoming visual, the NFP shall announce "Visual front left/right" "Taking Over" and the flight crew will complete the hand over take over drill in the normal manner.
9	The old NFP now becomes the FP and can then call Air Traffic Control that they are now " Visual and confirm the change of category to NVFR NVG".
10	The old FP will, after relinquishing control, then announce "goggling up front left/right" and go through the goggle up procedure so that the entire crew is now operating using NVGs.
11	It is the Aircraft Captain's (AC) decision as to who should continue to act as the FP and NFP in the normal manner.
12	The flight will now continue as an NVG flight.

Transition from NVG Flight to NVFR Flight

Step	Action
1	Because all NVG flights originate as NVFR flights, there is no requirement to notify Air Traffic Control unless, as a courtesy, if climbing to an altitude that will now conflict with other traffic or enter controlled airspace. The transition procedure is one for the crew so that they have a mental shift in the procedures and rules that now apply to the flight and manage the flight as an NVFR flight and not an NVG flight. In practical terms, there are very few reasons to stop using the NVG and revert to unaided NVFR flight; however, the procedure does need to be documented.
2	Assuming this is a planned transition (not an inadvertent or accidental flight into IMC or an NVG failure), then prior to making the decision, the Aircraft Captain (AC) should initiate a discussion among the entire crew as to the reason why and all should agree before the command to transition to NVFR flight is given.
3	Before the transition from NVG to NVFR flight, the crew shall: - If required, contact Air Traffic Control on the Area Frequency and notify them of the requirement to change category and ask for a Transponder Code and, if applicable, an Airways Clearance before going NVFR if controlled airspace is going to be entered or is close. This should be made easier if the NVG flight had a flight plan lodged prior to departure. - Configure the helicopter for NVFR, tuning, identifying and testing the applicable navigation aids and readying the lighting if there is going to be a change. - Ready the appropriate maps and charts as applicable. - Consider when to initiate a climb to LSALT or above and then when to commence the transition procedure. - Once the decision is made and the Airways Clearance is received (if applicable), the Aircraft Captain will issue the command "Transition to NVFR flight".
4	All members of the crew are to acknowledge the command with the response "Roger".
5	The FP then commences the Attitude, Heading, Torque Airspeed (AHTA) drill to commence the climb using Instrument flight (IF) techniques with the NVGs still in the goggled up or down position.

Step	Action
6	Once the helicopter reaches the LSALT The NFP will then announce "de-goggling front left/right" and de-goggles, at which point the NFP will announce "de-goggled front left/right".
7	The NFP commences using NVFR and Instrument flight techniques by scanning outside the cockpit unaided as well as a cross reference instrument scan on the inside and when ready should commence taking control of the helicopter by running through the usual "Hand Over / Take Over" (HOTO) drill.
8	At this point the helicopter is considered to be now operating under the NVFR and the lighting can be set as required for NVFR.
9	The new NFP if required can then confirm with Air Traffic Control the change from NVG to NVFR.
10	When control of the helicopter is transferred to the new FP then the new NFP is to announce "de-goggling front left/right" and de-goggles. The new NFP will then resume an instrument scan and NFP duties under the NVFR whilst assisting the FP.
11	The remaining NVG crew members should continue to use the NVGs and visual scanning techniques until such time that the helicopters is at a height that the NVG are no longer of any practical use. At that time the crew may individually de-goggle and notify the remaining crew by announcing "de-goggled back left/right" etc.
12	It is the Aircraft Captains (AC) decision as to whether other crew members in the back are to remain goggled up or not if there are operational reasons to do so.
13	It is the Aircraft Captains (AC) decision as to who should continue to act as the FP and NFP in the normal manner.
14	The flight will now continue as a NVFR flight.

Transition from NVFR Flight to NVG Flight

Step	Action
1	Assuming this is a planned transition and all weather minima and fuel requirements have been met and planned for, then, prior to making the decision, the Aircraft Captain (AC) should initiate a discussion among the entire crew as to the reason why and all should agree before the command to transition to NVG flight is given.
2	Before the transition from NVFR to NVG flight, the crew shall: ■ Contact Air Traffic Control and notify them of the requirement to change. This should be relatively easy as being an NVFR flight you should already have a flight plan in the system. ■ Configure the helicopter for NVG, adjust the lighting as applicable and any other operational requirements for NVG operations. ■ Ready the appropriate NVG maps and charts as applicable. ■ Consider when to initiate a descent below LSALT and then when to commence the transition procedure.
3	Once the decision is made, Air Traffic Control has been notified, and if applicable, a clearance for the descent is received, the Aircraft Captain will issue the command "Transition to NVG flight".
4	All members of the crew are to acknowledge the command with the response "Roger".

Step	Action
5	The NFP will then announce "goggling up front left/right" and goggles up, at which point the NFP will announce "goggled up front left/right".
6	The remaining crew members will also announce "goggling up front/back left/right" and go through the goggle up procedure. Once goggled up, they will all in turn announce "goggled up front/back left/right" as applicable.
7	The FP then announces and commences a descent to the LSALT. It is important to note that the FP is not yet goggled up but is still flying the helicopter under the NVFR. The NFP is also cross-checking the instruments under the goggles on descent but is also bringing his scan outside looking to confirm visual reference with the ground as are the other crew members.
8	The FP will then either level of at the LSALT and wait for the NFP to call visual (possibly with the assistance and confirmation of other crew members) or if the crew do not become visual, they may have to remain under the NVFR and initiate a climb and return to base (after communicating this with Air Traffic Control).
9	Once reaching the LSALT and becoming visual, the NFP shall announce "Visual front left/right" "Taking Over", and the flight crew will complete the hand over take over drill in the normal manner.
10	The old NFP now becomes the FP and can then call Air Traffic Control that they are now "Visual and confirm the change of category to NVG".
11	The old FP, after relinquishing control, will announce "goggling up front left/right" and go through the goggle up procedure so that the entire crew is now operating using NVGs.
12	It is the Aircraft Captain's (AC) decision as to who should continue to act as the FP and NFP in the normal manner.
13	The flight will now continue as an NVG flight.

NVG Emergencies

When using NVGs, the helicopter and crew can encounter any emergency situation as they could under the Day VFR, NVFR or IFR categories.

Emergencies such as a generator failure, hydraulic failure, instrument lighting failure or even an engine failure or fire in flight may be applicable, but we are not going to discuss those types of emergencies here as the appropriate response when the crew are using NVGs would be consistent with the response required during the Day, NVFR or when IMC. What we will discuss here are emergencies specific to the NVGs.

In general, the use of NVGs at night during any emergency will assist with improved situational awareness. This gives the crew the ability to identify obstacles and emergency landing areas that would otherwise be hidden by the darkness. They allow the crew to make better decisions and give them more options than to simply accept that the ground is "somewhere" underneath them.

Helicopter Emergencies With NVGs In General

The use of NVGs generally improves the likelihood of successfully dealing with helicopter emergencies during night-time operations.

However, because NVG operations are routinely conducted at lower levels than unaided night operations (NVFR), this can result in the helicopter being in closer proximity to the ground and surrounding terrain and obstacles. When faced with helicopter emergencies or malfunctions when using NVGs, the Aircraft Captain should prioritise the crew's actions as follows:

1. Use NVG visual cues to maintain control over the helicopter's attitude and flight parameters, and confirm this with instrument crosschecks;
2. Use NVG visual cues to remain clear of obstacles and establish a safe flight path for the helicopter;
3. Allocate tasks to the crew to identify the malfunction and carry out any immediate actions; and
4. Use the established procedures to complete the checklist actions before revising the planned task or amending the flight plan.

There may be some circumstances where the Aircraft Captain may have to decide that the use of NVGs during certain emergency situations may not be appropriate, and the relevant crew member may have to de-goggle to conduct the required response.

Either way, both the Aircraft Captain and the crew need to work together to resolve the emergency. Prior training and practice will ensure a better outcome compared to crews coming together without any thought as to how to handle normal emergency situations.

NVG Specific Emergencies

Radio Altimeter (RADALT) Failure

A RADAR altimeter is an electrical device that will display to the crew the helicopter's height above the ground in real-time. A serviceable RADALT with an audible warning is a mandatory requirement for all NVG operations. Should the RADALT fail in-flight, the crew shall:

1. Maintain visual separation from the ground by looking outside with the crew calling obstacles and terrain as they come into the field of view;
2. Not deviate from the planned sortie flight path when below LSALT unless forced to do so;
3. The Aircraft Captain shall notify the crew and have the NFP complete the checklist actions; and
4. The Aircraft Captain shall decide to either:
   (a) Climb to LSALT and return to base. If at or above LSALT, this can be done either under the NVFR or IFR. If transitioning to NVFR procedures and at or above the LSALT, the crew may remain goggled up or de-goggled at the Aircraft Captain's discretion depending on the operational needs, OR
   (b) If due to operational reasons such as bad weather or altitude restrictions due to controlled airspace, then the Aircraft Captain may, providing it is safe to do so, remain under the NVG procedures but must return to base or divert to the nearest practical aerodrome.

Goggle Failure Drill

If either of the flying pilots suffers a total failure of the NVG, experiences an unacceptable defect or significant performance reduction of either or both of the NVG monocular tubes, this will constitute an "**NVG failure**". In the case of a single tube failure, reduced visual cues may still be available. However, all cases of NVG failure should be dealt with by going through the following drill.

Flying Pilot Goggle Failure

Step	Action
1	The FP will announce "*Goggle Failure front left/right, Handing Over*". Because the NFP will typically be navigating or conducting other non-flying duties he may not be in a position to immediately affect a Take Over; therefore the FP should be prepared to conduct the AHTA drill and turn away from know obstacles and terrain until the NFP is able to complete the handover, takeover drill.
2	NFP announces "Taking over", with the response from the FP being "you have control".
3	The FP will then attempt to rectify the failure by changing from the Primary batteries to the Secondary batteries, confirming all power leads are secured, and/or changing the goggles with a serviceable set.
4	If the goggles are then restored, the old FP will announce the cause of the failure and announce "goggles restored front left/right. Based on the reason for the failure, the Aircraft Captain will decide to either continue with the sortie or recover to the nearest suitable location.
5	If the goggles cannot be restored and there is not a spare set of NVGs available, the Aircraft Captain will decide to either: (a) Climb to LSALT and transition to NVFR or IFR, or (b) If LSALT cannot be achieved due to weather and operational reasons, the crew will consult together to determine the best course of action, remembering safety is the main priority, and they may return to base with only one NVG equipped pilot, who shall be the FP.

Non-flying Pilot Goggle Failure

Step	Action
1	The NFP will announce "Goggle Failure front left/right" The FP will then acknowledge by announcing "Roger taking up the scan".
2	The NFP will then attempt to rectify the failure by changing from the Primary batteries to the Secondary batteries, confirming all power leads are secured, and/or changing the goggles with a serviceable set.
3	If the goggles are then restored, the NFP will announce the cause of the failure and announce, "Goggles restored front left/right." Based on the reason for the failure, the Aircraft Captain will decide to either continue with the sortie or recover to the nearest suitable location. If the goggles cannot be restored and there is not a spare set of NVGs available, the Aircraft Captain will decide to either - Climb to LSALT and transition to NVFR or IFR, or - If LSALT cannot be achieved due to weather and operational reasons, the crew will consult together to determine the best course of action, remembering safety is the main priority, and they may return to base with only one NVG equipped pilot, who shall be the FP.
4	If the operation is being flown as a multi-crew, then if only one set of NVGs remains serviceable, the mission may be continued with the FP using the serviceable NVGs. In this case, the flight profile must be adjusted to comply with the single pilot NVG operational requirements.

Step	Action
5	It is important to note that the FP can continue below LSALT until the NFP has, within a reasonable time, been able to either restore the goggles or announces that they are unserviceable. If appropriate, at any time, the FP can elect to conduct the AHTA drill and climb to LSALT.

Single Tube Failure

This is an unusual emergency with not many documented cases of just one tube failing. It is more common for both tubes to go at the same time, usually due to a power failure of some sort. Also, because there are usually two pilots up front, each with a set of goggles it is very easy to just hand over to the other pilot.

In Australia, it is a requirement to practice and conduct a circuit and a landing with only one tube operational on the NVGs. This is because we are actually allowed to go out single-pilot NVG in some situations. It is considered, in this circumstance, better to use the single tube to get home and land rather than revert to NVFR or IFR, which may not be available.

Step	Action
1	If the NVGs only achieve single tube functionality, the affected crewmember is to announce "Single tube NVG failure front/back left/right".
2	If the operation is flown multi-crew then continue the drill as per the normal goggle failure stated above.
3	If the operation is flown single-pilot then: 1. Switch from Primary batteries to Secondary batteries in the hope this may fix the problem. 2. Jiggle the mount and electrical cables, remembering that if you make the situation worse and lose the good tube, you will immediately have to affect the AHTA drill. 3. If the goggles cannot be restored to their full functionality, then the single pilot will decide to either: (a) Climb to LSALT and transition to NVFR or IFR, or (b) If LSALT cannot be achieved due to weather and operational reasons, either abort the sortie and return to base or divert to the nearest practical landing area using the remaining single NVG tube to assist. Which decision you make will be dependent on the circumstances you are in. The preferred curse of action is to climb to LSALT and revert to NVFR procedures.
4	Changing NVGs in-flight following an NVG failure should only be conducted by a 2-pilot crew or in an autopilot equipped helicopter. A single pilot with no autopilot should recover unaided and land prior to changing goggles or continue the task unaided if appropriate. It is important to note here that if you are a single pilot and using an autopilot, you should not attempt to change the goggles with the autopilot flying the helicopter until you are at or above LSALT.

Night Vision Goggles *for Helicopter Pilots*

Inadvertent IMC (IIMC) Procedure

Unintentional (accidental) flight into conditions where the crew no longer have any visibility is referred to as "Inadvertent Instrument Meteorological Conditions" (IIMC).

This is an undesirable condition that can creep up on you without warning as the NVGs themselves can mask deteriorating visibility conditions, especially for the uninitiated. One moment you could be visual with the ground, the surrounding terrain or external lighting, the next moment, you may be looking at a blank green screen. There are several scenarios that may lead to the IIMC condition.

- While flying straight and level, you may be flying into deteriorating weather conditions and encounter a rainstorm, snow, sleet, fog, mist, haze or cloud. You could also encounter smoke or dust, or pollutants.
- While on approach or on take-off, the downwash from the helicopter could stir up the ground, causing dust and dirt to create a brownout or snow and sand to cause a white out.
- Flying into an area of very bright light can temporarily overload the goggles.
- Another interesting scenario is if descending or climbing through an inversion the helicopter's windscreen could instantly fog up as condensation forms on the window, and this creates its own IIMC situation.

Whatever the reason, inadvertently losing your in-flight visibility is not a good thing. There are often small tell tales or hints that there is a pending problem and discovering what these are is why gaining experience on NVGs is important. Additionally, having an IIMC recovery plan determined and agreed to by all the crew during the pre-flight brief is essential to a good outcome, as making the plan up at the time of the event is the first error that could lead to a combination of errors and ultimately an accident or incident.

In general, the following procedures for an IIMC event shall apply.

If during normal flight (not on take-off or landing) and any crew member notices reducing visibility, they will:

1. Announce "Reducing visibility front/back left right" followed by an indication of the direction and distance from the helicopter and what they think the issue may be. This is a warning that IIMC may be imminent and, if possible, avoiding action shall be taken early by the FP.
2. Actions taken may include:
    (a) Descending to avoid cloud and getting closer to the ground for better contrast and use of IR or white light.
    (b) Turning away from the area of reducing visibility, or doing a 180-degree turn to come back the way you have just come from, which was previously not affected by reducing visibility.
    (c) Reduce speed to have better control and manage the flight better.
    (d) Make a precautionary landing into an HLS Standard or Basic.
    (e) Climb to get above the area of reduced visibility.
    (f) Continue as the reducing visibility is not below the minimum required.

The Aircraft Captain shall make these decisions.

> **Example**
>
> *For example*: Consider a helicopter at 300 ft AGL with a ground speed of 60 KIAS. The NFP notices that the halo from a house approximately 1 NM away is getting bigger and that the discernible horizon is disappearing. He correctly determines that there is a small shower on the front left of the helicopter and that the continued track may put the helicopter into the shower and an IMC situation is imminent. The correct statement from the NFP would be:
>
> "*Caution; reducing visibility front left, 1 o'clock 1 NM shower of rain suggest a right turn*".
>
> The FP will respond with "*Roger turning right*' or "*Roger sighted*".

Entering IMC (IIMC)

If inadvertently entering IMC (IIMC) and losing flight visibility, either the FP or the NFP shall announce "Entry into IMC".

The FP (or the Aircraft Captain will direct the FP) will immediately commence the IIMC procedure by initiating the AHTA drill with sole reference to the cockpit instruments.

A	Attitude	Roll helicopter level (evidenced by rolling the wings level on the AI) and set the climb attitude with reference to the instruments (AI).
H	Heading	Initially, maintain the initial heading or adopt a safe heading. Once a climb is established, select a heading that will provide the best obstacle clearance.
T	Torque	Set climb power or 100% torque depending on the performance required.
A	Airspeed	Adjust the attitude to set the best climb speed.

The FP will climb to the pre-planned LSALT, or level out if above LSALT.

AHTA Drill

The AHTA drill is completed when either:

- visual reference has been regained below LSALT, whereby the crew can return to NVG ops, or
- level off at or above LSALT, where the crew will then go through the transition to IFR procedure.

During IIMC

During the IIMC event and while the FP is conducting the AHTA drill, the NFP will:

1. Assist the FP in managing the AHTA drill until LSALT is reached
2. Monitor the instruments and read out the required heading, torque, and airspeed parameters
3. Occasionally scan outside to see if visual reference is restored, if it is, then the NFP shall announce "Visual front left/right", and the crew can return to NVG operations
4. Make the appropriate radio calls and change category to IFR, notifying Air Traffic Control (ATC) of inadvertent IMC
5. Confirm the IIMC recovery plan discussed during the Pre-flight and direct and assist the FP in making good the plan.

Once above LSALT, the Aircraft Captain can decide if all or some of the crew de-goggle. It may be wise to keep one crew member goggled up so that if the helicopter flies into clear air again, they can announce visual and recover visually instead of having to complete the IIMC recovery plan if that is desired.

If the crew members are NVFR rated but not IFR rated, and VFR conditions cannot be established at LSALT, the crew shall make an appropriate radio call to Air Traffic Control and commence instrument flight techniques. The pilot should then attempt to re-establish VFR conditions. This may be able to be achieved by:

- climbing higher to achieve cloud break
- asking for radar vectoring to cloud break (where applicable)
- tracking using a suitable navigation aid towards a location that offers VFR conditions, or
- descent to a lower LSALT in an area that offers this option.

It is important to remember that if the crew are not IFR qualified, inadvertent flight into IMC is an emergency warranting a MAYDAY call. Based on the crew's experience and situation, this may or may not be appropriate, but either way, clear communication with Air Traffic Control is essential.

Loss of Visual Reference (Brownout/Whiteout)

The emergency procedure for loss of visual reference in a landing or manoeuvring area during a lift-off, take-off or approach and landing is designed to minimise the likelihood of a helicopter striking obstacles.

Like the IIMC recovery procedure, there are often tell tails or hints that there is going to be an issue if the helicopter continues on its current path. This is usually articulated by one of the crew members giving a "Caution" statement such as "Caution dust" or "Caution snow", etc.

If the helicopter then starts to influence the ground, a crew member may then continue by saying, "Caution losing visual reference front/back left right".

If nothing is done at this point, this could lead to a total loss of visual reference with the ground where one of the crew members will announce "RIFTO RIFTO RIFTO".

As we know, the term RIFTO refers to a Reduced (or restricted) Instrument Flight Take-off where the visibility is reduced, so an instrument type take-off with reference to the cockpit instruments is required. This simply means that the FP shall commence a vertical climb using the cockpit instruments until clear of the bad visibility or at least until obtaining a safe height and then commence a transition into a forward climb.

On hearing the statement "RIFTO RIFTO RIFTO", the FP will either:

- If still visual with the ground, decide to continue with a landing to the surface and acknowledge the crew member's call by stating, "Roger continuing with the landing", or
- Initiate a Reduced Instrument Take-off (RIFTO) profile using the AHTA drill.

A	Attitude	Using available visual cues but primarily relying on the position of the AI adopt and maintain a hover attitude
H	Heading	Maintain the current heading with reference to the HSI and turn indicator
T	Torque	Set climb power or 100% for better performance to commence a ROC
A	Airspeed	Once established a ROC and clearing the surface obscurants created by the downwash and at a height that is safe, adjust the attitude to obtain best climb speed

or

- Climb as appropriate until visual reference is regained, or the decision is to revert to IFR flight as you would for the IIMC procedure followed by the transition from NVG to IFR procedure.

Landing Techniques

If making a landing into an area with a known issue, the crew can set themselves up for this so that there is nothing unexpected.

In general, the FP can usually see between his feet. The downwash of the helicopter pushes the dust or snow away from the helicopter, so looking out the front and side can be worse than looking straight down. This is why the FP can decide to ignore crew members calling RIFTO and make their own decision to conduct a landing.

In this case, the NFP shall shadow the controls so that if the FP completely loses visual reference and himself calls a RIFTO, the NFP can take over and use instrument flying techniques to commence the AHTA drill.

With the diagrams below, a good knowledge of what the downwash will do and with the help of wind, you may be able to beat the RIFTO event.

If the RIFTO event commences and if the crew are quick enough, they could commence the climb and stay above and out of the problem area.

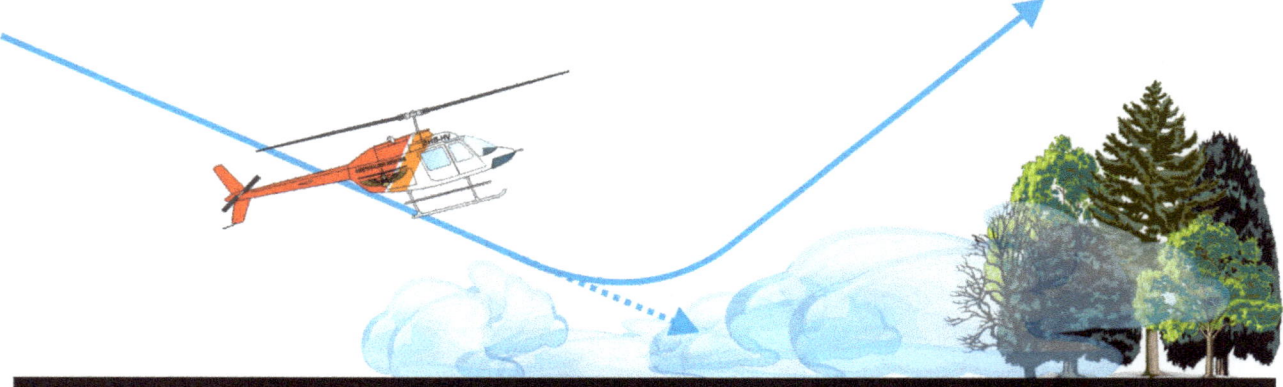

If the helicopter can stay ahead of the downwash, they may avoid a RIFTO while affecting the landing.

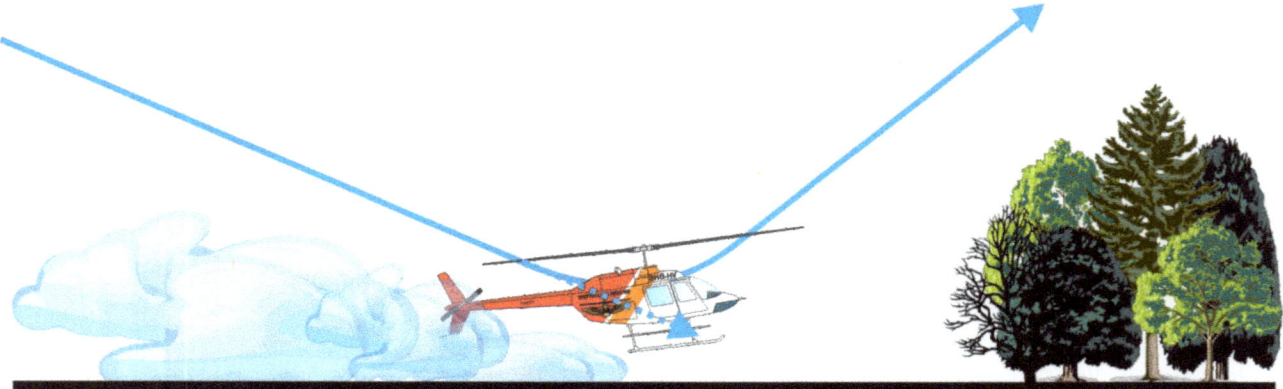

Night Vision Goggles *for Helicopter Pilots*

Take-off Techniques

When coming into an HLS or prior to departing, it is always a good point for the crew to note the height of the obstacles they need to clear on take-off before they commence the lift-off. Although this may sometimes be the crew's best guess, in the event of a RIFTO on take-off, they are able to use the RADALT to gauge when they are clear of the obstacle and commence a transition into forward flight even if they are still inside the obscurants.

The transition to forward flight may be conducted on instruments, or visually if external visual reference has been regained. Establishing forward flight will reduce the risks of inadvertent drift and heading changes during the manoeuvre but should only be commenced when the helicopter has climbed above any obstacles in the immediate area.

The procedure requires a steep climb through OGE. Pilots conducting an approach or manoeuvring in an area where they may be subject to brownout/whiteout conditions must confirm the helicopter has a suitable power margin to climb away expeditiously in the event of a RIFTO situation. Do not attempt or continue to land without adequate visual reference.

The NFP or other aircrew member shall assist the pilot by monitoring and calling relevant information such as:

1. Helicopter attitude and rate of climb
2. Power setting
3. When external visual reference is regained, and
4. Terrain and/or obstacles.

The NFP may also come on the controls to assist the FP, if the FP does not recognise an unsafe helicopter attitude.

RIFTO Departures

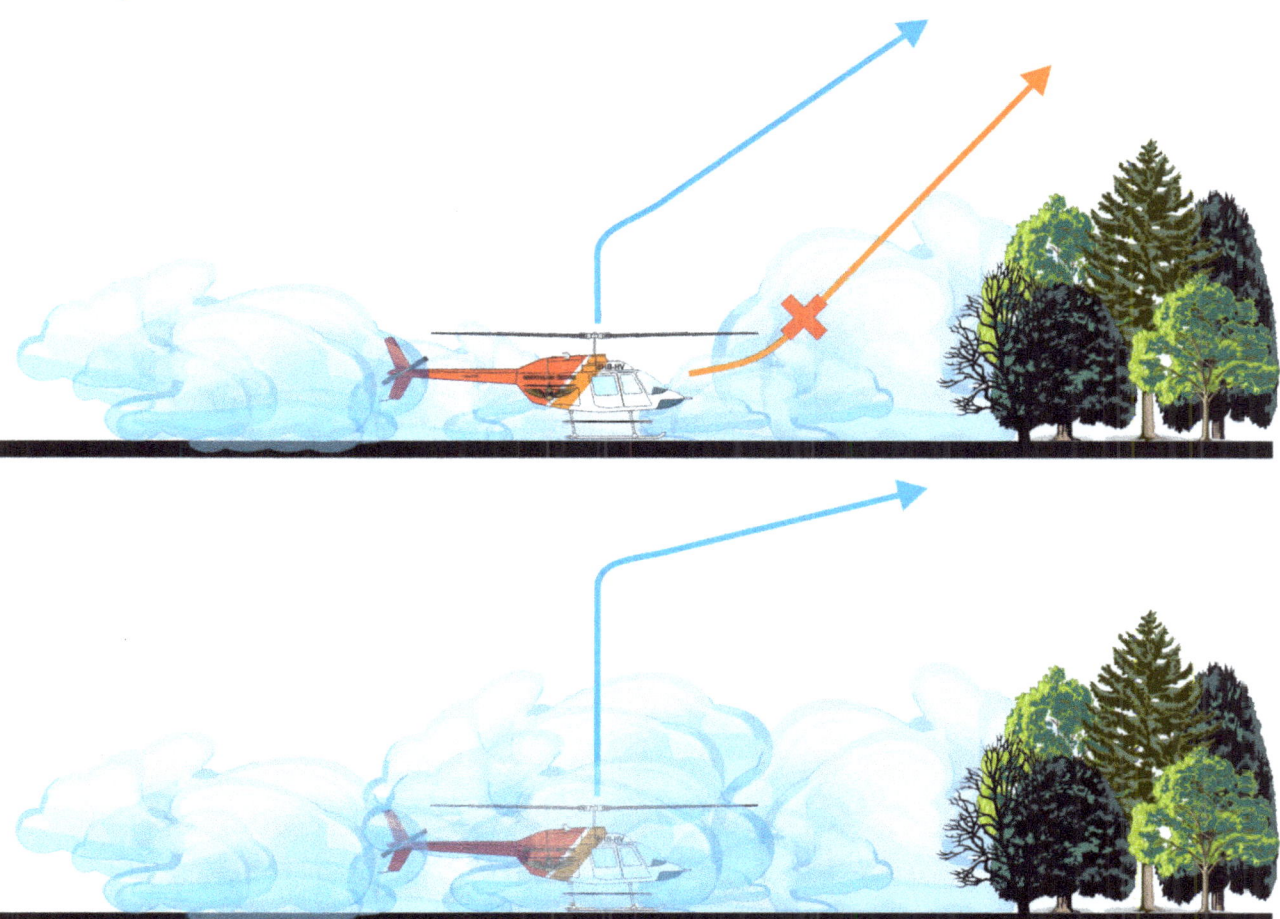

Mike Becker

Planning an NVG Flight

Flight planning for an NVG sortie is no different from any other flight under the VFR, NVFR or IFR; in that, the NVG crew needs to collect all relevant information, particularly with regards to the weather, the route, the destination, and information on the type of mission or what the actual purpose of the flight is. The crew then need to apply this information, check it against the regulations and make a **GO / NO GO** decision.

Add to this the responsibilities of ensuring that the aircraft and the crew are suitably qualified and current and fit to fly, specifically for the NVG flight, have all been briefed, and that any ancillary equipment and personnel are in place, and the planning of an NVG flight can then start to get complex.

For an NVG flight, there are some additional NVG specific elements to consider, including:

- The amount of ambient light available
- additional or Reduced Flight Planning Weather Minimums (RFPWM) for NVG that may be NVFR or IFR specific
- flight below LSALT, and
- a more detailed assessment of the:
  - route flown to consider more carefully obstacles such as wires and towers, and
  - the impact adverse weather may have on the flight at night at low level.

The secret is to look at the flight in the planning stages as being conducted while using NVG, but also assume that if the NVGs fail and you need to revert to NVFR or IFR at any time, this has been considered and planned for.

As we know, the key to any flight is to start with the end in mind. If there are no clear objectives for the flight, then planning becomes superfluous or seemingly unnecessary. The NVG flight should be very well planned and thought out.

There is no room for guesswork and just *"winging it"*. When the goggles fail, and you find yourself inadvertently in cloud, in the dark, below LSALT, guesswork will only lead to disaster.

Much of this planning information can all be coordinated through the use of a good NVG specific checklist.

NVG Checklist

The checklist given in this chapter is an example only. It is included in the helicopter's normal and abbreviated checklist data and is an aid to help crews plan and conduct an NVG sortie.

Each of the main headings categorises a specific area that needs to be looked at, while the items under the heading highlight specific items that the crew need to consider and have an answer for.

1. NVGs

1	Serviceable and released
2	Mounted to Helmet
3	Focused
4	Battery life
5	Backup if required

2. AIRCRAFT

1	Serviceable and released
2	NVFR or IFR approved
3	Instruments and lighting are serviceable
4	Configuration (Hoist, Incendiaries, Belly tank, etc.)
5	RAD ALT
6	GPS Data card
7	Fuel and oil
8	Ancillary equipment as required (fuel pump, tools, emergency equip, etc.)
9	C of G calculated

3. CREW

Note: These criteria may differ depending on each country's regulatory requirements.

1	Rested and within Flight and Duty Times
2	Stop time calculated
3	If less than 50 hours NVG, then: ■ 3 hours NVG in last 3 months or a Competency Check Flight (CCF) ■ CCF completed last 6 months
4	If more than 50 hours NVG, then: ■ 3 hours in last 6 months or CCF ■ CCF completed last 12 months
5	NVFR 3 take-offs, circuits and landings in last 90 days (NVG flights count)
6	NVFR 1 take-off, circuit and landings in last 6 months (NVG flights count)
7	NVFR 1 hour NVFR in last 12 months (NVG flights count)

4. MISSION

1	Mission outline / purpose / desired outcome / Go or No-go criteria
2	Flight timings
3	Start / Airborne / working time / Landing / Reporting cycle
4	Airspace co-ordination for NVG
5	Aerial work activity discussed (SAR, Incendiaries, FFS, Belly Tank)

5. ROUTE

1	Route and working area selected and assessed
2	Terrain appreciation (Low contrast, mountains, over water?)
3	LSALT calculated
4	Wires and obstacles noted (wire/obstacle map markings)
5	IIMC recovery plan and route discussed
6	Maps, DAPs and ERSA current

6. WEATHER

1	TAFs valid for Departure and Arrival
2	No more than 4/8s cloud at less than 1500 ft AGL and visibility (8k for NVFR and 5k for NVG)
3	ARFOR and RFPWM (NOTED AS PER AIRCRAFT CERTIFICATION NVFR/IFR) ■ NVFR cloud no more than 4/8s below 2000 ft AGL within 2 NM of track, visibility 5 KM ■ IFR cloud no more than 4/8s below 1000 ft AGL within 2 NM of track, visibility 5 KM
4	NOTAMs assessed
5	Cloud base noted
6	Visibility noted
7	Freezing level noted
8	Alternates and Holding fuel determined
9	Moon phase, position and illumination determined

7. FLIGHT PLANNING

1	Navigation flight log completed – one per flight crew
2	Mud Map drawn – briefed and one per flight crew
3	Submit flight plan to ATS and nominate a SARTIME or Company Flight note
4	Crew briefing and co-ordination
5	Risks and Threats discussed
6	IMC recovery plan determined and agreed upon
7	NVG Sortie Crew Plan

8. POST FLIGHT

1	SARTIME cancelled
2	Aircraft secured
3	NVGs returned to equipment room and signed in
4	Debrief of crew

Explaining the NVG Checklist

1. NVGs: Checklist Explained

Serviceable And Released

There is no point in planning a flight, unless the NVGs themselves are serviceable and have been released for service. This can normally be confirmed by reading the NVGlog card and noting any defects that may have been entered by the previous user, and sighting the "Green" release tag, which should be inside the NVG case.

Mounted To Helmet And Focused

Attach the NVGs to your helmet; ensure they are working correctly, that they are focused and that the low power warning indicator is working.

Battery Life

Ensure you have confirmed the remaining battery life in the power pack. The Primaries may be part-life with the NVG log book helping you calculate this information, but the Secondaries should be new. It is a good idea to take a spare set of new batteries with you in your top pocket.

Backup If Required

If possible and available, take a spare set of NVGs as a backup.

2. Aircraft: Checklist Explained

Serviceable And Released

The Maintenance Release (MR) or Aircraft Technical Log (which one will depend on the Operator's maintenance procedures) will confirm that the aircraft is serviceable and has been released for service. Review this document and check that there is sufficient time remaining to complete the sortie and there are no outstanding maintenance issues.

NVFR or IFR Approved

Confirm which category the helicopter is approved for. It must be, as a minimum, either NVFR or IFR certified. This information will be checked on the top of the maintenance release. Based on the crew's qualifications and the aircraft configuration, either NVFR or IFR procedures may be planned for.

Confirm that this aircraft is also approved for NVG operations. This information would not normally be listed on the top of the maintenance release or tech log, but the helicopter flight manual will have a supplement allowing for NVG operations. Each individual aircraft must be approved for NVG operations regardless of its configuration (NVFR/IFR).

Pre-flight Inspection

Go and do a full pre-flight of the aircraft and turn on all the lights; this includes the NVG compatible cockpit lighting, as well as the external position and landing lights.

Make sure the RADAR Altimeter and the steerable searchlight are functioning properly.

Ensure the GPS data card is current.

Have the aircraft refuelled and configured for your flight.

Ancillary Equipment

Ensure any ancillary equipment required for the flight is operational and, if it has an effect on NVGs, is on the approved NVG list as being compatible equipment allowed to be used when the crew are on NVGs. The approved list would normally be found within the Operator's operations manual and is more applicable to equipment that will emit some form of light, such as a phone, iPad, torch, computer, etc.

Based on the mission and the route, ancillary equipment required may include, but is not limited to:

- Portable ground-based lights for use at a remote HLS
- Lifejackets and life raft
- Survival equipment and water
- Additional communication equipment (satellite phone, HF radio, portable GPS, emergency beacon, etc.)
- Refuelling equipment
- Tools
- Equipment required for the aerial work task

Weight And Balance

Ensure that once all the equipment is loaded, the helicopter is refuelled, and the crew details are known, an accurate weight and balance (C of G) calculation is completed.

3. Crew: Checklist Explained

Rested And Within Flight And Duty Times

Prior to the flight, all crew members should be well-rested. Different organisations may use varying tools to help crews manage fatigue to ensure adequate rest between flights. A common system in use by some operators at present is the **F**atigue **R**isk **M**anagement **S**ystem (FRMS), which is usually written by organisations to take into account their specific aircrew requirements. It incorporates information taken from universities and sleep studies, as well as information from the organisation, that will then put up a safety case to the relevant aviation authority and propose their Fatigue Risk Management System (FRMS).

Stop Time Calculated

The FRMS system usually incorporates a scoring system and a stop time for operations and is computer-based. It will not be discussed in detail here except to say that prior to an NVG flight all crew members need to ensure that they are:

- adequately rested
- in reasonable health with a good fitness level and have a good balanced diet
- not suffering from an illness, especially a cold or flu virus
- have nominated a stop time for operations and that each crew member is aware of the others' fatigue levels

Because NVG operations are done outside the normal day/night circadian rhythm, crews can suffer from psychological and physiological stress. It is up to the operator and the individuals to monitor themselves and their crew members and to speak up if fatigue symptoms are observed.

Currency And Recency

Prior to the flight ensure that the Pilot-In-Command (PIC) and crew have the required NVG recency and qualifications. Obviously, if you are a student, you will not have the qualifications, but your instructor will. In Australia, unless otherwise approved by CASA, NVG trainees must meet the NVG training pre-requisites as stated in the regulations.

Additional to NVG recency, if the planned flight is going to be conducted under the NVFR, then the crew members are required to have all the recency requirements for an NVFR flight.

If you have been doing the majority of your night sorties using NVGs, then the lift-offs and landings and the time in the air will count towards your NVFR recency. Remember, NVG is just an addition to NVFR.

Additional to the NVG recency, if the planned flight is going to be conducted under the IFR, or the IIMC recovery plan for a NVFR flight is to transition to the IFR category, then the crew members are required to have all the recency requirements for an IFR flight.

For a NVG qualified pilot with less than 50 hours of NVG total time, then prior to a flight where you will be the PIC you are required to have completed a minimum of 3 hours NVG in the last 3 months or have completed a Competency Check Flight (CCF).

Regardless of the number of hours you have done in the last 3months, if you have less than 50 hours NVG, you have to do a CCF at least every 6 months. A CCF shall be a minimum of a 1-hour flight.

For a NVG qualified pilot with more than 50 hours of NVG total time, then prior to a flight where you will be the PIC you are required to have completed a minimum of 3 hours NVG in the last 6 months or have completed a Competency Check Flight (CCF).

Regardless of the number of hours you have done in the last 6 months, if you have more than 50 hours NVG you have to do a CCF at least every 12 months. A CCF shall be a minimum of a 1-hour flight.

If you are going to apply the NVFR Reduced Flight Planning Weather Minimums (RFPWM) to an NVFR category flight, then you need to ensure that the operator has the applicable approval from CASA to do this.

If you have an instrument rating and are flying an IFR aircraft and you wish to take advantage of the IFR RFPWM, then you need to ensure that the operator has the applicable approval from CASA to do this. Additionally, the crew need to ensure that their IFR recency is current. This also applies to whatever instrument approach you may have elected to nominate in the event of an IMC recovery exercise involving an instrument approach.

4. Mission: Checklist Explained

Purpose

Prior to the flight, it is important that each crew member has a good understanding of just what the intention of the flight is: What are you trying to achieve, the purpose, the desired outcome, the end goal. Having a clear picture of this makes for coordinated crew members who will be striving for the same thing and will lead to a more successful outcome.

This can be as simple as the crew sitting down over a coffee before departure and talking through the flight.

Example
For example: Consider an Incendiary operation at night using NVG. The two pilots at the front have to co-ordinate with the navigator and the bombardier in the back. They need to: ■ know how and when the incendiary equipment is operating,   ■ know they are dropping in the right area,   ■ be communicating and working with crews on the ground,   ■ know how long they can stay in the area,   ■ discuss what will happen if there is a problem with the incendiary device,   ■ discuuss what will happen if the flight crew go IMC and are effecting a recovery and the incendiary device is still going, etc.   A good crew discussion and pre-planning prior to the mission are critical.   This philosophy should be the same for a training SAR, Incendiary, Firefighting Support, military or any other mission.

Flight Timings

Calculating timings can be important because this has ramifications on fuel available, weather requirements and crew duty times. Writing down and discussing when you will depart, how long it will take to get to an area, how long you can work in that area before returning back to base, making sure you arrive with all reserves intact, including an inadvertent IMC recovery if applicable, all set you up for a successful flight and a successful recovery if conditions deteriorate. Remember even the best-laid plan will not work if you run out of fuel.

Example		
Consider a helicopter with a total fuel endurance of 3 hours on a firefighting support mission to drop incendiaries. The flight timings may be considered prior to the flight and noted on a kneeboard as shown:	Walk time	18:00 hrs
	Start time	18:20 hrs
	Departure time	18:30 hrs
	Transit time to work area	20 mins
	Holding fuel (INTER, TEMPO)	30 mins
	IIMC recovery plan	30 mins
	Fixed reserve	30 mins
	Transit time back to base	20 mins
	Effective work time	50 mins
	Return to base time	20:00 hrs
	Stop time for crew	23:30 hrs

In the previous example, all fuel requirements have been considered, but the timings are based on the flight out and back plus the work time. The remaining fuel should remain in the tank unless used because of the operational requirements (INTER, IIMC, etc.).

Airspace

As discussed previously, your flight may take you in and out of controlled airspace. Planning this ahead of time and even contacting the relevant authorities before the flight will make for a smooth transition with no delays. If people know you are coming, you will find that you will be accommodated much more efficiently compared to if you just turn up unannounced.

This is very relevant as part of the IIMC recovery plan. Even if the entire flight was originally planned to be outside controlled airspace and a Company SAR is being held, if the flight details have been submitted to Air Traffic Control, then in the event that you did go IIMC and had to either climb in cloud to LSALT or you intend to change category to IFR, when you contacted Air Traffic Control and ask for a clearance all your details would already be in the system, and you will find that they are able to respond to your requests much faster when compared to a flight about which they had no prior knowledge. When inadvertently flying into IMC conditions, time is of the essence as fuel is limited and your options are reducing, so anything that can speed up the process will be to your advantage.

Example
Consider a simple training sortie to conduct circuits at a non-towered airfield 20 NM away from home base with an instrument approach. A fog and a thick band of stratus cloud that was not forecast rolls in and the crew have to go IIMC. They commence a climb to an LSALT of 5500 feet but very quickly have to contact Air Traffic Control asking for a change of category from VFR to IFR and a clearance. There are other IFR aircraft in the area, so time is critical because you do not know if you are climbing into the path of another IFR aircraft. If a plan had been submitted to Air Services, then all your details will be available to the controller, and he/she will be able to accommodate your request much sooner compared to if you had no details in the system and then had to start passing them on through the radio. All NVG flights should at least submit their planned details to Air Services. The SARTIME can be kept locally.

Mike Becker

Aerial Work Activity

The actual task needs to be discussed. Flying from point A to B and back to A is often just a small part of the entire sortie and not necessarily a sortie on its own.

Any aerial work activity approved by CASA (or the relevant aviation regulatory authority that the operator is able to conduct will be described in detail in the Operator's operations manual.

The crew all need to understand their role in the sortie and conduct it in accordance with the company's directions.

5. Route : Checklist Explained

Route And Working Area Selected and Assessed

When selecting a route, you need to consider the reason for the task as this may have a bearing on the route you select.

Are you simply doing a navigational training exercise? Are you choosing a route in order to get to an area of operations to conduct a firefighting operation or SAR or an insertion or extraction? As previously discussed, the mission can determine the route.

Typically, civil NVG operations may allow a direct route at a higher altitude (500 ft AGL or above), whereas military NVG operations may require an indirect route at a lower altitude (500 ft AGL and below). Either way, route selection when using NVG should consider the following, in addition to that already considered for NVFR and IFR.

Terrain Appreciation

Now that we can see at night and because we can operate below LSALT, selecting the best terrain to fly over is more important.

Try to select a route that keeps you as low as possible going from a known point to a known point. For civil operations, the route should be planned no lower than 500 ft AGL. Military operations will be as required for the mission.

Often the most direct route is not the most efficient as it may be better to navigate to a known point before tracking to the actual destination. For example, consider tracking to a small Basic NVG HLS 10 NM west of a regional airport. It may be easier to track first to the airport to positively fix your position, then track to the entrance to a valley, avoiding the ridges, then track to the HLS, rather than just trying to track direct to the HLS from your original departure aerodrome.

If you are going to fly over areas of low contrast, you may have difficulty pinpointing your position. The same could occur if you are over areas of high cultural lighting or possibly over low lying cloud layers. The harder the course you will fly, the more time you may have to spend with your head inside the cockpit trying to relate the ground to your map. By making the best use of key features and radio navigation aids, and GPS, you can reduce this workload considerably.

Plan to negotiate large valleys on the illuminated side with respect to the moon's position. This will avoid shadows cast by the moon and facilitate silhouetting of terrain features for navigation. Shadows may hide rising terrain or obstacles. Whenever possible, transit at height instead of close to the ground.

Avoid a route that heads directly into a low rising or setting moon. Instead, plan to fly in a zigzag advance across the route of flight to offset the distraction of the moon.

Anticipate wires by always assuming a wire will follow a road or a cut line through trees and bush. Look for poles - remembering that poles can often have guy wires. By reading the hardware on a pole, you can determine the direction of the wires. When a pole is located, always plan to fly over it.

Anticipate towers on the top of hills and peaks - remember that if the tower or obstacle is less than 360 ft, it does not necessarily have to be shown on a map.

Determine some checkpoints which will help monitor your progress along a route. In general, checkpoints should be obvious, unique, natural or man-made features that are easily detectable and identifiable.

Select a route that makes the best use of airspace. This may be to enter controlled airspace, or it may be to avoid it. This will depend on your specific task.

Weather will also influence the route, which includes, as usual, cloud base, visibility, freezing level, wind strength, atmospheric disturbances such as rain, dust, smoke, fog, haze, the moon phase, etc., which will affect the route you choose.

Being NVG the preference is not to go into inadvertent IMC but to remain VMC; therefore, a lower route with escape routes and alternates is preferred.

Is the Reduced Flight Planning Weather Minimums (RFPWM) going to be used? In which case, the route may also have a 2 NM boundary drawn on it to help visualise the area in which it will apply.

LSALT Calculated

At any point along the route, if you inadvertently fly into IMC, then you shall know what the LSALT is and have an IMC recovery plan. This simply means that the crew has put some thought into what height to climb to, how to transition from NVG de-goggle and operate NVFR or IFR, make appropriate radio calls and gain clearances and then divert to an alternate where a visual or instrument approach can be used to make a landing.

Ensure all maps, DAPS, and the ERSA is current for the route being flown.

Have all the relevant information for your destination landing area. In some cases, this information can be made into a Landing Site Card which can be hand-drawn or taken from Google Earth, as shown below.

Figure 109 Landing site card (hand-drawn)

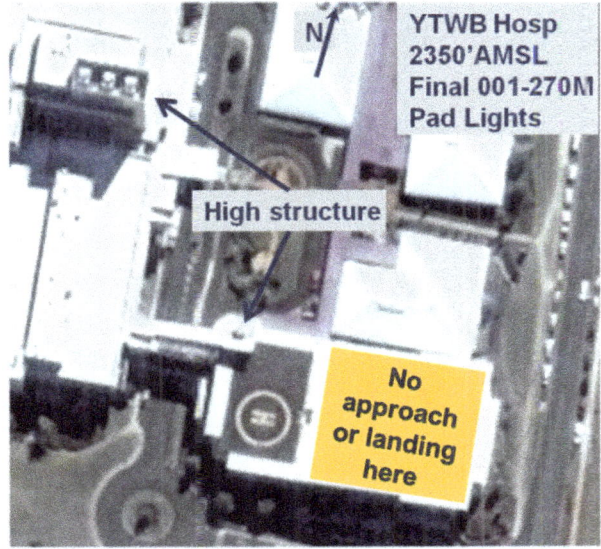

Figure 110 Landing site card (Google Earth)

For HLS in Australia, most SAR/EMS organisations have created a database of available HLS so that operators can quickly get a picture of what the HLS will look like if they have never been there before. This information can be found at www.helipads.org.

Wires And Obstacles Noted

This is covered in both the Mission and the Route part of the checklist because it is very important. All known wires and obstacles will be placed on either a topographical or mud map. In some cases, where the crew want to specifically identify a certain obstacle, they may also enter it as a waypoint in the GPS.

During the mission part of the checklist, wires and obstacles are discussed that are relevant to the operating area of the particular task, which is usually conducted below 500 ft AGL, whereas wires and obstacles for the route are relevant to the navigation phase of getting to and going from the area of operations which is usually conducted at least 500 ft AGL for civil operations.

There are several rules to remember when operating low level, both day and night, and particularly with NVGs:

1. **All roads have wires**
2. All buildings have wires going to them
3. All valleys and rivers have wires strung across them
4. If in doubt, there is a wire there

The only sure way to know there is not a wire in front of you is if you have been through the same area before. Otherwise, wires for the low-level pilot, and particularly the low level NVG pilot, can be a real killer. A reconnaissance by day and local knowledge are a pilot's best friend.

Wires can be almost impossible to see; it takes the right amount of illumination, the right angle of light and the right background to visually see and detect a wire. Normally all these things do not come together at once, so instead, we have to use proven techniques and procedures to avoid wires that we cannot see.

The diagram below was taken under a full moon high in the sky. There are no shadows, but there is a lot of illumination. Inside the black circle is a large hi-tensile power line tower. It is one of a line of towers with wires running from left to right. For all intents and purposes, it is practically invisible.

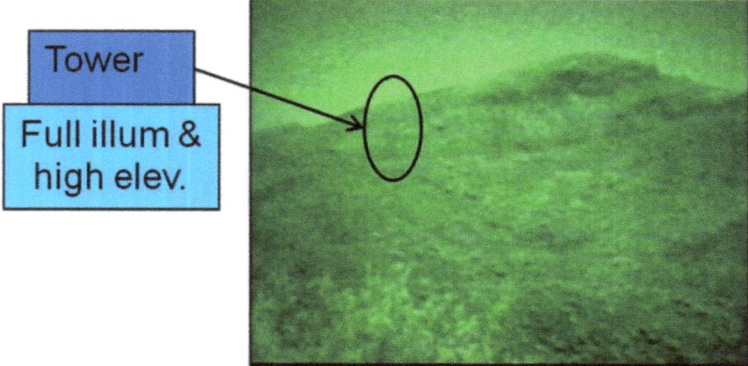

Wires can come in various disguises, shapes and sizes, including large high tensile distribution cables to smaller power lines, phone lines, guy wires, stays, fences, flying foxes, electric fences, and cables, to name a few.

Figure 111 Flying fox

Best Way To Look For Wires

The best way to find a wire is to not look for the wire itself, but for the evidence that there is a wire there, this includes looking for:

- Roads, railway lines and watercourses. Just assume that all roads and railway lines have wires running parallel to them and that all watercourses (rivers) have wires cutting across them.

Night Vision Goggles *for Helicopter Pilots*

Road	Railway line	River

Figure 112 Road   Figure 113 Railway line   Figure 114 River

- Buildings. Just assume all buildings have wires running to them. It is often a good bet that if there is a road nearby, there will be a wire running from the road somewhere to the building. Assume there are wires running between adjacent buildings. All towns, villages, factories, etc., will have wires running to them and away from them in various directions.
- If you are flying inside a valley (below the ridge tops) that you have no local knowledge of, you can only assume there is a wire strung across it somewhere, and you should not be there.
- Cut lines, where the vegetation has been cut down showing a clear path across the ground where a wire might be.

- Poles. Assume every pole has a wire. Once you have seen a pole, fly over it or at least be higher than it, as it is unlikely that a wire is going to be higher than a pole. When you find a pole, look at the cross members and the conductors on it. This is referred to as the "equipment" or the "hardware". If you read the equipment or hardware carefully, you can get an indication of where the wire may be going.
- Assume all high peaks have a tower on them, remembering that any tower or obstacle below 360 ft does not have to be lit or marked on a map.

- At any other time, if you are low level and you are not sure if there is a wire or obstacle, then you must assume there is one and climb to avoid it.

Negotiating Wires and Obstacles

Once a wire or obstacle is identified, or the crew knows it is there but cannot see it, then the safest way to avoid it is to remain clear of it. If this is not possible, then the next best option is to fly over the highest pole or tower or obstacle by at least 100 ft.

Even during the day, depth perception to a wire is extremely difficult, so at night using NVGs, it is practically impossible. So, parallel tracking along a wire at less than 100 meters laterally should be avoided and is considered to be dangerous due to the possibility of secondary wires tracking off at 90 degrees to the main wire.

As a general rule, if operating low level on a particular task, plan to be 100 feet above the highest pole or tower within a 1000 meter (1km) radius of the helicopter.

Flying under a wire should, where possible, be avoided and only conducted in an emergency. If there is no other option and you must fly under the wire, then the following needs to be considered.

1. Confirm the height of the helicopter AGL by use of the RAD ALT and visual cues.
2. If possible, use white light and have one crew member de-goggle so that they are able to have better depth perception.
3. Utilise all crew members to call and confirm distances.
4. Transit under the wire at a slow hover taxi speed.
5. Cross near a pole, taking into account:
   (a) The wires will sag towards the centre of the span, and the amount of sag can vary with temperature. High temperatures result in a bigger sag; cold temperatures result in a small sag. In technical terms, the sag of a wire is referred to as its catenary and can be affected by the amount of electricity passing through it.
   (b) The pole or tower may have guy wires.
   (c) There may be secondary wires you have not seen, so read the hardware on the pole.
   (d) The highest part of the helicopter is usually the tip of the main rotor blades and/or the top of the tail rotor or rear fin.
6. If possible, land and have a crew member walk under the wire and visually check and confirm the route.

Wire Maps

Once a wire or obstacle is discovered within the operating area or route, then they can be placed on a wire map. This will build up the local knowledge that a pilot or operator may have in an area and allow NVG flight to occur with confidence, knowing that there are no wires in the area of operations or if there is a wire, the crew know where it is. If operating outside of the wire map area and outside of the local knowledge a pilot may have, then flights should be planned to be at a higher altitude (500 ft AGL as a minimum).

Wire maps can either be overlaid on a topographical map or, if the area of operations is small enough, form part of a mud map. Remember that at night, unless being viewed with white light, colours are difficult if not impossible to see, so use dark (black) thick pen or pencil to make it easy for the crew to see at a glance.

Below is an example of a master wire map that is placed on the wall in the operations room for a training area. This can then be used by crews to transpose the relevant wires onto their own maps.

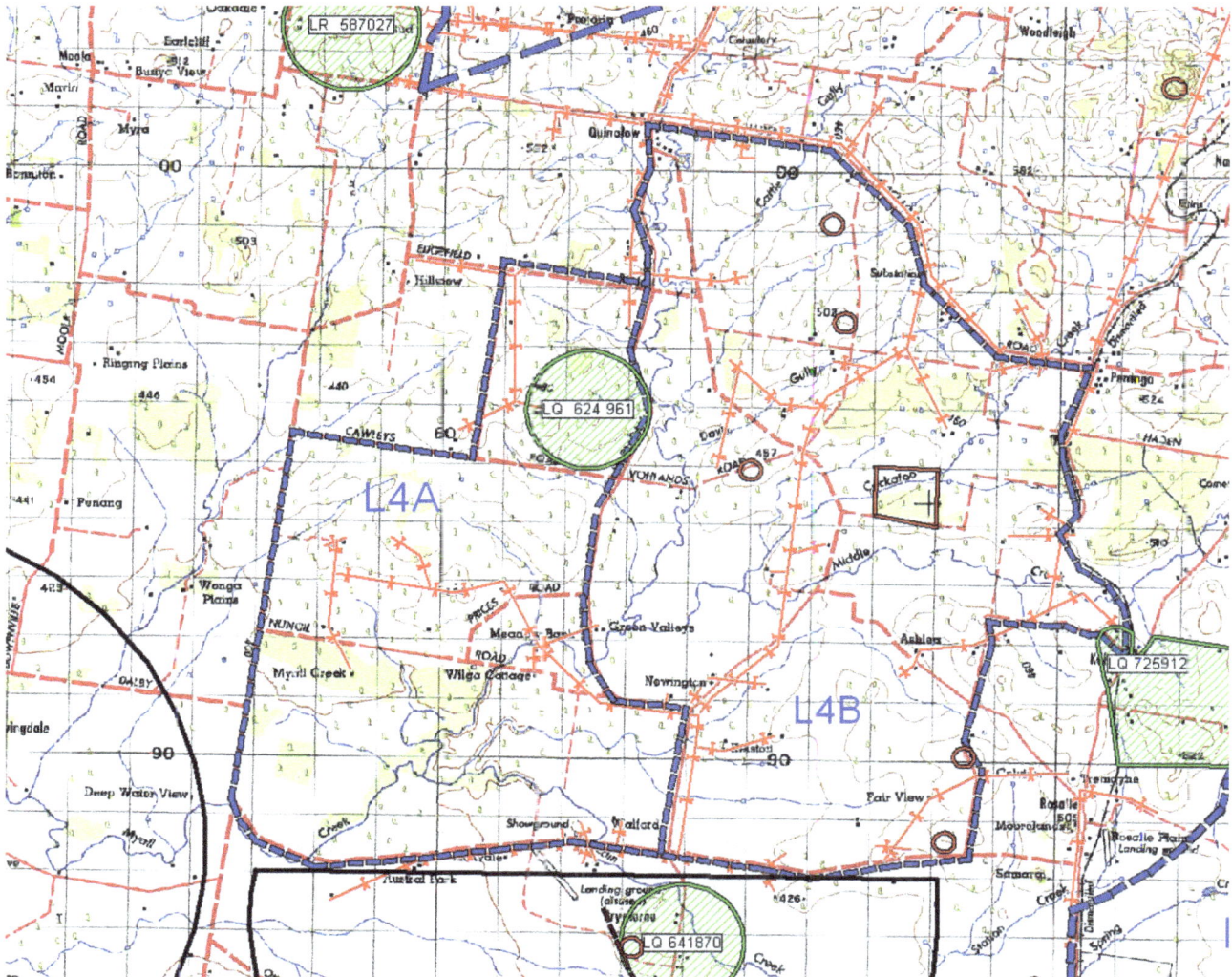

6. Weather : Checklist Explained

This can be an interesting part of your preparation, as interpreting the weather and NOTAMS for your particular route can lead to varying opinions among the crew. These opinions can come from the various crew members who have varying experience levels and varying levels of comfort when flying at night or under the IFR. This is one area where a commercial imperative can lead crews to make decisions they may not otherwise make.

Careful consideration needs to be given to the reasoning why a particular flight can or cannot go due to weather. Do not let emotion or commercial imperative drive you in these decisions. As a general rule for aviation, apply the following:

IF IN DOUBT, THERE IS NO DOUBT, DON'T GO

There are also other sources of information that will help in making decisions. These include using the weather radar on the internet, weather cams, asking other flight crews who may have just returned from a flight in the same area, being able to ask a responsible person on the ground at your destination or en-route for the local weather, actually looking outside and seeing if the forecast has any resemblance to what you can actually see and, of course, local knowledge, just to name a few.

The weather must then be applied to the route and the area of operations. Often the weather can be good at the departure point but below the limitations en-route or at the destination or vice versa. There is no doubt that weather interpretation and application of the information can be a very controversial crew discussion.

Australia: For NVG Operations, The Following Weather Requirements Will Apply And Are The Legal Minimums Within Australia

- You must obtain a valid TAF for departure and arrival that describes the cloud being no more than 4/8s at less than 1500 ft AGL with a flight visibility of 8 km reduced to 5 km when using the NVGs.
- If a TAF is not available, then an Area Forecast (ARFOR) will be sufficient but the cloud shall be no more than 4/8s at less than 1500 ft AGL with a flight visibility of 8 km reduced to 5 km when using the NVGs.
- If the Operator has an approval from CASA to utilise a Reduced Flight Planning Weather Minimum (RFPWM), then for:
    - NVFR flights, the cloud shall be no more than 4/8s below 2000 ft AGL within 2 NM either side of the planned track and a visibility of 5 km; and for
    - IFR flights, cloud shall be no more than 4/8s below 1000 ft AGL within 2 NM either side of the planned track and a visibility of 5 km.
- The purpose of the RFPWM is to allow the NVG equipped helicopter to manoeuvre in mountains and valleys where the cloud is obscuring the tops of the mountains, but the helicopter crew because they are able to fly below LSALT, can visually remain clear of the terrain. The danger here is ensuring that regardless of the terrain flown over, the crew can maintain a cloud base of 2000 ft AGL.
- Another consideration with regards to the weather is the category of flight to which you can revert if the NVGs fail or if you inadvertently go IMC. In either of these cases you need to be able to recover to either NVFR or IFR.
- If recovering to NVFR, then you need to climb to the route LSALT remaining clear of cloud.
- If recovering to IFR, then you can enter the cloud but you must have considered how the cloud base is going to affect the decent minima for the instrument approach you were considering using as a contingency.

Example

For example: Consider a flight in an IFR helicopter with an IFR qualified pilot. The cloud base is overcast at 1600 ft and a visibility of 5 km, so you are good for NVG. However, the LSALT is 3500, the freezing level is 3000, and the MDA on the instrument approach is 1700 ft due to a hill close to the airfield. In the event of inadvertent IMC, a climb to LSALT is not going to be a good thing due to flight into icing conditions and the fact that you may not reach the MDA when on approach, so the NVG flight should not proceed in the first place, unless you can be assured of remaining visual at all times.

- NOTAMS are considered part of the weather brief because Air Services Australia will collate the NOTAM information and print it along with the weather. Although a typical helicopter operation may not usually have too many NOTAMS to be concerned about, the NVG pilot needs to take a closer look, as obstacles such as cranes, firework displays, and a change in the lighting conditions at the destination airport can all affect the low-level helicopter at night.

Five Key Elements Of The Weather

The following five key elements should be noted down as information the crew have available on their kneeboards.

No.	Item	Example on the kneeboard
1	Cloud	4/8 2000 overcast 5500
2	Visibility	10k
3	Freezing level	7500
4	Alternates and Holding	YBSU 30 mins holding
5	Light	86% illumination 30 degrees above the horizon East.

1. Cloud Amount and Base

If there is less than 4/8s (SCT) of cloud below 1500 ft AGL at the departure or destination aerodrome on the TAF then you can go. This can also be looked at the other way around in that if there is more than 4/8s (SCT) of cloud below 1500 ft AGL at the departure or destination aerodrome on the TAF then you cannot go.

If there is less than 4/8s (SCT) of cloud below 2000 ft AGL within a 2 NM radius on either side of your route on the ARFOR and you are in an NVFR helicopter, then you can go. This can also be looked at the other way around in that if there is more than 4/8s (SCT) of cloud below 2000 ft AGL within a 2 NM radius or either side of your route on the ARFOR and you are in an NVFR helicopter, then you cannot go.

If there is less than 4/8s (SCT) of cloud below 1000 ft AGL within a 2 NM radius on either side of your route on the ARFOR and you are in an IFR helicopter, and the PIC holds a command instrument rating, you can go. This can also be looked at the other way around in that if there is more than 4/8s (SCT) of cloud below 1000 ft AGL within a 2 NM radius on either side of your route on the ARFOR and you are in an IFR helicopter, and the PIC holds a command instrument rating then you cannot go.

2. Visibility

- If the visibility is less than 8000 meters (8 km) at the departure or destination aerodrome on the TAF then you cannot go.
- If the visibility is less than 5000 meters (5 km) 2 NM radius either side of your route on the ARFOR then you cannot go.

3. Freezing Level

A helicopter cannot fly when there is known icing conditions. Icing conditions will exist when there is visible moisture in the air and when the temperature drops to zero outside or below. Additionally, it should be remembered that even if the outside air temperature is above zero, as air moves over rotor blades and the surface of the helicopter, a drop in air pressure that will produce lift will also cause a drop in temperature at that surface; therefore ice can form when the outside air temperature is still above zero degrees.

In the planning stages of a flight, the crew have to determine the weather conditions carefully and that if the helicopter inadvertently entered IMC necessitating a climb, would they fly into icing conditions. If icing conditions exist below LSALT, then the flight should not proceed unless the crew is certain they can remain VMC and below the freezing level. If the freezing level is above the LSALT, then the flight can proceed.

The importance of understanding and applying the freezing level in any NVFR, IFR and NVG flight cannot be over-emphasised.

4. Alternates and Holding Fuel

An alternate or holding fuel may be required if:

- the destination weather forecast is indicating that the required minima's will not be met
- there are INTERS, TEMPOS or FROMs
- there is an issue with NAVAIDS and lighting.

The flight may still proceed as long as the crew have made allowances for these "Operational Requirements" and carry additional fuel enabling a flight to the alternate HLS or holding fuel to wait out the event causing the delay.

Often helicopter crews forget to read NOTAMs carefully. A NOTAM could necessitate the operational requirement to plan for an alternate or have additional holding fuel. An example of this is if planning on flying into a busy international airport, because of the large volumes of traffic, there may be a temporary NOTAM telling aircraft to have an additional amount of fuel for holding because of the traffic delays. Although helicopters are not usually affected by this, it may still be a requirement in the planning stages of the flight.

5. Ambient Light

The ambient light needs to be considered. As we know, the darker it gets, the more difficult it is to see. This is also true with NVGs as they require ambient light to work, so any light that is available can improve NVG performance.

Because NVGs were, and still are, primarily used by the military, the ambient light is considered in a tactical sense. At times it would be a disadvantage to go out on a bright moonlit night as you would give away your tactical advantage of not being seen in the dark. From a civil perspective, it does not matter if we are seen; we are merely using the NVGs to enhance our ability to do a job that would normally be done NVFR. When considering ambient light, therefore, we need to first consider the mission and why the NVGs are being used.

If for a tactical use by the military, we would consider the best time to do the sortie, the best route, the best altitude, and speed to give the best advantage of being able to see but not be seen.

If as an aid to civil flying, then we are more concerned with being able to see sufficiently to identify obstacles and hazards so that we can fly from one point to another, land and then depart in the shortest possible time with the best levels of safety.

Ambient light has three main sources:

- Natural light from starlight, the moon and the sun
- Cultural (man-made) light from towns, factories, mills, roads and the helicopter itself and
- Reflected light from water sources such as lakes and rivers and alow cloud base

With regards to the three sources of light above, in the planning stages of the flight, it is important to consider:

- The time the sun rises and sets and how this relates to the time your NVG sortie is scheduled and in what direction. If tracking towards a setting or rising sun, the NVGs may receive too much light and make the terrain difficult to see, so a route may be chosen that has the sun beside or behind the helicopter.
- The moon's illumination, what time it rises and sets, what phase it is in and how much illumination it will be providing. Like the sun, a low bright moon is not desirable to be flying directly into. In general, the illumination is considered low if less than 23%, preferred at 23-80% and optimum at 40-60%. Consider the moon's illumination along your route, how high will you be flying, where will it place the shadows if flying low in the mountains. When selecting a route, it is best to have the moon behind the helicopter. If that is not possible, then the next best is with the moon on either the left or right. The worst place is for the moon directly in front.
- If there is no moon, then you will be relying on starlight illumination which in turn can be greatly affected by cloud cover.
- Cultural light can be both a benefit and a hindrance. Excessive cultural lighting can actually provide too much light and particularly too much IR light that can cause blooming of the NVGs. Major cities, large factories, sports grounds, prisons all provide excessive light where it may actually be better to de-goggle and fly unaided. Smaller towns, major roads, and smaller factories provide good navigation waypoints. Cultural lighting can also hide obstacles, as shown in the image below. On the left is the NVG image, where it is very difficult to see the high rise building the helicopter is about to fly over. On the right is the unaided image. In this case, it is actually better to be flying unaided.

Night Vision Goggles *for Helicopter Pilots*

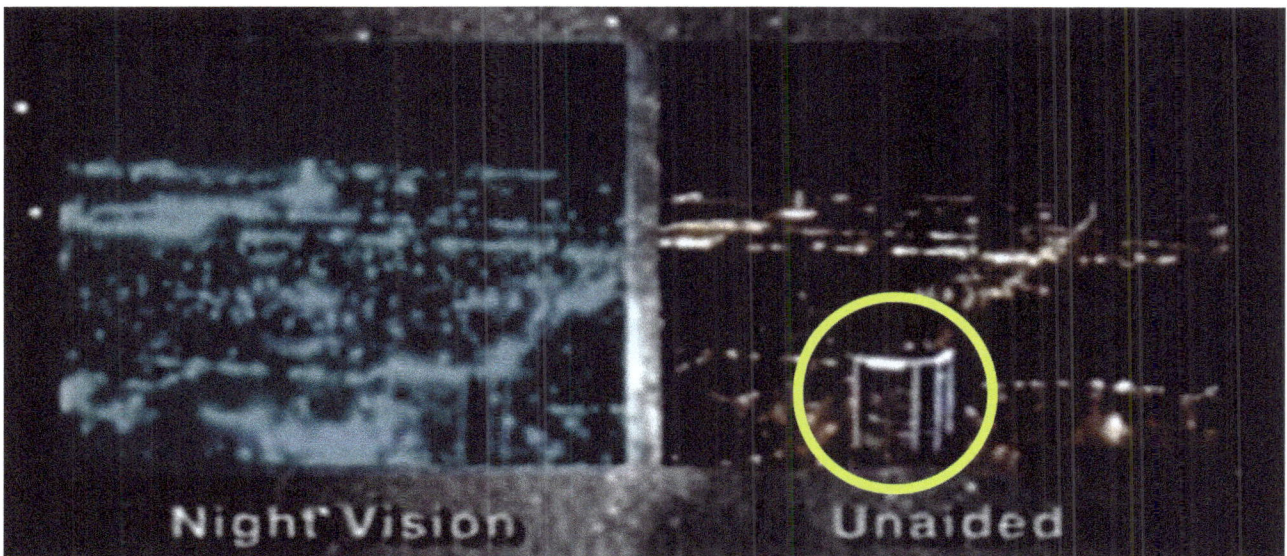

- Reflected light can be by either natural or cultural sources. If there is a thick cloud cover, then if it is low (below 5000 ft AGL), it will reflect any cultural lighting helping the NVG performance; it can make an otherwise dark night quite bright. If it is high (above 5000 ft AGL), then there is less reflected light and, obviously, no starlight, so you can be assured of a very dark night.
- Any water source, whether that be a lake, river, pond, swimming pool, reservoir, etc., are excellent reflective light sources and make for good navigation waypoints. Remember, they need to reflect light, so they will be of no use on a dark night.
- The weather, including haze, mist, fog, cloud and humidity, as well as atmospheric obscurants, such as dust, smoke, salt, etc., can affect ambient light and needs to be considered.

A good trick to use in the planning stages of a flight is to place a torch on your map where you think the major light source (the moon) is going to be in relation to your route. This will help you gain an understanding of where the light is going to be and where your shadows are going to be.

7. Flight Planning: Checklist Explained

Flight Log

Once you have collected all the relevant information, it needs to form part of a flight plan.

Mud Map

Where applicable, transpose this information onto a mud map in the same way as for an NVFR flight. This just makes the information easier to retrieve and use.

Flight Plan With Air Traffic Services (ATS).

Submit a flight plan to Air Services. It is Company policy at Becker Helicopter Services to do this. A SARTIME can either be submitted to Air Services at the same time, or a Company SARTIME can be held. The choice for this is with the crew dependent on who can support them back at base (or not) while the NVG flight is conducted.

Crew Briefing and Co-Ordination

All the applicable crew members, both flying and non-flying, are then to go over the flight and brief each other so that they all have the same mental model and expectations with regards to:

- Roles and responsibilities, both normal and in the event of an emergency
- The goal for the NVG flight and the expected outcomes
- Each crewmember is to participate in identifying, discussing and resolving any expected risks or threats applicable to the flight
- IMC recovery plan is determined, documented and planned for
- RIFTO drills and crew co-ordination is discussed

All crew shall become familiar with their own and other crew members' personal items such as torches, finger lights, lip lights, portable GPS, ELTs, mobile phones, iPads, etc. This personal equipment is your responsibility, so ensure that the batteries are fresh and the equipment is working.

Additionally, if you are using equipment that is not part of the aircraft, it must have been approved by the Chief Pilot or his delegate as equipment that is allowed to be used during NVG operations as it has the potential to conflict with the NVG technology. The Operator will keep a registered list of approved NVG supplemental equipment as an addition to the operations manual.

If a new piece of equipment is to be introduced to the cockpit, then it first needs to be trialled and accepted by the Chief Pilot or Senior NVG pilot before use on an operational sortie.

Risks and Threats Discussed

In general, the crew shall attempt to identify any risks and threats that may be relevant to the flight. These could be threats and hazards external to the helicopter, or they could be internal.

External threats could relate to the operating environment, such as terrain and obstacles, the weather, or other items that the crew think could adversely affect the flight.

Internal threats could come from helicopter equipment or the crew themselves.

Because pilots may train at different organisations, it is important that prior to the flight, all crew have agreed on the standard words and phrases used in the cockpit to affect the different procedures. These have all been covered in the Crew Resource Management and Phraseology chapter and include a good knowledge the following.

- The use of standard phraseology
- Crew scanning responsibilities
- The goggle up and de-goggle procedure
- The use of light
- Goggle failure drill
- Inadvertent IMC drill
- The transition from NVG to NVFR flight
- The transition from NVG to IFR flight
- The transition from NVFR flight to NVG flight
- The transition from IFR flight to NVG flight
- The actions and words used when encountering low contrast situations
- Managing the searchlight
- Managing entering and departing an HLS, including the RIFTO drills

IIMC Recovery Plan

The IIMC Recovery Plan will be an agreed course of action the crew will take in the event of an IIMC event.

It will include the determination of an LSALT, a recovery procedure which may be to a designated aerodrome or HLS; it may involve the change of category to NVFR with a visual recovery and approach or IFR with an instrument approach. It shall be decided which member of the crew is going to conduct the flying and who is going to do the administration (radio calls, reading the instrument approach plate, etc), and a discussion on when and how to de-goggle, etc.

NVG Sortie Crew Plan

Based on all this information and all the discussion between the crew, an NVG Sortie Crew Plan will become evident. Remember, the goal is to have all crew members singing to the same song sheet with the same "*Mental model*".

8. Post Flight: Checklist Explained

Post-flight actions that all crew are responsible for include:

1. Cancellation of the SARTIME. If this is held with ATS, then either a radio call in the circuit or a phone call on the ground is required.

2. Once landed, the helicopter is secured and put away for the night, documentation completed, refuelling completed.
3. NVG equipment is to be individually packed away, logbooks completed, and the NVGs locked in a secure cabinet.
4. The crew shall then have a debrief as part of the consolidation and improvement process for NVG operations.

Mike Becker

NVG Map Hints and Tips

Maps

There are various differing scales, colours, types of information and sizes of maps. In general, you need to look at all the maps and take what information you need from each. Which map you choose to use will depend on the mission and the route.

> **Example**
>
> *For example*: Consider departing an aerodrome for a 30-minute flight to a work area to commence some NVG HLS practice. You may select a VTC to get there and then a 1:100,000 map to mark out wires within your area of operations. The use of modern aids such as Google Earth and an iPad may also be considered.

Maps can be difficult to see under cockpit, lip or torch lighting. Colours may not stand out, and contour lines may be difficult to see. Below is an example of how a VTC may appear if viewed using green lighting on the left compared to white lighting as seen on the right.

Green lighting   White lighting

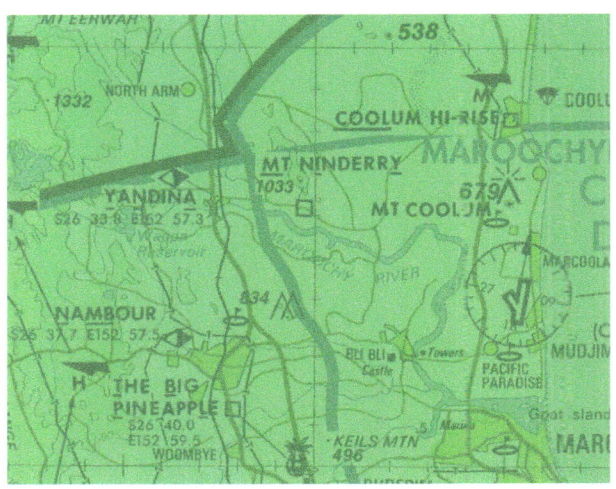 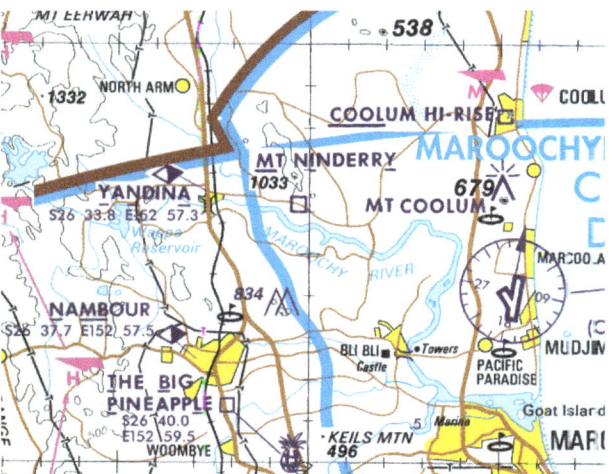

Always mark the map with pencil. The use of pens or markers is not recommended as they can be affected if the map gets wet or is smeared by fingerprints.

Map Marking

Let's look at a simple 1:100,000 map and start building information on it that can be used for an NVG flight. Below is an unmarked map as seen during the day.

The added pencil marks highlight the obvious contours that may affect your flight (below).

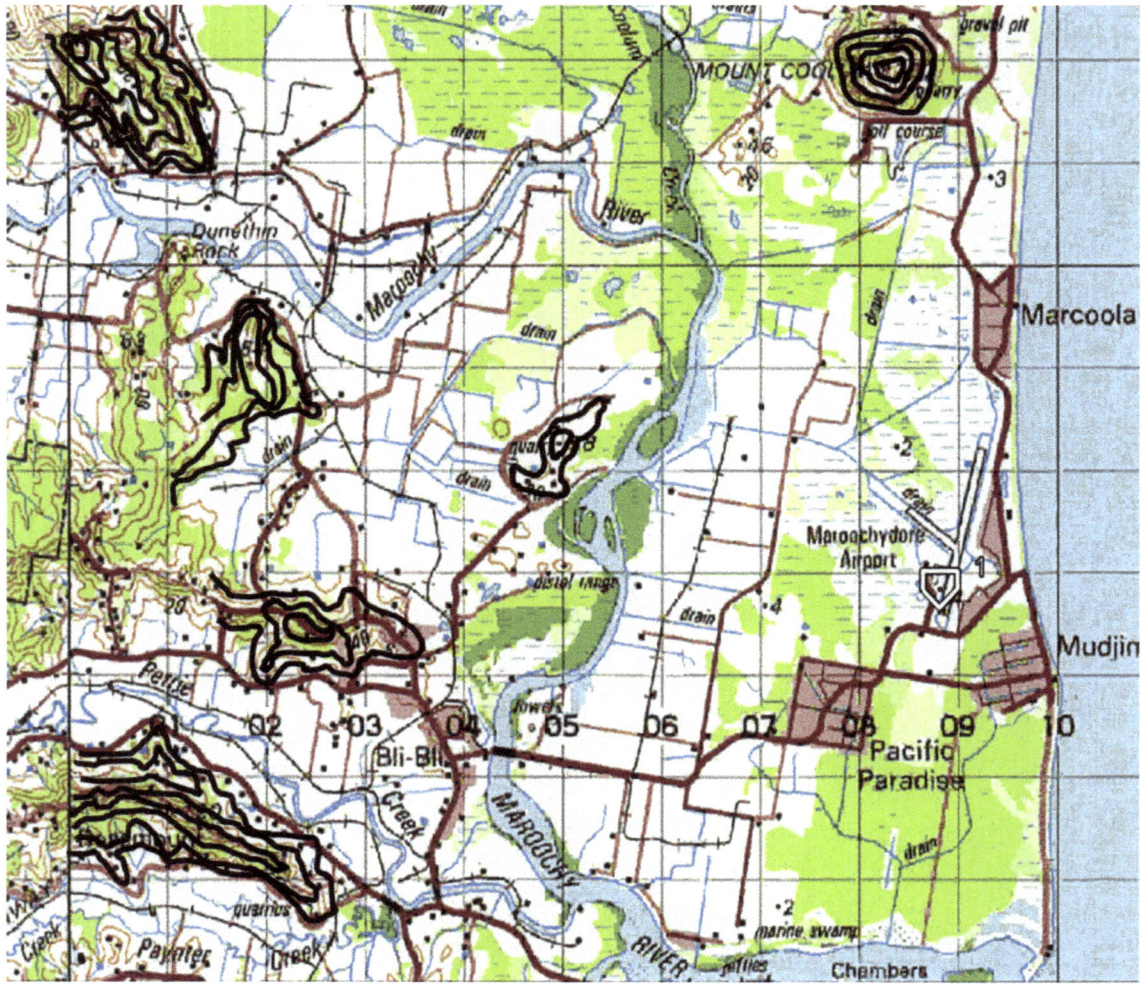

Next add in the known wires that may affect your flight and consider any "avoid" areas due to population, industry, restricted areas and noise abatement.

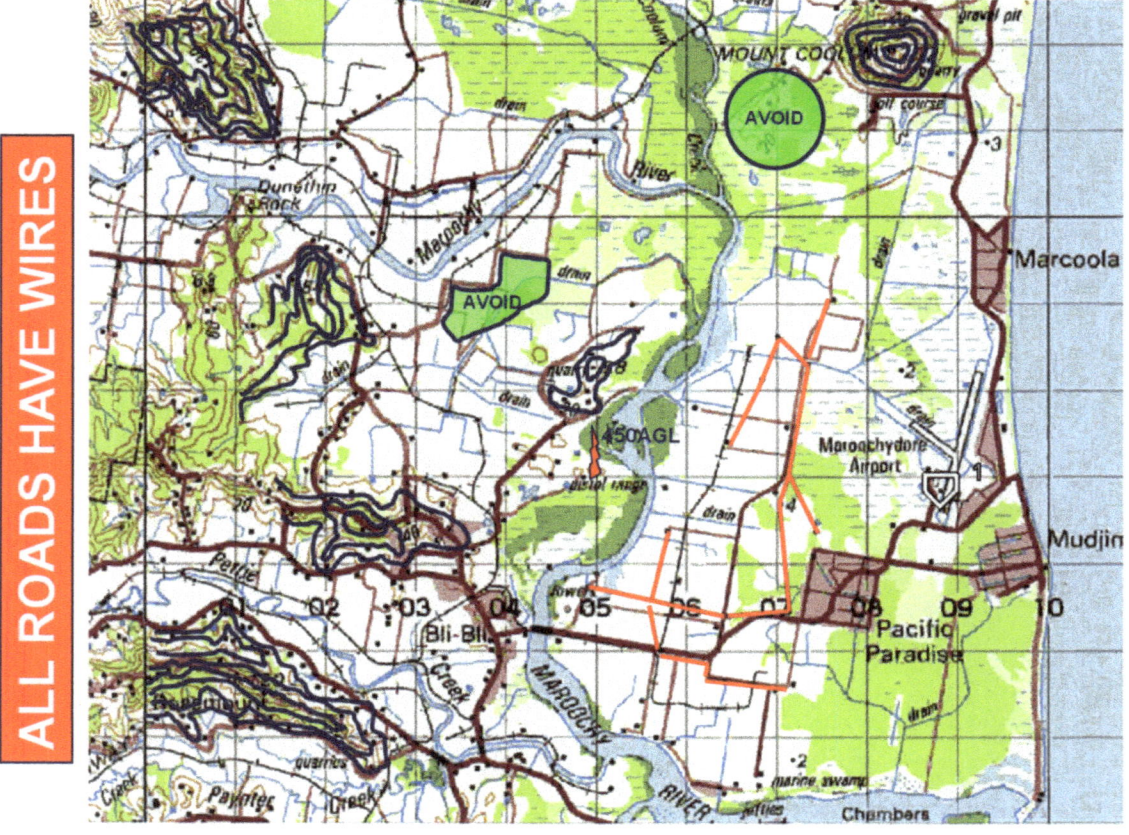

Night Vision Goggles *for Helicopter Pilots*

Add the route and rocket boxes

Compile all this onto a flight plan form.

Creating A Mud Map

A mud map is a simple way of putting relevant information onto a single sheet of paper. It can take all the key elements from the actual map and de-clutter it into a simple and easy to read the outline of the route.

Below is an example of a mud map:

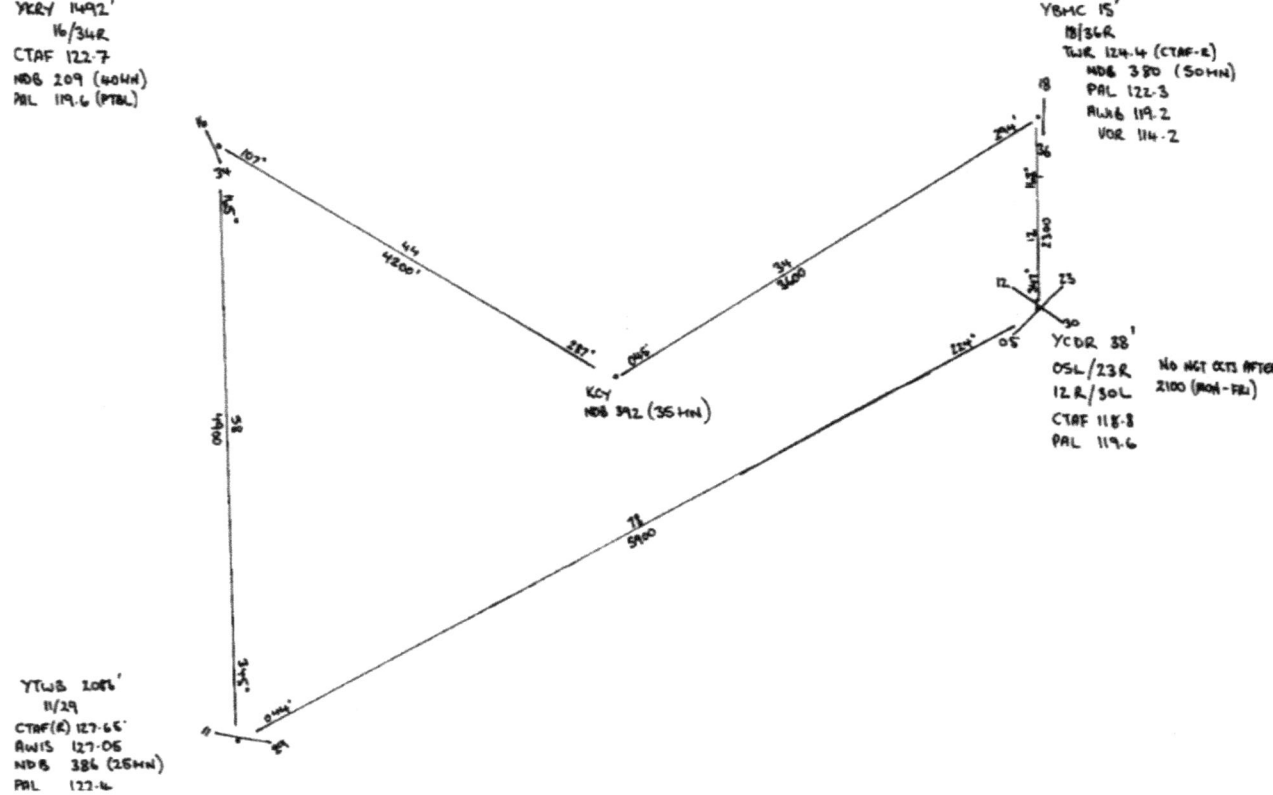

Abbreviations

AC	Advisory Circular
ADF	Australian Defence Force
ADF	Automatic Direction Finder
AFRU	Aerodrome Frequency Response Unit (also known as a 'beepback' unit)
AGL	Above Ground Level
AIP	Aeronautical Information Publication
AIP ENR	Aeronautical Information Publication enroute section
AIP ERSA	AIP En-route Supplement Australia
ALA/HLS	Aircraft Landing Area/Helicopter Landing Site
ALARP	As Low as Reasonably Practical
ALT	Altitude
ANVIS	Aviator Night Vision Imaging Systems
AO	Air Operator
AOC	Air Operator's Certificate
AOCM	Air Operator Certification Manual
AOPA	Aircraft Owners and Pilots Association
ARN	Aviation Reference Number
AS	Australian Standard
ASEPTA	Approved Single-Engine Power Turbine Aeroplane
ASI	Air Speed Indicator
ATC	Air Traffic Control
ATO	Authorised Testing Officer
ATS	Air Traffic Services
AWK	Aerial Work (Air work – general aviation)
BCN	Beacon (aeronautical ground light)
BKN	Broken
C/A	Course Acquisition

CAA	Civil Aviation Authority (of the UK)
CAAP	Civil Aviation Advisory Publication
CAO	Civil Aviation Order
CAP	Civil Aviation Advisory Publication (UK)
CAR	Civil Aviation Regulations 1988
CASA	Civil Aviation Safety Authority
CASR	Civil Aviation Safety Regulations 1998
CB	Cumulonimbus (meteorological)
CDI	Course Direction Indicator
CFI	Chief Flying Instructor
CFIT	Controlled Flight into Terrain
CG	Centre of Gravity
CHTR	Charter
COM	Communications
CONOPs	Concept of Operations
CP	Chief Pilot
CRM	Crew Resource Management
CTA	Control Area
CTR	Control Zone
DME	Distance Measuring Equipment
DOD	Department of Defence
DOT	Department of Transportation
DR	Dead Reckoning
EFIS	Electronic Flight Instrumentation Systems
EMS	Emergency Medical Service
ERC	En-route Chart
ERSA	En-route Supplement Australia
ETA	Estimated Time of Arrival
ETI	Estimated Time Interval

FAA	Federal Aviation Administration (of the USA)
FAAAC	Foreign Aircraft Air Operator's Certificate
FDS	Flight Director System
FLIR	Forward Looking Infrared
FOI	Flying Operations Inspector
FOM	Figure of Merit
FOR	Field of Regard
FOV	Field of View
FRMS	Fatigue Risk Management Systems
ft	foot/feet
G	Gravity
G/S	Groundspeed
GAAP	General Aviation Aerodrome Procedures
GDOP	Geometric Dilution of Precision
GEN	General
GNSS	Global Navigation Satellite System
GPS	Global Positioning System
GPSN	Global Positioning System Navigation
HDG	Heading
HF	High Frequency
HLS	Helicopter Landing Site
HUD	Heads Up Display
ICAO	International Civil Aviation Organisation
ICAO PANS	ICAO Procedures for Air Navigation Services
ICUS	In Command Under Supervision
IF	Instrument Flight
IFR	Instrument Flight Rules
IMC	Instrument Meteorological Conditions (other than VMC)
INTER	Intermittent/Intermittently (meteorological)

IR	Infrared
IRM	Immediately Reportable Matters
JAA	Joint Aviation Authorities (of the UK)
JAR-OPS	Joint Aviation Requirements Operations (of the UK)
LIF	Light Intensity Filter (LIF)
LL	Lower Limit
LSALT	Lowest Safe Altitude
M.02	Mach.02
MCC	Multi-crew Coordination
MCP	Microchannel plate
METAR	Aviation Routine Weather Report (in Aeronautical Meteorological Code)
MIL-STD	Military Standard
MOPS	Minimum Operational Performance Standard
MTOW	Maximum Take-off Weight
MTTF	Mean Time To Failure
NAIPS	National Aeronautical Information Processing
NAS	National Airspace System
NAV	Navigation
NDB	Non-directional Beacon
NM	Nautical Miles
NOTAM	Notice to Airmen
NPA	Non-precision Approach
NTSB	National Transport Safety Board (of the US)
NVD	Night Vision Device
NVED	Night Vision Enhancement Devices
NVFR	Night Visual Flight Rules
NVG	Night Vision Goggle (refers to a singular monocular goggle)
NVGs	Night Vision Goggles (refers to a set of binocular goggles)
NVG CCF	NVG Capability Check Flight

NVIS	Night Vision Imaging Systems
NZS	New Zealand Standard
OBS	Omni Bearing Selector
OEM	Original Equipment Manufacturer
PAL	Pilot Activated Lighting
PAPI	Precision Approach Path Indicator
PC	Personal Computer
PCATD	PC-based Aviation Training Device
PDOP	Positional Dilution of Precision
PIC	Pilot-in-command
PICUS	Pilot-in-command Under Supervision
POH	Pilot Operating Handbook
PRD	Prohibited, Restricted, and Danger areas
PVT	Private
R/T	Radio Telephone
RAIM	Receiver Autonomous Integrity Monitoring
RIFTO	Restricted Instrument Flight Take-off
RPM	Revolutions per minute
RPT	Regular Public Transport
RRM	Routine Reportable Matters
RTB	Return to Base
RTCA	Radio Technical Commission for Aeronautics
SA	Situation Awareness
SAR	Search and Rescue
SARTIME	Time search action required
SARWATCH	Search and Rescue Watch
SC	Special Committee
SCT	Scattered (meteorological)
SOP	Standard Operating Procedure

TAF	Aerodrome Forecast
TCO	Training and Checking Organisation
TEM	Threat and Error Management
TEM	(Illustrated) Tool and Equipment Manual
TEMPO	Temporary/temporarily (meteorological)
TFR	Temporary Flight Restrictions
TMG	Track Made Good
TS	Thunderstorm (followed by RA = rain; SM = snow; PE = ice pellets; GR = hail; GS = small hail and/or snow pellets or combinations thereof, e.g. TSRASN = thunderstorm with rain and snow)
TSO	Technical Standard Order
UFIT	Uncontrolled Flight into Terrain
UK	United Kingdom
USA	United States of America
VA	Visual Acuity
VFR	Visual Flight Rules
VHF	Very High Frequency (30 – 300 MHz)
VHF COM	VHF Communications
VMC	Visual Meteorological Conditions
VOR	VHF Omni Range
VSI	Vertical Speed Indicator
W/V	Wind Velocity
WAC	World Aeronautical Charts
WGS84	World Geodetic Standard 1984
WPT	Waypoint

Glossary

Absorptance	The ratio of the radiant energy absorbed by a body to that incident upon it.
Adverse Event	Means any event or incident in which life, health or property is: - lost or damaged in, on, or by a helicopter in which NVG are used; or - at significant risk of loss or damage in, on or by a helicopter. Note: The following are some examples of significant risks: a near miss; NVG equipment failure, malfunction or abnormal operation; the failure, malfunction or abnormal operation of NVG-related or affected equipment; unintentional I.M.C. penetration; inadvertent loss of visibility; abnormal degree or accelerated onset of fatigue.

Aerial Firefighting	Means an operation, in an operational area for a fire, to fight the fire from the air using:
	
	- a flight crew of at least 1 pilot and 1 aircrew member; and
	- either:
	  - incendiaries for controlled burning dropped from the helicopter by a person specifically carried for that purpose, provided that the operation is supported by an operational safety case approved in writing by CASA; or
	
	Note: If acceptable to CASA, an operational safety case may be in the form of, or include, relevant additions or supplements to the operator's operations manual for the aerial firefighting.
	
	  - a helicopter equipped with a belly tank that is filled and refilled with water, fire retardant or similar substance taken from:
	    - a source on the ground while the helicopter is on the ground; or
	    - a portable tank at a standard HLS with ground lighting while the helicopter is in the hover using the helicopter's on-board pump; or
	
	Note: For standard HLS, see CAAP 92-2. This is not a HLS-NVG standard.

Aerial Firefighting Support	Means an operation for: - the tactical insertion or extraction of firefighting crews in an operational area for a fire; or - the carriage of persons to map, locate or observe fires, or to control or direct firefighting operations. Note: In CAO 82.6 aerial firefighting support does not include aerial firefighting in the form of, for example, water bombing.
Aeroplane/aircraft/helicopter is balanced	The skid ball in the balance indicator is less than a quarter of the ball diameter from the centre.

Aided flight	Means a flight in which NVG are used in an operational position by trained personnel to enhance night vision. Note: Aided flight is associated with the procedure of goggle-up where the crew member places NVG in the operational position.
Aircraft is trimmed/Trims aircraft	The aircraft is trimmed within 10 seconds of achieving stabilised and balanced flight, after an attitude, power or configuration change, so that no control input is required from the pilot to maintain this state.
Aircrew member	A crew member of a helicopter (other than a supernumerary crew member) assigned by the operator: ■ to assist the pilot in the operation of the helicopter; ■ to operate the winch on the helicopter; or ■ to supervise rappelling or sling-load operations; or ■ to supervise or assist a medical, paramedical or rescue crewmember in the performance of his or her duties on the helicopter; or ■ to use the auto-hover system to position/reposition the helicopter via inputs through an auto-hover trim control (crew hover).
Albedo	The ratio of the amount of light reflected from a surface to the amount of incident light.
Approved checklist	A checklist derived from information set out in the Flight Manual/POH, placards or other documents provided with the aircraft, necessary to ensure the safe operation of the aircraft.
Approved NVG flight simulator	Means a flight simulator or synthetic training device approved by CASA for NVG initial qualification training by a trainee who holds an endorsement for the aircraft which is simulated.
Approved operator	Means an operator who has the approval mentioned in subparagraph 1 (c) (iii) of Appendix 1 of CAO 82.6 to use NVG for the trial.
Automatic Brightness Control (ABC)	One of the automatic gain control circuits found in second and third generation NVG devices. It attempts to provide consistent image output brightness by automatic control of the micro channel plate voltage.
Automatic Gain Control (AGC)	Comprised of the automatic brightness control and bright source protection circuits. Is designed to maintain image brightness and protect the user and the image tube from excessive light levels. This is accomplished by controlling the gain of the intensifier tube.

Autogating	Autogating is a feature found in many image intensifier tubes manufactured for military purposes after 2006, though it has been around for some time. Autogating will completely turn the electricity on and off at the photocathode, but it will do this at such a high speed (measured in nanoseconds which is a billionth of a second) that the viewer will not notice. In effect the light is gated or shut off at the entrance to the tube. As the gating occurs at high frequency and by varying the duty cycle to maintain a constant current draw from the microchannel plate, it is possible to operate the tube during brighter conditions, such as daylight, without damaging the tube or leading to premature failure. Autogating of image intensifiers is militarily valuable as it allowed extended operational hours giving enhanced vision during twilight hours while providing better support for soldiers who encounter rapidly changing lighting conditions, such as those assaulting a building.
Baro-aiding	When the GNSS receiver uses barometric data to calculate RAIM.
Blackbody	An ideal body of surface that completely absorbs all radiant energy falling upon with no reflection.
Blooming	Common term used to denote the "washing out" of all or part of the NVG image due to de-gaining of the image intensifier tube when a bright light source is in or near the NVG field of view.
Bright Source Protection (BSP)	Protective feature associated with second and third generation NVG that protects the intensifier tube and the user by controlling the voltage at the photo cathode.
Brownout	Condition created by blowing sand, dust, etc., which can cause the pilots to lose sight of the ground. This is most commonly associated with landings in the desert or in dusty locations.
CAR 1988	Means the Civil Aviation Regulations 1988 (Australia).
Civil Nautical Twilight	The time when the true altitude of the centre of the sun is six degrees below the horizon. Illuminance level is approximately 3.40 lux and is above the usable level for NVG operations.
Class	Is a terminology used to describe the filter present on the NVG objective lens. The filter restricts the transmission of light below a determined frequency. This allows the cockpit lighting to be designed and installed in a manner that does not adversely affect NVG performance.
Class A	NVG that incorporate a filter, which generally imposes a 625 nanometre cut-off. Thus, the use of colours in the cockpit (e.g., colour displays, colour warning lights, etc.) may be limited. The blue-green region of the light spectrum is allowed through the filter. Often referred to as 'minus blue'.
Class B	NVG that incorporate a filter that generally imposes a 665 nanometre cut-off. Thus, the cockpit lighting design may incorporate more colours since the filter eliminates some yellows and oranges from entering the intensification process.

Closure rate	The apparent speed at which a helicopter or gyroplane moves towards a specified point or object.
Controlled corrective action	Timely and coordinated use of controls, without abrupt manoeuvring, is made to achieve specified performance.
De-goggle	Means the action of transferring from NVG flight to non-NVG (unaided) flight by removing the NVG from a usable position. Note: The expression is also used as a command and is opposite to goggle-up.
Devoid of surrounding cultural lighting	Means that at 500 ft above the terrain, and any object on it, in an area there is insufficient ground lighting to maintain an unaided visible horizon.
Diopter	A measure of the refractive (light bending) power of a lens.
Electroluminescent (EL)	Referring to light emission that occurs from application of an alternating current to a layer of phosphor.
Electro-Optics (EO)	The term used to describe the interaction between optics and electronics, leading to transformation of electrical energy into light or vice versa.
Emergency Medical Services	An operation where transportation is required to facilitate emergency or medical assistance by an aircraft carrying one or more of the following: - medical personnel; - medical supplies (including equipment, blood, organs or drugs); and - ill or injured persons, and other persons directly involved in, or associated with, their retrieval or care.
Evacuated	To empty or remove the contents of. To create a vacuum in.
Fatigue	The dynamic balance between competing forces; forces producing fatigue and forces reversing the effects of fatigue (recovery). There are a number of different definitions of fatigue, including: - 'Weariness from bodily or mental exertion' (Macquarie Essential Dictionary; 1999:282); - 'The consequences of inadequate restorative sleep' (Centre for Sleep Research); and - 'The increasing difficulty to perform physical or mental activities' (Baker, Fletcher and Dawson; 1999:8).
Figure of Merit (FOM)	FOM is an abstract measure of image tube performance, derived from the number of line pairs per millimeter multiplied by the tube's signal-to-noise ratio. Tubes manufactured in the USA with a FOM greater than 1600 are not exportable outside the USA.
Foot-Candle	A measure of illuminance; specifically, the illuminance of a surface upon which one lumen is falling per square foot.
Foot-Lambert	A measure of luminance; specifically the luminance of a surface that is receiving an illuminance of one foot-candle.

Full panel	Flight instrument array of at least an artificial horizon (AH), stabilised heading indicator, vertical speed indicator, altimeter, turn and balance indicator/turn coordinator and engine power indication.
Gain	When referring to an image intensification tube, the ratio of the brightness of the output in units of foot-lambert, compared to the illumination of the input in foot-candles. A typical value for a GEN III tube is 25,000 to 30,000 Fl/fc. A "tube gain" of 30,000 Fl/fc provides an approximate "system gain" of 3,000. This means that the intensified NVG image is 3,000 times brighter to the aided eye than that of the unaided eye.
Gating	Gating is a means by which an image intensifier tube may be switched on and off, like an electronic gate. See autogating.
Generation	Refers to the technological design of an image intensifier. Systems incorporating these light-amplifying image intensifiers were first used during World War II and were operationally fielded by the US military during the Vietnam era. These systems were large, heavy and poorly performing devices that were unsuitable for aviation use, and were termed Generation I (Gen I). Generation II devices represented a significant technological advancement and provided a system that could be headmounted for use in ground vehicles.

Generation III devices represented another significant technological advancement in image intensification, and provided a system that was designed for aviation use.

Although not yet fielded, there are prototype NVG that include technological advances that may necessitate a Generation IV designation if placed into production.

Because of the variations in interpretations as to generation, NVG will not be referred to by the generation designation. |
| **Goggle-up** | The action of transferring to NVG flight by placing the NVG in a position where it may be used by the crew.

Note: The expression is also used as a command and is opposite to de-goggle. |
| **HLS operations** | For a helicopter means:

- take-off or landing at a Helicopter Landing Site (HLS); or
- operations at a HLS that do not involve a landing on skids or wheels; or
- HLS similar operations:
    - that are approach to the hover, winching, sling load operations, rappelling, hovering, deplaning, emplaning or similar types of operations; and
    - for the conduct of which each relevant crewmember is qualified. |
| **HLS-NVG basic** | Means a Helicopter Landing Site (HLS) that:

- does not conform to the guidelines contained in CAAP 92-2 (1) for standard HLS night operations; and
- is unlit or unprepared. |

HLS-NVG standard	Means a Helicopter Landing Site (HLS) that: - conforms to the guidelines contained in CAAP 92- 2 (1) for NVG standard HLS night operations; - is unlit; and - does not require a windsock.
Human factors	Human Factors aims to optimise the relationships within systems between people, activities, and equipment.
Illuminance	Also referred to as illumination. The amount, ratio or density of light that strikes a surface at any given point.
Image Intensifier	An electro-optic device used to detect and intensify optical images in the visible and near infrared region of the electromagnetic spectrum for the purpose of providing visible images. The component that actually performs the intensification process in a NVG. This component is composed of the photo cathode, MCP, screen optic, and power supply. It does not include the objective and eyepiece lenses.
Incandescent	Refers to a source that emits light based on thermal excitation, i.e., heating by an electrical current, resulting in a very broad spectrum of energy that is dependent primarily on the temperature of the filament.
Infrared	That portion of the electromagnetic spectrum in which wavelengths range from 0.7 microns to 1 millimetre. This segment is further divided into near infrared (0.7-3.0 microns), mid infrared (3.0-6.0 microns), far infrared (6.0-15 microns), and extreme infrared (15 microns-1 millimetre). A NVG is sensitive to near infrared wavelengths approaching 0.9 microns.
Irradiance	The radiant flux density incident on a surface. For the purpose of this document the terms irradiance and illuminance shall be interchangeable.
Law enforcement	for an operation, means an operation for the enforcement of the laws applying in Australian territory, including, customs, waterways or border protection laws.
Limited panel	Flight instrument array of at least a magnetic compass, air speed indicator, vertical speed indicator, altimeter, turn and balance indicator/turn coordinator and an engine power indication.

Limiting Resolution	Tube resolution is measured in line pairs per millimetre or lp/mm and is a measure of how many lines of varying intensity (light to dark) can be resolved within a millimetre of screen area. Limiting Resolution is a measure of the modulation transfer function and is typically defined as the point at which the modulation transfer function becomes 3% or less. The higher the value, the higher the resolution of the tube. Note: this is based on the physical screen size in millimetres and is not proportional to the screen size. As such, an 18 mm tube with a resolution of around 64 lp/mm has a higher overall resolution than an 8 mm tube with 72 lp/mm resolution. Resolution is usually measured at the centre and at the edge of the screen, and tubes often come with figures for both. Military Specification or '*milspec*' tubes only come with a criterion such as "> 64 lp/mm" or "Greater than 64 line pairs/millimetre".
Line up checks	Line up checks are performed before take-off when lined up in the runway or take-off direction. The checks should include: ■ Compass checked and aligned with take-off direction; ■ Engine instruments indicating engine within operating limits.
Look under/under view	Is the ability of operators to look under or around the NVG to view inside and outside the aircraft.
LSALT, or lowest safe altitude	Means not less than 1 000 feet above the highest obstacle located within 10 miles of the helicopter in flight, except when take-off or landing is necessary.
Lumen	A measurement of luminous flux equal to the light emitted in a unit solid angle by a uniform point source of one candle intensity.
Luminance	The luminous intensity (reflected light) of a surface in a given direction per unit of projected area. This is the energy used by NVGs.
Lux	A unit measurement of illumination. The illuminance produced on a surface that is one metre square, from a uniform point source of one candle intensity, or one lumen per square meter.
Marine pilot transfer	Means an operation, in accordance with Civil Aviation Order 95.7.3, to transfer a marine pilot from: ■ land to ship; ■ ship to land; or ■ ship to ship.
Mean Time To Failure (MTTF)	A value, expressed in operational hours, for how long a tube typically should last. Typical examples of tube life are: ■ First Generation: 1000 hrs ■ Second Generation: 2000 to 2500 hrs ■ Third Generation: 10000 to 15000 hrs. Many recent high-end second-generation tubes now have MTTFs approaching 15,000 operational hours.

Mesopic Vision	Mesopic vision is experienced at dawn, dusk, and during full moonlight. Vision is achieved by a combination of the rods and the cones, however, as available light decreases the cones become less effective decreasing the ability to discern colour and sharp image interpretation.
Microchannel Plate	A wafer containing between 3 and 6 million specially treated microscopic glass tubes designed to multiply electrons passing from the photo cathode to the phosphor screen in second and third generation intensifier tubes.
Micron	A unit of measure commonly used to express wavelength in the infrared region; equal to one millionth of a meter.
Minimum NVG crew	The minimum number of NVG aided and NVG qualified crew members required for a particular flight or operation. Note: CASA approval is not required for a person to use NVG for observation or surveillance only - the primary means of terrain avoidance for safe air navigation using visual surface reference external to the aircraft. However, a person engaged in such unapproved use is not part of the minimum NVG crew.
Modified Class B	NVG incorporates a variation of a Class B filter and also incorporates a notch filter in the green spectrum that allows a small percentage of light into the image intensification process. Therefore, a Modified Class B NVG allows operators to view a fixed heads up display (HUD) symbology through the NVG without the HUD energy adversely affecting NVG performance.
Modulation Transfer Function (MTF)	Found on the image intensifier, it is a measure of the output amplitude of dark and light lines on the display for a given level of input from lines presented to the photocathode at different resolutions. It is usually given as a percentage at a given frequency (spacing) of light and dark lines.
Nanometer (nm)	A unit of measure commonly used to express wavelength in the visible and near infrared region; equal to one billionth of a meter.
Night	The time between the end of evening civil twilight and the beginning of morning civil twilight as published in the American Air Almanac.
Night Vision Device (NVD)	General Definition: An electro-optical device used to provide a visible image using the electromagnetic energy available at night. For example, a night scope on a rifle is a non aviation example of a NVD. Aviation Definition: In aviation, a NVD means night vision enhancement equipment fitted to, or mounted in or on, an aircraft, or worn by a person in the aircraft, and that can: - detect and amplify light in both the visual and near infra-red bands of the electromagnetic spectrum; or - provide an artificial image representing topographical displays.

Night Vision Goggle (NVG)	Aviation Definition:
	When referring to NVGs used for aviation purposes; a headmounted, lightweight, self-contained binocular system consisting of two independent monocular intensifier tube assemblies.
	NVGs are a type of Night Vision Device.
	Note: NVGs can also be used for other purposes, for example, NVGs can be worn by soldiers. However, these are not mounted to a helmet.
NVG aircrew member	A person who:
	■ has successfully completed NVG aircrew member training and is qualified in accordance with CAO 82.6; or
	■ is an NVG aircrew member instructor; or
	■ is an NVG pilot, an NVG flight instructor, an NVG FOI or an NVG testing officer who has complied with the aircrew member training and competency requirements of Appendix 3 of CAC 82.6.
NVG aircrew member instructor	A person qualified in accordance with CAO 82.6 to instruct air crewmembers.
NVG CCF, or NVG capability check flight	Means:
	■ if carried out by a training or checking organisation (TCO) - an NVG proficiency check flight to test aeronautical skills and knowledge for use of NVG, carried out in accordance with:
	■ the requirements of CAO 82.6 for an NVG capability check flight (CCF);
	■ the operator training and checking manual;
	■ otherwise — an NVG base check flight to test aeronautical skills and knowledge for use of NVG, carried out in accordance with: and
	■ the requirements of CAO 82.6 for an NVG CCF; and
	■ Part C of the operator operations manual.
NVG compatible lighting	Aircraft interior or exterior lighting with spectral wavelength, colour, luminance level and uniformity, that has been modified, or designed for use with NVG, and does not degrade or interfere with the image intensification capability performance of the NVG beyond acceptable standards.
NVG flight instructor	A NVG pilot who is a flight instructor qualified in accordance with this order and approved in writing by CASA to conduct NVG training.
NVG flight time	The flight time gained by an NVG aircrew member or pilot, or a person receiving NVG flight training, or during an NVG operation.
	Note: NVG flight time must be logged in the specialist column of the aircrew flying logbook.
NVG FOI	A CASA flying operations inspector appointed to carry out some, or all, of the duties of an NVG FOI or an NVG testing officer.
NVG initial training	Training to qualify a person for an NVG pilot or NVG aircrew member qualification.

NVG operation	A permitted NVG operation under subclause 5.1 of Appendix 1 of CAO 82.6.
NVG operator	An operator approved by CASA under clause 2 of Appendix 1 of CAO 82.6 to conduct NVG operations.
NVG pilot	A person who: ■ has successfully met the requirements of this Order for the issue of an initial NVG endorsement and had his or her log book endorsed accordingly; or ■ is an NVG flight instructor, an NVG training and checking pilot, an NVG FOI or an NVG testing officer.
NVG testing officer	A person appointed in writing by CASA to be an authorised testing officer to: ■ conduct NVG flight tests; and ■ issue endorsements for NVG qualifications based on those flight tests.
NVG training	Training undertaken by a pilot, or aircrew member, for NVG flight in accordance with the relevant training requirements and competency standards mentioned in CAO 82.6.
NVG training and checking pilot	A NVG pilot who is training and checking pilots for a TCO, qualified in accordance with CAO 82.6 and approved in writing by CASA to conduct training and checking.
NVG training provider	Means: ■ a training organisation in Australia approved by CASA to provide NVG initial training for CAO 82.6; or ■ a training organisation outside Australia approved by the relevant national aviation authority, recognised by CASA, to provide NVG initial training. Note: The National Aviation Authorities, recognised by CASA, are listed on page 21 of this CAAP.
NVG trial	The controlled trial of NVG in accordance with an order by NVG operators approved by CASA.
NVIS, or night vision imaging system	The system in which all of the elements required to operate an aircraft effectively and safely using NVG are integrated, including NVG and associated equipment, NVG compatible lighting, other associated aircraft components and equipment, associated training and recency requirements and continuing airworthiness. Note: NVIS is synonymous with aviator night vision imaging systems, sometimes called ANVIS.
OMNIBUS	Refers to a US Army contract vehicle that has been used over the years to procure NVG. Each successive OMNIBUS contract included NVG that demonstrated improved performance. There have been five contracts since the mid 1980s, the most current being OMNIBUS VII. There may be several variations of NVG within a single OMNIBUS purchase, and some NVG from previous OMNIBUS contracts have been upgraded in performance to match the performance of goggles from later contracts.

Operational requirements	The effects that weather forecasts, availability and serviceability of radio navigation aids and aerodrome lighting status have on the determination of fuel, holding and alternate aerodrome requirements.
Photocathode	A cathode that emits electrons when exposed to radiant energy and especially light.
Photon	A quantum (basic unit) of radiant energy (light).
Photopic Vision	Vision produced as a result of the response of the cones in the retina as the eye achieves a light adapted state (commonly referred to as day vision).
Radiance	The flux density of radiant energy reflected from a surface. For the purposes of this manual the terms radiance and luminance shall be interchangeable.
Reflectivity	The fraction of energy reflected from a surface.
Resolution	The capability of NVG to present an image that makes clear and distinguishable the separate components of a scene or object.
Review and Brief	During instrument approaches, to study the instrument approach chart, interpret the instructions and self-brief or brief any crew members/assessors about the conduct of the approach procedure.
RTCA/DO-275	Means the document titled Minimum Operational Performance Standards for Integrated Night Vision Imaging System Equipment, referenced RTCA/DO- 275, dated 12 October 2001, of RTCA Inc., Washington, USA.
Safe/safely	Means that a manoeuvre or flight is completed without injury to personnel, damage to aircraft or breach of aviation safety regulations while meeting the flights standards specified.
Scotopic Vision	That vision produced as a result of the response of the rods in the retina as the eye achieves a dark-adapted state (commonly referred to as night vision).
Search and rescue	An operation by an aircraft to search, locate, rescue, or provide immediate assistance to, a person threatened by a grave and immediate danger or a hostile environment.
Sensitivity	The sensitivity of an image intensifier tube is measured in Micro-Amperes per Lumen (µA/lm). It defines how many electrons are produced per quantity of light that falls on the photocathode. This measurement is made at a specific colour temperature, such as 'at a colour temperature of 2854 K". The colour temperature used tends to vary slightly between manufacturers. Additional measurements at specific wavelengths are usually also specified, especially for Gen II devices, such as at 800 nm and 850 nm (infrared). Typically, the higher the value, the more sensitive the tube is to light.
Situational Awareness (SA)	Degree of perceptual accuracy achieved in the comprehension of all factors affecting an aircraft and crew at a given time.

Starlight	The illuminance provided by the available (observable) stars in a subject hemisphere. The stars provide approximately 0.00022 lux ground illuminance on a clear night. This illuminance is equivalent to about one-quarter of the actual light from the night sky with no moon.
Stereopsis	Visual system binocular cues that are used for distance estimation and depth perception. Three dimensional visual perception of objects. The use of NVGs seriously degrades this aspect of near-depth perception.
TCO or training and checking organisation	A training and checking organisation approved by CASA under subregulation 217 (1) of CAR 1988.
Termination point	The 'termination point' associated with a landing.
Transmittance	The fraction of radiant energy that is transmitted through a layer of absorbing material placed in its path.
Type	Refers to the design of the NVG with regards to the manner in which the image is relayed to the operator. A Type 1 NVG is one in which the image is viewed directly in line with the image intensification process.
A Type 1 NVG is also referred to as 'direct view' goggle.
A Type 2 NVG is one in which the image intensifier is not in-line with the image viewed by the operator. In this design, the image may be reflected several times before being projected onto a combiner in front of the crewmember's eyes. A Type 2 NVG is also referred to as an 'indirect view' goggle.
Ultraviolet	That portion of the electromagnetic spectrum in which wavelengths range between 0.1 and 0.4 microns.
Unaided	Term used to describe those times when NVGs are not being used (i.e., normal night vision is not being aided).
Unaided flight	Means the NVG is in a non-operational position when night vision is not being enhanced by any other means.
Note: Unaided flight is associated with the de-goggle procedure where the crewmember places the NVG in the non-operational position.
Use, in relation to NVG	Means use as the primary means of terrain avoidance for safe air navigation by means of visual surface reference external to the aircraft.
Wavelength	The distance in the line of advance of a wave from any one point to the next point of corresponding phase; is used to express electromagnetic energy including IR and visible light.
Whiteout	A condition similar to brownout but caused by blowing snow.

Bibliography

Boutot, JP, Eschard, G, Polaert, R, and Duchenois, V, A Microchannel Plate with Curved Channels: An Improvement in Gain, Relative Variance, and Ion Noise for Channel Plate Tubes, Laboratiroes d'Electronique et de Physique Appliquee, Paris, in Morgan, BL (ed.), Photo-Electronic Image Devices, e-book, Google Books, viewed 12 July 2013, books.google.com.au/books?id=bG1xAj9w5TgC&pg=PA103

Department of the Army, 1988, Night Flight Techniques and Procedures, Training Circular 1-204, 27 December 1988, Headquarters, Department of the Army, US Army, Washington DC.

Department of the Army, 2007, Fundamentals of Flight, Field Manual FM 3-04.203, 7 May 2007, Headquarters, Department of the Army, US Army, Washington DC.

Department of the Army, 2009, Aeromedical Training for Flight Personnel, Field Manual FM 3-04.301(1-301), 29 September 2009, Headquarters, Department of the Army, US Army, Washington DC.

Grosvenor, C 2010, How Did Colonial People Make Candles, viewed 20 June 2013, candles.lovetoknow.com/How_Did_Colonial_People_Make_Candles

Hoffman Engineering Corp., 1997, *ANV-20/20 and ANV-20/20C NVD Setup Reference for Infinity Focus and Performance Verification*, Stamford.

J.-M. Hasenfratz, J.M., Lapierre, M, Holzschuch, N, and Sillion, F., 2003, A Survey of Real-time Soft Shadows Algorithms, online article, viewed 21 November 2011, artis.imag.fr/Publications/2003/HLHS03/

Photonis.com, viewed 20 June 2013, www.photonis.com/en/nightvision/75-xr5.html

Point Trading, 2009, *Aviation Night Vision Imaging System NL-94-AU Operations Manual*, Point Trading, Melbourne.

The Engineering Toolbox, online table, viewed 30 July 2013, www.engineeringtoolbox.com/light-level-rooms-d_708.html

Turpin, T, 2001, Night Vision Goggles (NVGs) and NVG Equipment with Market Potential, FAA, pg 35.

United States Army Aviation Warfighting Center, 2008, Initial Entry Rotary Wing Aviator, TH-67, Primary Phase (Objective), April 2008, United States Army Aviation Warfighting Center, Fort Rucker.

Williams. B. 1999, Footcandles and Lux for Architectural Lighting, Ed. 2.1, online article, viewed 11 November 2011, www.mts.net/~william5/library/illum.htm#7

Index

A

absorption - atmospheric ... 136
acceptable defects ... 73
active infrared ... 99
adjustment
    eye span distance ... 84
    fore and aft adjustment knob ... 84
    problems ... 86
    tilt adjustment lever ... 83
    vertical ... 83
aeromedical
    ears ... 119
    fatigue ... 112, 119
    field of regard ... 110
    fitness ... 122
    helmet fitting ... 120
    night adaptation ... 113
    proprioceptive system ... 119
    side effects ... 122
    stress ... 112
    visual illusions ... 115
AHTA (attitude, heading, torque, airspeed) ... *See* drill
aided flight - definition ... 155
airborne obscurants ... 138
aircraft configuration ... 141
airframe icing ... 138
albedo - terrain reflectivity ... 130
altered planes of reference – visual illusion ... 117
alternates – flight planning ... 205
ambient light
    flight planning ... 206
    scanning ... 112
ancillary equipment – flight planning ... 195
anode – electrical supply ... 66
anti-collision light ... 163
approach profile ... 168
    pinnacle ... 172
    PSWATP ... 168
    standard ... 169
approval - flight planning ... 194
arcs of responsibility - scanning ... 154
artificial light - scanning ... 112
astronomical twilight ... 128
atmospheric influence ... 138
atmospheric obscurants ... 135
    absorption ... 135, 136
    reflection ... 137
    refraction ... 137
    scattering ... 136
atoms ... 15
    energy, light and heat ... 22
aurora ... 126
autogain ... 69
autogating ... 70
autokinesis ... 117
automatic brightness control ... 68

B

barrel distortion ... 51
barrier - ion barrier film ... 58
battery
    lithium ... 79
    low battery indicator ... 80
    rechargeable ... 79
    usage plan ... 79

battery compartment ... 77
binocular housing ... 38
black ... 20
black spots ... 74
blooming ... 67
breakaway – mounting system ... 85
bright source protection ... 68
bright spots ... 73
brownout ... 187
brownout/whiteout ... 167
BSP (bright source protection) ... 68

C

calibration - USAF 1951 calibration chart ... 43
candle
    candlepower ... 26
    foot-candle ... 27
    spermaceti candle ... 26
candlepower ... 26
cathode – electrical supply ... 66
chart - USAF 1951 calibration chart ... 43
checks ... 161
    hover checks ... 161
    instrument performance checks ... 162
    NVG operations ... 191
    power wind plan statement ... 162
    pre-liftoff and pre-landing ... 161
    PWPWOH ... 162
chicken wire ... 74
civil twilight ... 128
classification ... 101
clouds (atmospheric influence) ... 139
cockpit
    class A and B filters ... 46
    class A and B lighting ... 45
    NVIS Green A ... 45
    NVIS Green B ... 45
    temperatures ... 138
cockpit design ... 143
cockpit lighting ... 142
coherent – laser property ... 34
collimated – laser property ... 34
collimation – adjustment problems ... 86
colours
    black ... 20
    grey ... 21
    tints, shades and tones ... 21
    white ... 20
communication (phraseology) ... 152
consequence rating ... 147
contrast (terrain) ... 131
crater illusion ... 118
crew resource management ... 152
    eyes inside/outside drill ... 153
    HLS operations ... 172
    low contrast situations ... 167

D

defects
    acceptable ... 73
    black spots ... 74
    bright spots ... 73
    chicken wire ... 74
    conditional ... 73
    edge glow ... 72

emission points 72
fixed pattern noise 74
flashing 73
flickering 73
honeycomb 75
intermittent operation 73
scintillation 75
shading 71
unacceptable defects 71
de-goggle 163
procedure - in the air 166
procedure - on the ground 165
de-goggle - phraseology 155
departure profile 166
constant angle 167
RIFTO 167
standard airfield 167
diopter 40
dioptric lens 39, 46
distortion
barrel distortion 51
fibre optic inverter 65
fisheye effect 51
geometric distortion 51
halo effect 68
pincushion distortion 51
s-distortion 65
sheer distortion 66
drill
AHTA 172, 174, 184, 186
eyes inside/outside 153
hand over/take over 177, 179, 180, 181
IIMC 161
PSWATP 168

E
ears 119
edge glow 72
edge shading 71
electrical circuit 80
electrical connection 85
electrical supply (intensifier tube) 66
electricity (history) 13
electromagnetic waves 17
elements - periodic table of 62
emergencies 181
goggle failure 182
inadvertant IMC 185
landing techniques 188
loss of visual reference 187
RADALT 182
emission points - defect 72
energy 15
environmental factors 123
ergonomics (cockpit design) 143
error (threat error management) 151
eye span adjustment knob 84
eyepiece 46
eyes
astigmatism 47
corrective lenses (glasses) 114
eye factors 112
eyes inside - phraseology 156
eyes outside - phraseology 156
fatigue 112
field of regard 110
field of view 108
long-sighted 47
monochromatic adaptation 119
night adaptation 113
short-sighted 47
stress 112
visual illusions 115

F
false horizons 115
fascination 115

fatigue
aeromedical factors 119
flight planning 195
fibre optic inverter 64
distortion 65
fibre optics - what is it 64
field of regard
aeromedical factors 110
scanning 153
field of view
affected by mounting position 84
eyes when using NVGs 108
low level 175
maximising 84
figure of merit (FOM) 76, 77, 103
filters 44
class A and B filters 46
light intensity filter 45
minus blue 46
fisheye effect 51
fitness - aeromedical factors 122
fitting
aeromedical factors 120
helmet 120
fixation 115
fixed pattern noise 74
flashing - defects 73
flicker vertigo 115
flickering - defects 73
flight planning 190
aircraft 194
ambient light 206
ancillary equipment 195
checklist 191
crew 195
crew briefing 207
IIMC recovery 199
IIMC recovery plan 208
mission 196
NVGs 194
route 198
sortie crew plan 208
terrain 198
weather 203
wire map 202
wires and obstacles 199
FLIR (forward looking infrared) device 24
fluorescent 61
focus
focus lane 43, 88
focus ring 43
hoffmann box 88
hoffmann box procedures 94
fog 140
fogging 138
FOM (figure of merit) 77, 103
foot-candle 27
foot-lambert 28
fore and aft adjustment knob 84
FOV .... See field of view
frame of reference 176
fuel holding 205

G
gain 48
system gain 49
tube gain 48
gallium arsenide - generation III 100
gated filmless technology 100
gegenscheins 126
generations 97
generation 0 99
generation I 99
generation II 100

generation III 100
generation III omnibus X 100
generation III plus 100
generation IV 100
summary 106
super generation II 100
terms 102
XR5 100
geometric distortion 51
glasses
corrective lenses 47
eyes using NVGs 114
goggle up 163
procedure - on the ground 164
grey 21
greyscale - snellen pattern 92

H
halo effect 68
halos 138
hazard 144
NVG flights 145
haze 140
heads up display 46
HEFFR 161
height perception illusion 117
helmet
balance 121
centre of gravity 121
fitting 120
helmet mounting 81
history
electricity 13
intensifier tube 14
night vision device 12
HLS operations
arriving 173
departing 172
pinnacle 172
hoffmann box 43, 88
controls and indicators 89
focus lane 87
focusing procedures 94
minimum resolution 91
resolution pattern 91
honeycomb 75
hover checks 161
HUD (heads up display) 46
hydrogen 15

I
icing 138
IFR
transition to IFR 177
transition to NVG 178
IIMC (inadvertent instrument meteorological conditions) 138
illuminance 30
illumination 123
levels of 124
night sky 126
infinity - NVG focus 43
infrared
aeromedical factors 118
infrared light 22
night sky 125
radiation 22
spectrum 18
instrument performance checks 162
intensifier tube
anode and cathode 66
autogain 69
autogating 70
automatic brightness control 68
bright source protection 68
components 48
defects 71
electrical circuit 80
electrical supply 66
fibre optic inverter 64
figure of merit (FOM) 77
gain 48
history 13
light control 67
mean time to failure 49
microchannel plate 54
phosphor screen 61
photocathode 50
photocathode photosensitivity 53
resolution 76
signal to noise ratio 76
interpupillary adjustment knob 84
ion barrier film 58
ITT 97

L
landing techniques 188
laser 34
classification 35
green laser dazzler 45
hazards 35
labels 36
protection for NVDs 35
type and wavelength 36
lens
compound lens 42
concave lens 41
convex lens 40
diopter 40
dioptric focus lens 46
dioptric lens 39
diverging lens 41
image inversion 40
objective lens 39
planar lens 42
LIF (light intensity filter) 45
light
aeromedical factors 118
ambient light 206
artificial sources 129
aurora 126
history 12
infrared 18, 22
laser 34
light spectrum 18
measurements 26
natural sources 124
noctilucent cloud 127
science of light 15
solar influence 128
source of light 15
speed of light 19
starlight 126
visible spectrum 18
wavelengths 34
zodiac light 127
light control
blooming 67
halo effect 68
intensifier tube 67
light intensity filter 45
light measurements
candlepower 26
foot-candle 27
lumen or lux 28
light pollution 142
light terminology
illuminance 30
luminance 31
radiance 30
summary 33
lighting
aircraft configuration 142
anti-collision 163
cockpit 142
external 143

external lighting	162
finger light	*163*
landing light/search light	163
lip light	163
position lights	162
strobe	163
torch	163
lightning	140
likelihood rating	148
locking pin	82
loss of visual reference	187
low battery indicator	80
low contrast situations	167
low level flight	175
low temperatures	138
lumen	28
luminance	31
lumination	124
luminescence	
phosphor screen	61
lux	28

M

maps	210
map marking	211
mud map	214
matter	15
MCP (microchannel plate)	54
mean time to failure	49
mental model	152, 207, 208
microchannel plate	54
curved MCP	55
generation II	100
ion barrier film	58
parabolic MCP	55
mist	140
monochromatic	
adaptation	119
image	112
laser	34
moon – natural sources of light	125
mount assembly	81
mounting system	81
breakaway	85
electrical connection	85
MTTF (Mean Time To Failure)	49

N

nanometres	18
nautical twilight	128
navigation	175
low level	175
Newton's inverse square law	29
night adaptation - aeromedical factors	113
night sky illumination	125
night vision device	
history	12
lasers	35
noctilucent cloud	127
NVD (night vision device)	25
NVFR	
transition from NVFR	180
transition to NVFR	179
NVG	
autogain	69
autogating	70
binocular housing	38
biocular	38
calibration	43
cockpit lighting	45
components	37
defects	71
displaced	98
field of regard	110
field of view	108
filters	44
focus ring	43
full face	98
glasses	47
light intensity filter	45
monochromatic image	112
monocular	38
objective focal adjustment	43
NVG operations checklist	
aircraft	194
crew	195
flight planning	207
mission	196
NVGs	194
route	198
weather	203

O

objective lens	39
omnibus	97
operational defects	71
operations checklist	191
optical image differences	87

P

passive systems - generation I	99
performance family	101
periodic table of elements	62
phosphor screen	61
periodic table of elements	62
the making of	64
phosphorescence	61
photocathode	50
generational change	53
geometric distortion	51
photomultiplier	51
photosensitivity	53
the making of	52
vacuum chamber	54
photomultiplier	51
photons	16
photosensitivity	53
phraseology	152, 158
hover and taxi	159
identifying and avoiding obstacles	160
in flight	159
take off and landing	161
pincushion distortion	51
pinnacle operations	172
plan - risk management plan	145
position lights	162
visual illusions	118
power supply	77
power wind plan statement	162
pre-flight brief - threat error management	151
pre-flight inspection	194
pre-liftoff and pre-landing checks	161
primary battery	194
proprioceptive system	119
postural right reflex	119
vestibular ocular reflex	119
PSWATP - approach drill	168
PWPWOH checks	162

R

radiance	30
rain	140
reflection	137
refraction	137
resolution	76
minimum	91
resolution pattern	
greyscale	92
hoffmann box	91

reversible perspective illusion 118
RIFTO - restricted instrument flight take-off 167
risk 144
risk management
    consequence rating 147
    content of RMP 145
    likelihood rating 148
    NVG flights 145
    NVG operations 145
    overview 144
    process 145
    risk management plan 145
    risk management plan example 149
    risk matrix 147

S

scanning
    arcs of responsibility 111, 154
    eyes inside/outside drill 153
    patterns 111
    procedures 153
    techniques 110
    unaided 111
scattering - atmospheric 136
scintillation 75, 138
s-distortion 65
shades 21
shading 71
shadowing - terrain 134
sheer distortion 66
signal to noise ratio 76
size distance illusion 117
snellen pattern 91
    greyscale 92
sniperscope 99
snooperscope 99
snow 140
SNR (signal to noise ratio) 76
solar influence 128
spatial disorientation - scanning 153
spectrum
    laser 36
    light spectrum 18
standard
    phraseology 152
    words and phrases 155
starlight 126
strobe lighting 163
structural illusion 117
sun
    astronomical twilight 128
    civil twilight 128
    nautical twilight 128
    solar influence 128
surface contrast 134
system gain 49

T

takeoff techniques 189
taking over - phraseology 157
TEM - threat error management 150
terrain 129
    albedo 130
    contrast 131
    reflectivity 130
    shadowing 134
terrain factors 123
thermal imaging 23
    colour 24
threat - definition 150
threat error management 150
    error 151
thunderstorms 140
tilt adjustment lever 83
tints 21
tones 21
torch 163
transition flight categories 177
transition metal compounds 62
tube gain 48
twilight 128

U

USAF 1951 calibration chart 43

V

vacuum chamber 54
verbal communication (phraseology) 152
vertical adjustment 83
vestibular system - scanning 153
visible spectrum 18, 19
visual illusions 115
    altered planes of reference 117
    autokinesis 117
    confusion of ground lights 116
    crater 118
    false horizons 115
    fascination (fixation) 115
    flicker vertigo 115
    height perception 117
    lack of motion 116
    relative motion 116
    reversible perspective 118
    size distance 117
    structural 117
    waterfall 117
    wave drift 116

W

waves 17
weather 135
    ambient light 206
    cloud 205
    elements 204
    freezing level 205
    fuel holding 205
    terrain and environmental factors 137
    visibility 205
weather requirements 204
white 20
white light 18
whiteout 187
wind 141
windshield 141
wires 199
    map 202

X

XR5 100

Z

zodiac light 127

www.ingramcontent.com/pod-product-compliance
Lightning Source LLC
Chambersburg PA
CBHW042016090526
44588CB00024B/2882